CHEROKEE EDITOR

THE WRITINGS OF

ELIAS BOUDINOT

CHEROKEE EDITOR

THE WRITINGS OF ELIAS BOUDINOT

Edited, with an Introduction, by
THEDA PERDUE

Brown Thrasher Books
THE UNIVERSITY OF GEORGIA PRESS
Athens and London

Published in 1996 as a Brown Thrasher Book
by the University of Georgia Press, Athens, Georgia 30602
www.ugapress.org

Set in 11/12 Caledonia

Printed digitally in the United States of America

Library of Congress Cataloging-in-Publication Data

Boudinot, Elias, d. 1839.
Cherokee editor : the writings of Elias Boudinot / edited by Theda Perdue.
x, 243 p. ; 22 cm.
"A Brown thrasher book"—T.p. verso.
Originally published: Knoxville : University of Tennessee Press, © 1983.
Includes bibliographical references and index.
ISBN 0-8203-1809-4 (pbk. : alk. paper)
1. Boudinot, Elias, d. 1839. 2. Cherokee Indians—History—Sources. 3. Cherokee Indians—Biography.
I. Perdue, Theda, 1949– . II. Title.
E99.C5B735 1996
973'.04975—dc20
[B] 95-23379

ISBN-13: 978-0-8203-1809-7

British Library Cataloging-in-Publication Data available

Frontispiece: Portrait of Elias Boudinot, OHS Glass Plate Collection. Reproduced by permission of the Archives and Manuscripts Division of the Oklahoma Historical Society, 19615.43.

For Charles Crowe

CONTENTS

PREFACE

The story of the Cherokee Indians, who in the early nineteenth century adopted many aspects of Anglo-American "civilization" only to be removed west of the Mississippi, has long captured popular and scholarly interest. In less than three decades, the Cherokees built a network of schools and churches, developed an alphabet, published a bilingual newspaper, organized libraries as well as literary, temperance, and benevolent societies, and instituted written laws and a constitutional republican government. In addition, they made plans for a museum and a national academy. A kind of utopianism permeated all of these accomplishments, a utopianism perhaps best expressed in the writings of Elias Boudinot, editor of the *Cherokee Phoenix*. But the great experiment in Indian "civilization," at least in the southeastern United States, came to an end in the 1830s when whites, motivated more by materialism than idealism, forced the Cherokees from their homeland. Elias Boudinot signed the removal treaty believing that Cherokee "civilization" could be saved if the Cherokees went west. Willing to part with the land, he could not part with the dream.

This study of Elias Boudinot and the collection of his published writings grew out of research on utopianism and American Indian policy which a fellowship of the Rockefeller Foundation made possible. In this volume, I have included all the publications of Elias Boudinot which I have located except repetitious and nonanalytical editorials from the *Cherokee Phoenix*.

I would like to thank William McLoughlin and Peter Wood for their critical readings of the entire manuscript and F. N.

Boney, Charles Crowe, and Neal Salisbury for their comments on the introduction. I also appreciatively acknowledge the assistance of staff members of the American Antiquarian Society, the Library of Congress, the Newberry Library, the Maryland State Law Library, the Oklahoma Historical Society, the Univesity of Georgia Library, and the Western Carolina University Library.

In this edition of the published writings of Elias Boudinot, capitalization has been normalized. Errors which seem to be typographical have been silently corrected. Punctuation has not been altered.

Theda Perdue
Cullowhee, North Carolina
April 23, 1982

CHEROKEE EDITOR

THE WRITINGS OF
ELIAS BOUDINOT

Oh, what is a man who will not dare to die for his people? Who is there here that will not perish, if this great Nation may be saved?

—Elias Boudinot
New Echota,
Cherokee Nation
December 29, 1835

INTRODUCTION

The expansion of Europe through exploration, conquest, colonization, and commerce characterizes modern history. Whether European military and economic power has been so overwhelming that the disintegration of other cultures was inevitable or whether the supposed superiority of European culture has made it irresistibly attractive to other peoples, Western "civilization" has invaded most of the globe. The transformation of indigenous cultures and the adoption of Western values and lifesyles by individuals within those societies often have been agonizing experiences. For many native peoples, physical survival has seemed to dictate cultural destruction. Leaders who perceive this to be the case face a difficult choice: fight to the bitter end or accommodate the intruders and promote the acculturation of their people. Those who choose to struggle against overwhelming odds often posthumously become heroes, even to the enemy, by appealing to the romantic element in Western culture. On the other hand, native leaders who embrace Western "civilization" frequently suffer repudiation in their own time and condemnation by later generations.[1] Elias Boudinot was a Cherokee Indian who advocated acculturation. He himself received an English education, converted to Christianity, married a white woman, edited a newspaper, and, finally, under pressure from whites, signed the treaty by which Cherokees relinquished their homeland in the southeastern United States. Throughout his life, Boudinot maintained that the preservation of his people depended solely upon abandonment of their own traditions, culture, and history.

Elias Boudinot was born about 1804 at Oothcaloga in northwestern Georgia near the present-day town of Calhoun.

Oothcaloga was a relatively new settlement established about 1800 by "progressive" Cherokees such as Boudinot's father, Oo-watie, and his uncle, Major Ridge. Oothcaloga, with its widely separated, single-family homesteads, differed markedly from Hiwassee, the town in southeastern Tennessee where Boudinot's immediate ancestors had lived. In Hiwassee, multigenerational households surrounded the council house and square ground, beyond which lay fields of corn and beans. The women in such traditional towns did most of the farming while men hunted and went to war, and the matrilineal kinship system dominated social interaction by determining possible marriage partners, distinguishing friends and enemies, regulating comportment, and protecting rights through retaliation and retribution.[2]

In the eighteenth century Hiwassee was an important trading town where whites located their stores and exchanged European ammunition, hoes, knives, hatchets, kettles, blankets, and other goods for Indian deerskins and war captives. This trade brought significant changes to Cherokee society. Successful hunters and warriors began to accumulate wealth from the sale of skins and slaves, and an economic class system began to emerge. Contributing to the inequality in wealth were the children of white traders and Indian women; such children inherited the mother's tribal affiliation along with the father's property. The warriors and descendants of traders began to dominate politics as well as economics. Previously, every man (and some women) had a voice in government, and leaders only advised and never coerced. But because Europeans desired the alliance of warriors and communicated more easily with the bilingual descendants of traders, political power came to be concentrated in the hands of an economic elite.[3]

During the American Revolution, many Cherokees including Major Ridge allied with the British, and the rebelling colonists invaded the Cherokee territory. Since the Cherokees were concentrated in towns along riverbanks, they were far more vulnerable to an invasion than a nomadic people would have been. The troops destroyed towns and burned fields and orchards while inhabitants fled to the forests. Famine and epidemic followed, and those who survived were reluctant to rebuild their desolated settlements. When the Cherokees (except for the Chickamaugans in northeast Alabama) made peace with the Americans, towns lost any defensive function they might have possessed, and Cherokees began to abandon their villages and establish scattered homesteads such as those in the Oothcaloga valley.[4]

The U. S. government encouraged this move away from traditional towns as part of an overall program to "civilize" the Cherokees. The ultimate objective was to locate each family on a self-sufficient farm so that the tribe would cede hunting grounds that it presumably no longer would need. The government appointed agents to implement other aspects of the program, which included the introduction of fences, plows, and the principles of animal husbandry to men, and cotton cards, spinning wheels, and looms to women. In the interest of furthering Indian "civilization," the government offered assistance to Protestant denominations and missionary societies in the establishment of schools and churches in the Cherokee Nation.[5]

Oo-watie was one of those Cherokees who took advantage of the government's "civilization" program. Along with his brother, Major Ridge, Oo-watie left Hiwassee and settled at Oothcaloga, where he cleared and fenced fields, built a log cabin, and planted orchards in the manner of the whites. Oo-watie's wife, Susanna Reese, gave birth to nine children at Oothcaloga. The first child, a son called Gallegina or "Buck," eventually would take the name Elias Boudinot; the second, a son named Stand, would also play a major role in Cherokee history as a politician, planter, and Confederate general. The children born at this Oothcaloga homestead entered a family and community very different from the ones Oo-watie had known as a boy. They lived a far more isolated and individualistic existence than their father had, sharing their home only with parents and siblings. The adoption of "Watie" as a surname by all the children except Boudinot indicated a move away from matrilineality, and the absence of traditional relationships with kinsmen divorced the Waties from their Indian heritage.[6]

In 1811 Oo-watie enrolled his oldest son in the Moravian mission school at Spring Place east of present-day Chatsworth, Georgia. Buck found his cousins, John and Nancy Ridge, and a number of other Indian children already in attendance. The Moravians had been ministering in the Cherokee Nation since the beginning of the nineteenth century and first received Cherokee children at their mission school in 1804. The curriculum at Spring Place included reading, writing, arithmetic, history, geography, and religion. But according to the Moravians, the instruction of Indian children involved far more than a formal curriculum. Insisting that children don European clothing, the missionaries endeavored to teach them the "arts of civilization"—hoeing, plowing, chopping wood, spinning, weaving, cooking, and sewing. Although they aimed primarily to save the souls of their charges, the missionaries believed that conversion was intrinsically linked to "civilization." In order to prevent their students from lapsing into "savage" ways while out of their care, the Moravians tried to house all Cherokees on the premises and severely limited vacation periods.[7] Consequently, when Buck began his formal education at the age of six, he left behind even that remnant of Cherokee culture which existed at Oothcaloga.

Except for a brief and unsatisfactory tenure with a private tutor hired by his uncle, Buck remained at Spring Place until 1817, when Elias Cornelius of the American Board of Commissioners for Foreign Missions, an interdenominational missionary society headquartered in Boston, invited him and several other promising scholars from the mission to further their education at the American Board school in Cornwall, Connecticut. Oo-watie gave his consent, and Buck and another boy decided to accompany Cornelius and American Board treasurer Jeremiah Evarts on their return to New England. Other Cherokees including John Ridge would soon follow. While on the way to Connecticut, Cornelius and the Cherokees visited the elderly Elias Boudinot, American Bible Society president, member of the Continental Congress, and proponent of the theory that American Indians were the lost tribes of Israel. Following the ancient Cherokee custom of changing names and the more recent practice of adopting the names of prominent whites and benefactors, Buck chose to take the old man's name, and so when he arrived in Cornwall, Buck Watie enrolled in the Foreign Mission School as Elias Boudinot.[8]

Elias Boudinot joined about twenty other students who came from various American Indian tribes and from such exotic places as Tahiti, Hawaii, and China. The American Board had established the Foreign Mission School in 1817. The board stated that its purpose was to prepare young men "who come to this favored land, from amidst the darkness and corruptions and miseries of paganism to be sent back to their respective nations with the blessings of civilized and christianized society." Providing academic, religious, and practical instruction, the school prepared students for professional training as physicians, teachers, interpreters, and ministers so that they could "communicate to the heathen nations, such knowledge in agriculture and the arts as may prove the means of promoting Christianity and civilization."[9]

A few white Americans training for the mission field enrolled in the school, but most students were native American or foreign. In general, the atmosphere at the school was a mixture of fascination with and rejection of "savagery." A guest at the Foreign Mission School in 1821 wrote a friend in Ohio:

> We had an excellent exhibition before a crowded house, this spring, which is annual, and answers very well to commencement with you. After the exercises of prayer, singing, and a sermon by Mr. Blair, a number of single pieces were spoken, and then a Cherokee council was held on the subject of war with the Osages. After a consultation in their own language, a Choctaw appears as interpreter, and gives his advice. A messenger comes and informs them, that Governor Miller [of Arkansas territory] has mediated a peace between their countrymen at the west and the Osages. They all join in a song. Also, a dialogue among the Owhyheans [Hawaiians], on information brought them of the renunciation of idolatry among their countrymen; together with an exhibition of a *real idol* brought this spring from Owhywee. This idol is carved in wood of a dark brown colour, mounted on a pedestal—the whole two feet high, with silver plates for eyes. The house was filled completely, every aisle, stair, &c. All expressed the highest gratification. Numbers of the Owhyheans are genteel young men; and also the Cherokees, among whom the appearance and performance of Elias Boudinot, John Ridge, and David Brown, the Brother of Catharine, would have done credit to the best white young men

> of their age. Elias Boudinot, in a declamation, confuted the idea more completely by his appearance than his arguments, that savages are not capable of being civilized and polished.[10]

In 1821 Adam Hodgson, an English merchant traveling in the United States, stopped by the mission school in Cornwall. He met Boudinot and reported that he "had gone through a course of history, geography, and surveying, had read some books of Virgil, and was then engaged in studying Enfield's philosophy, over which, indeed I afterwards found him, when I visited the school. I also saw his trigometrical copy-books." Apparently, Boudinot excelled as a student. The principal of the school published letters he penned in the *Religious Remembrancer* and the *Missionary Herald* and sent a calculation he made of lunar eclipses to Jedidiah Morse, the Yale geographer.[11]

Boudinot had converted to Christianity in 1820, and he came to exhibit such piety that the American Board made arrangements for him to study at Andover Theological Seminary, a center of Protestant evangelicanism. The missionaries entertained high hopes for Boudinot and David Brown, who also planned to attend Andover. As native ordained ministers, they could preach to the Cherokees without the risk of error; they also could baptize converts and serve them communion. The presence of men who could minister directly to the Cherokees without the assistance of interpreters had a number of benefits, including the lower cost and a lessened urgency for white missionaries to learn the Cherokee language. David Brown enrolled at Andover and went on to master Greek (and, some said, lose Cherokee). However, Boudinot's health prevented his immediate matriculation, and in 1822 he returned to the Cherokee Nation. On his way home, he and several other Cherokee youths visited Charleston, South Carolina. The annual report of the American Board commented: "The impression made upon this city, by the visit of so many improved, intelligent, and pious young men, taken but a few years since from the forest, and educated by Christian benevolence, was very favorable to the missionary cause. Liberal contributions were received, and the same effects were produced at Augusta, and other places, through which the company passed."[12]

While he was a student in New England, Boudinot began to develop many of the ideas that would shape his career. As a convert to an evangelical Christianity, he was not content with merely his own spiritual well-being. Instead, he assumed responsibility for the welfare of his people and felt that he personally must help to bring them the blessing of Christian "civilization." He did not believe that such an undertaking should be an individual effort but insisted that all Christians had a moral and religious obligation to assist the transformation of "savage" societies. Consequently, Boudinot often appealed to whites for aid ranging from prayer to financial assistance. The warm hospitality accorded Boudinot and other students at first by the white citizens of Cornwall and the generosity of benefactors of the school had indicated to the young Cherokee that many white Americans were deeply committed to "civilizing" the Indians and other "primitive" peoples and kindled in him a fervent optimism for the future of the Cherokees.

Events that occurred shortly after Boudinot left the Foreign Mission School dampened his optimism. When his cousin John Ridge married Sarah Bird Northrup, daughter of the school's white steward, in 1824, Boudinot discovered that just beneath the philanthropic surface of American society lurked a virulent racism. Voicing Cornwall's indignation over the interracial marriage, Isaiah Bunce, editor of the *American Eagle*, claimed that the match was "the fruit of the *missionary spirit* and caused by the conduct of the clergymen at that place and its vicinity who are agents of the school." He described the "affliction, mortification, and disgrace of the relatives of the young woman . . . who has thus made herself a *squaw*, and connected her race to a race of Indians."

The furor over the Ridge-Northrup marriage had barely subsided when Harriet Ruggles Gold asked permission of her father, a Cornwall physician, to marry Elias Boudinot. The young woman felt divinely called to be a missionary and believed that she could best answer that call as the wife of Boudinot. Her father refused his permission and wrote his daughter's suitor forbidding the marriage. When Harriet became critically ill that winter, her father relented and agreed to the marriage. The outraged citizens of Cornwall met on the village green and burned the couple in effigy. Distraught over the possible ramifications of another marriage between a white woman and an Indian, the agents of the school branded the people involved in the courtship as "criminal." But reaction was so strong that not even condemnation of the interracial marriage could save the institution, and the Foreign Mission School soon closed its doors. Gradually the town's anger dissipated, and in the spring of 1826 Elias Boudinot and Harriet Gold married uneventfully in Cornwall.[13]

The impact of this episode on Elias Boudinot was profound. He had believed that conversion and education would erase all differences between Indians and whites, yet he found himself treated as an outcast by the very people he had tried to emulate. Sartre described a twentieth-century Jew as facing a similar dilemma: "He has been reduced to pursuing the impossible dream of universal brotherhood in a world that rejects him."[14] Following this traumatic experience, Boudinot's first impulse seems to have been to repudiate "civilization." Concerned missionaries reported that shortly after he learned of Cornwall's reaction to his cousin's marriage and his own engagement, he attended a Cherokee ballgame, an event frequently accompanied by all-night dancing, drinking, and gambling. Soon their convert returned to the fold, but he had altered somewhat his goals for Cherokee society.[15]

Boudinot continued to be an ardent advocate of "civilization," but so completely did he embrace the tenets of Western culture that he seems to have accepted the dominant white attitudes toward Indians. He began to exhibit racial consciousness, and he abandoned the notion that "civilization" would, in any practical sense, make all men one. The "civilization" he now envisioned for the Cherokees would not eliminate them as a distinct people; rather, they would develop their own separate "civilized" institutions. Boudinot rarely even considered the possibility of Cherokees' being assimilated into white society, and when he did entertain such a thought, he apparently could conceive only of the incorporation of the Cherokees as a unit into a political system dominated by whites. As editor of the Cherokee newspaper several years after his marriage, he wrote:

> We do not expect ever to be a great nation, in the common sense of the word, for our population is too trifling to entitle us to that appellation. We may, nevertheless, by our improvement in the various departments of life, gain the respect and esteem of other nations. Or, should we blended with the United States (which perhaps may be the case,) we shall enjoy the privileges of her citizens and receive in common, the regard due her from abroad.[16]

Furthermore, during the removal controversy of the 1830s, Boudinot totally rejected a proposal by the principal chief that the Cherokees remain in their homeland and become subject to the laws of the states in which their territory lay.[17] His resistance to the absorption of the Cherokees into white society probably stemmed from a belief that Indians and whites could never be equals. At very least, Boudinot's encounter with and perhaps subconscious acceptance of white racism reduced to an afterthought the idea of Indian assimilation.

Boudinot came to believe that the progress of "civilization" among his people depended upon the preservation of the Cherokees as a corporate group. This belief found expression in a letter written in the late 1820s appealing for support in the Cherokees' battle against removal: "As long as we continue as a people in a body, with our internal regulations, we can continue to improve in civilization and respectability." The achievements of the Cherokees, particularly those he perceived to be unique, became a favorite topic. Boudinot contributed an article to the *American Annals of Education*, for example, which detailed the untutored Sequoyah's invention of the Cherokee syllabary and its enthusiastic adoption by the Cherokees who, as a result, became "a reading and intellectual people."[18]

In the 1820s the Cherokees seemed to be moving rapidly toward "civilization." Many Cherokees adopted white farming techniques, and some such as Principal Chief John Ross, Major Ridge, and Joseph Vann owned large plantations graced by elegant houses. The fact that black slaves operated these plantations suggests the extent to which some Cherokees went in order to gain acceptance among southern whites by following their social and economic lifestyle.[19] The Cherokees exported livestock and grain, and they produced enough food and cotton for domestic consumption. Mills and blacksmith shops provided services, toll roads criss-crossed the Nation, commercial ferries transported vehicles across rivers, and inns offered accommodations to travelers.[20]

Methodist, Baptist, and Presbyterian as well as Moravian missionaries operated a network of schools, and Christianity seemed to be gaining wider acceptance than it had in the first decade of the century.[21] The missionaries began to rely on their converts to assist them, and Cherokees became teachers, translators, and exhorters. These Cherokees manifested their zeal for Christianity and "civilization" not only through their support of mission schools and churches but also by the organization of Bible study groups, prayer meetings, and self-help societies. Boudinot was a founder of and corresponding secretary for the Moral and Literary Society of the Cherokee Nation. The constitution which was adopted in 1825 pledged the members to the "suppression of vice, the encouragement of morality, and the general improvement of this Nation." The society also aimed to "unite in *fidelity* the citizens of this Nation to the true interest of their Country, and for supporting the government thereof" and to establish a library, in the interest of which Boudinot sought contributions from whites.[22]

In the early nineteenth century the Cherokees formalized their system of government and adopted such Anglo-American practices as written legislation and delegated political power. In 1808 they recorded their first law, which established a national police force for the protection of property, and two years later, representatives of the seven clans met to renounce the practice of blood vengeance. In 1817 the General Council of the Nation delegated power to a standing committee which would conduct the Nation's business when the Council was not in session, and in 1820 articles of government provided for the apportionment of representatives to the Council from various districts in the Nation. Finally, in 1827 the Nation ratified a constitution based on that of the United States.[23]

Even before the inauguration of the republican constitution, the Council made a move to obtain a printing press and types in the Sequoyah syllabary and to establish a national academy. In

1825 members authorized Elias Boudinot to travel throughout the United States to solicit donations for these projects. Departing in the spring of 1826, Boudinot delivered addresses in major cities such as Charleston, New York, Philadelphia, and Boston as well as in smaller towns and villages. He prefaced his appeal for contributions with a description of Cherokee progress and a summary of his views on human beings and their societies. While in Philadelphia, he published his speech in the pamphlet "An Address to the Whites."[24]

Although Boudinot's audiences may have been surprised by a fashionably dressed Indian speaking with eloquence in their churches and town halls, many of the ideas he expressed were probably familiar to them. Boudinot maintained that all human beings were fundamentally the same: "What is an Indian? Is he not formed of the same materials with yourself? . . . Though it be true that he is ignorant, that he is a heathen, that he is a savage; yet he is no more than all others have been under similar circumstances" The belief in a common humanity dominated both religious and secular thought in the late eighteenth and early nineteenth centuries, serving as the premise on which mission work among the American Indians was based. Hundreds of missionaries repeated the sentiment if not the words of Samuel Blatchford, who opened his sermon to the Oneidas in 1810 with "the same Great Spirit who made us, made you—he made all mankind—you are our brothers."[25]

Human societies, on the other hand, obviously differed. The missionaries had taught Boudinot to accept the basic European creed that societies existed at different levels of development with "savages" at the bottom and "civilized" peoples at the top of this hierarchy. "Savages" hunted for a living, relied on frequently brutal customs for their law, worshiped nature or idols, and lacked a written language. "Civilized" peoples had farms, republican governments, Christian churches, and systems of writing. As societies at the pinnacle of development advanced even further, those at the lower levels disappeared. The only alternative for individuals who lived "savage" existences was to "progress." Because of a common humanity, men and their societies could progress, and even the most "primitive" society could become "civilized."

Boudinot's speech echoed many eighteenth- and nineteenth-century works. In *Notes on the State of Virginia*, Thomas Jefferson wrote that Indians differed from northern Europeans before the Roman conquest in numbers alone and that with time, literacy, and an increase in population, the Indians might produce an individual comparable to Newton.[26] A Georgia schoolmaster expressed a similar view about the Cherokees in particular after a journey through the Nation in 1818: "We were pleased with the treatment which we received there, with the cheerful and happy faces we saw, and with the idea that the time was near when these hitherto untutored tribes were enjoying the benefits to be derived from a virtuous and useful education, and ere long there will arise among them Philosophers, Poets, Orators, Civilians, and Divines not inferior to those of any country."[27]

Most American Christian leaders of the period believed that they had an essential role to play in the "civilization" of the American Indians. Jonathan Edwards, the eighteenth-century Puritan divine, had proclaimed that "the conversion of the Indians is, undoubtedly, an object worthy of the greatest attention, especially as the Christianizing of them would be the most effectual way of civilizing them."[28] While Protestant denominations disputed whether "civilization" or Christianization should come first, they agreed that the two could not be separated. For example, Daniel Butrick of the American Board at his ordination in 1826 (the year of Boudinot's "Address to the Whites") was charged to "make the Indians English in their manners, their religion, and their language."[29]

Few doubted the missionaries' ultimate success. A fictional conversation in a popular American Board tract accurately presented the dominant view in the United States (and particularly New England) in the early nineteenth century. In this tract, a proper New England gentleman expressed doubt that the Indians could be "civilized." His astonished niece replied, "Why uncle, I thought the successful missionary experiments had long ago convinced almost everybody that the American Indians were as capable of making as great improvements in literature and the arts as any nation in the world."[30] Boudinot himself clearly concurred and even went so far as to suggest that God had commanded the Cherokees to become "civilized."

Boudinot returned from his fund-raising campaign determined to fulfill God's command. He taught briefly at the American Board mission at Hightower and served as clerk of the National Council, but a better opportunity to "civilize" the Cherokees soon presented itself. Boudinot's trip had been a success, and the Council appropriated $1,500 for the purchase of a press. The national leadership offered Boudinot the editorship of the paper, which was to be called the *Cherokee Phoenix*. At first, Boudinot refused because the Council proposed to pay the white printer more than the editor, but when Samuel Austin Worcester, the American Board missionary with whom Boudinot had been collaborating on a translation of the Bible, convinced the board to supplement the Council's appropriation, Boudinot agreed to become editor.[31] In return for the board's financial support, Boudinot translated and published religious matter including the New Testament, a Cherokee hymnal, and a tract, *Poor Sarah, or the Indian Woman*.[32]

In October 1827 the prospectus of the *Cherokee Phoenix* appeared.[33] The biweekly newspaper, according to the editor, would contain the following items in Cherokee and English:

1. The laws and public documents of the Nation.
2. Account of the manners and customs of the Cherokees, and their progress in Education, Religion and the arts of civilized life; . . .
3. The principal interesting news of the day.
4. Miscellaneous articles, calculated to promote Literature, Civilization, and Religion among the Cherokees.

Boudinot planned to print two hundred copies of each issue for circulation in the Nation, and he hired agents in a number of states to accept subscriptions from whites for the Cherokee Indian newspaper. By July, he could boast thirty to forty subscribers in Mobile, Alabama, and a like number in Troy, New York, as well as scattered subscribers throughout the United States. A year later, a copy of the *Phoenix* had even reached Baron William de Humbolt in Berlin. In 1829 Boudinot's father-in-law wrote that "he has about 100 newspapers sent him from different parts of the U. S. by way of exchange." Boudinot borrowed freely from these papers for United States and world news, and they sometimes reprinted editorials from the *Phoenix*. The Cherokee newspaper's wide circulation made it a powerful propaganda tool for the Cherokees.[34]

By publishing official correspondence and documents, legislation passed by the National Council, and notices of weddings, school examinations, meetings of temperance and other societies, and revivals, Boudinot not only informed Cherokee readers of events in the Nation but also demonstrated to white readers the remarkable accomplishments of his people. On the front page of an early issue, the editor printed a summary of the Cherokee census taken in 1824. He followed the observation that "if possessions can be considered as indicating the progress of civilization, some Districts are considerably farther advanced in improvement than others" with an impressive enumeration of the material evidence of "civilization"—slaves, livestock, plows, spinning wheels, looms, saw and grist mills, blacksmith shops, cotton gins, ferries, stores, public roads and turnpikes, and even a threshing machine.[35] Boudinot also reminded readers that the Cherokee Nation was a republic with a written constitution: "We are happy to learn that there is every prospect of punctual and general attendance at each of the precincts in this District, on our election day, which is to be next Monday. Preparatory meetings have been held in Coosewaytee, Pinelog, and other places. This augurs well for the success of our new Constitution."[36] And an editorial refuted charges of the U. S. senator from Georgia that the Cherokee masses were oppressed and exploited:

> Many of the people of the United States, who think with Mr. Forsyth that the Cherokee are *poor devils*, may be surprised to learn that among them are several societies for the spread of religion and morality, and what is still more astonishing, the chiefs of these people, "who grind the faces of the poor" and "keep them under, in poverty and ignorance," that "their avarice propensity may be gratified," generally take the lead and support them by their example and contributions. They have Missionary Societies, Tract Societies, Sunday School Societies,

Benevolent Societies, Book Societies and Temperance Societies.[37]

Most accounts of traditional Cherokee "manners and customs," which Boudinot published, suggested that these were either rapidly disappearing or being transformed into "civilized" practices. In an editorial about a communication of commissioners appointed by the United States to negotiate a removal treaty with the Cherokees, Boudinot challenged the title applied to the Nation's leaders:

> We are rather at a loss to know why the Gentlemen in the circulars, thought proper to address themselves to "warriors," when they might have known that we have no more such characters amongst us, and if there are a few such men who may consider such an appellation applicable to them, they have no voice in our councils, and are therefore not the proper persons to treat with. We hope the Savage appellation which we have determined to cast behind us, will no more be thrown upon us.[38]

To a scholar's inquiry about aboriginal Cherokee customs, he replied, "Traditions are becoming unpopular, and there are now but a few aged persons amongst us who regard them as our forefathers did."[39] Boudinot commented in a similar vein on the evolution of Cherokee political institutions: "They have had a government from time immemorial—this government has been in operation to the present day, and within the last thirty years has been changing from the savage to civilized; until it has finally assumed, in a great measure, the nature of *regular law*."[40]

Although Boudinot was concerned about other Indians, particularly the Choctaws and Creeks who along with the Cherokees were being pressured to remove, he often pointed out that the Cherokees had attained a much higher level of "civilization" than any other tribe. He wrote, "We have heard of late, in many of the Southern papers, the degraded state of our neighbors Creeks, and their rapid decline. This may be true, but we protest against associating the Cherokees with them under the general name of 'Southern Indians,' as we have noticed in some of the northern prints."[41] Boudinot also carefully distinguished between the Cherokees and those tribes which had been decimated by warfare and disease. On one occasion, for example, he pleaded that "the comparison between the Cherokees and the Indians of New York is likewise unjust. The situation of the Cherokees is very different from the few remnants in the northern states."[42] In particular, Boudinot denounced violent acts by plains Indians, referred to as the "American Arabs," who prided themselves on their relative independence from white culture. Cherokee society was said to have no place for the kinds of "atrocities" committed by tribes such as the Comanches, whose "massacre" of four whites was duly reported. Furthermore, removal would subject "civilized" Cherokees to similar attacks, he reminded readers in the report of a skirmish between Pawnees and Cherokees west of the Mississippi which left six Cherokees dead.[43]

Even though Boudinot frequently mentioned the superior achievements of the Cherokees, he never implied that other Indians could not follow the Cherokee example. In fact, he cited Cherokee accomplishments in order to demonstrate the capabilities of Indians in general, and in 1829 he renamed the newspaper *The Cherokee Phoenix and Indians' Advocate* as an indication of its enlarged scope. As editor, Boudinot defended all Indians by pointing to the Cherokees in particular. For example, he replied to an article in the *North American Review* which stated that no progress was being made in the "civilization" of American Indians because of an attachment to "practices and opinions which constitute the distinctive traits of their character" with the assertion, "One thing is certain, before the writer can establish his positions, he must prove that the *Cherokees* are not *Indians*."[44]

Boudinot also resented accusations that the accomplishments of the Cherokee Nation were the work of white men rather than Indians. An article in a North Carolina newspaper claimed that "the affairs of the Cherokee Nation are wholly managed by whites and half-breeds" because thirty-six of the fifty-six candidates for the General Council had English names. Boudinot countered that English names did not necessarily mean English ancestry and that "amongst the 56 were some half-breeds, but not a *single white man*."[45] The white men most often accused of exercising control over the Cherokees were missionaries. Boudinot informed his readers, "With most of the Missionaries among the Cherokees we are acquainted, & we can assure the public that they have no influence in political matters, nor do they wish to possess any, their object being the moral & religious improvement of the people among whom they are sent."[46] Since many whites refused to believe that an Indian could edit a newspaper, Boudinot frequently had to defend the integrity of the *Phoenix* and his own abilities to perform the responsibilities of his position. In a reply to the charge of a Tennessee Methodist periodical that Samuel Austin Worcester of the American Board was the real editor, Boudinot insisted, "It has already been stated to the public that the Phoenix was under Cherokee influence. It has never been, nor was it ever intended to be, under the influence of any Missionary or White man."[47]

While Boudinot generally presented a positive view of Cherokee society, he sometimes upbraided the Cherokees for what he perceived as shortcomings. Not long after the *Phoenix* began publication, the editor chastised a few of his fellow citizens:

> There appears to be a want of public spirit in some of our leading and wealthy citizens. Though they possess the means of doing much good, by encouraging education, and the general improvement of the Nation, they seem to stand aloof. This is our failing as a people, and we are sorry to say that some of the offices of our government have been and are filled by persons of this description. From such leaders, who pay more regard to the acquisition of wealth than the good and interest of our country, we have no reason to expect, any solid and permanent advantage. Is not our remark correct when it is considered that many (and some who were members of the Legislative body which established the press) possessing all requisite means, *will not subscribe for the Cherokee Phoenix*, which costs only two dollars and fifty cents a year. Who will encourage and uphold us, when our own citizens and *patrons* (they ill deserve the name) will not give us a helping hand?[48]

More serious than the recalcitrance of potential subscribers to the *Phoenix* was the prevalence of drunkenness and crime in the Nation. Following the notice of an execution, Boudinot declared that "intemperance has been the ruin of this man, as it has been with thousands of others."[49] He appealed to each reader to "employ his influence to discountenance the use of intoxicating liquors. Let the intemperate beware, & the dealer in spirits reflect and see whether they have been fostering an evil of no ordinary magnitude."[50] Boudinot feared that drunkenness and lawlessness would jeopardize Cherokee "civilization," and in order to aid the cause of law and order, the *Phoenix* editor published the name of one suspected thief along with a request that he be arrested and brought "to deserved punishment."[51]

Despite the foibles of some Cherokees, Boudinot firmly believed that the Cherokees as a people exhibited no greater failings than other peoples; he often printed news items in which the Cherokees actually benefited by comparison with neighboring whites or more remote Europeans. He reported the following Cherokee judicial proceeding for the purpose, clearly, of suggesting the relative inferiority of Georgia justice.

> At the last Circuit Court held in High Tower, three persons were convicted for stealing horses out of Carrol Co. Georgia & were sentenced to receive fifty lashes each. These persons, we are told, stole upon the principle of rendering evil for evil. How backward some of our neighboring whites may be to do justice to the Indians, we confess we feel a pleasure in noticing this instance of the impartiality of our courts. It would be well if the authorities of Carrol County (Gov. Forsythe's ministers) will look about and punish their offending citizens. It would be a sweeping work if they were to begin.[52]

Boudinot also observed that at the annual examination of the children at Brainerd mission school "we saw no one at whom we could point our finger and say, 'there goes a savage,' except one, and he happened to be a white man from Tennessee. We saw this man stand before the window, to the no small annoyance of civil Cherokees, leaning upon his *rifle*."[53] And he simply reprinted the following article from another journal without comment.

> After the battle of Waterloo, the bodies were first searched over for money, watches and clothes. Then came the purveyors of human hair, for the supply of the makers of false hair, wigs, curls

> and frizzettes; then came another class, who extracted from the dead bodies, all the sound teeth, for the supply of the dentists; and lastly when the flesh had putrified, the collectors of bones for manure searched the field for *their* harvest. This looks like barbarism. The idea is revolting to humanity.[54]

While Boudinot refrained from openly venturing a comparison, the intent of the article was clear.

Boudinot portrayed the Cherokees as a "civilized" people in part because he believed their society was in the process of complete transformation but also because he knew that a charge of "savagery" by whites might lead to their extermination. White southerners desperately wanted Cherokee land, and Boudinot was convinced that Georgians, in particular, would readily seize any excuse to dispossess the Indians. The creation of a constitutional republican government in 1827 provided Georgia with an issue, the violation of her sovereignty, which state politicians hoped would force federal compliance with the Compact of 1802. In this agreement to which the Indians were not a party, Georgia relinquished the western lands of her colonial charter in exchange for the federal government's promise to extinguish Indian land titles within her borders. Andrew Jackson's election in 1828 gave Georgia a staunch ally in the White House. The state promptly annexed a large section of Cherokee territory, extended her law over that part of the Nation, prohibited convening of the National Council, forbade Indians to mine gold discovered on Cherokee land near Dahlonega, required whites living in the Nation to take an oath of allegiance to the state, and threatened to arrest any Cherokee leader who spoke against removal of the Nation west of the Mississippi.[55]

When these laws went into effect in June 1830, whites streamed into the Nation to mine gold and seize Cherokee property within Georgia. The Nation was impotent: Cherokee laws had been abrogated, the judicial system dismantled, and the national police force relieved of all responsibility for maintaining order. Georgia courts offered little protection to Cherokees because a new Georgia law prevented Indians from testifying against whites. Boudinot condemned the Georgia legislation in the columns of the *Phoenix*.

> We entreat you, respected reader,—we implore you, to pause after perusing the above facts, and reflect upon the effects of *civilized* legislation over poor *savages*. The laws which are the result of this legislation, are framed expressly against us, and not a clause in our favor. We cannot be a party or witness in any of the courts where a white man is a party. Here is the secret. *Full licence to our oppressors, and every avenue of justice closed against us*. Yes, this is the bitter cup prepared for us by a *republican* and *religious* Government—we shall drink it to the very dregs.[56]

Jackson briefly sent federal troops to the area to keep peace but withdrew them when Governor John Forsyth indicated that the state preferred to rely on the Georgia Guard, a special militia organized to police the Cherokee territory which Georgia claimed. The Guard tended to harass rather than protect the Cherokees. The members did little to remove white intruders or protect the gold mines, but they seized every opportunity to steal or vandalize Cherokee property and insult or abuse Cherokee people. Boudinot often reported encounters between Cherokee citizens and the Guard and harshly criticized the behavior of the militia. He wrote:

> The object for which this military band was created by the last legislature was to defend the gold mines and to assist in enforcing the laws of the State. We considered their duties few and simple, and we thought we understood them, until they came and arrested Mr. Martin [the chief justice of the Cherokee Supreme Court] without a written precept, and without even alleging a charge. This put us in the dark, and we are utterly at a loss to account for such unprecedented proceedings. It is reported that a similar course will be pursued against other persons, such as the white men who have not taken the oath of allegiance. We shall soon know, however, how it will be. We hear many reports of what they intend to do—if half what we hear were true, it would be bad enough.[57]

The Guard's activities exceeded Boudinot's expectations. Not only were white residents and political leaders arrested, but the editor of the *Phoenix* himself was brought twice before the commander. Boudinot reported that the commander accused him of printing "a great many lies & abusive & libelous articles"[58] and threatened "to tie us to a tree and give us a sound whipping."[59] Insisting that the articles were not libelous because they were true, the editor challenged the Guard to disprove a single incident reported in the *Phoenix*. On both occasions, the commander released Boudinot without punishing him and finally decided to defend the Guard in a letter to the *Phoenix* which Boudinot published. In editorials he refuted the commander's charges, and he clearly considered his relatively light treatment to be a moral victory, however grudgingly the Guard conceded defeat: "We are threatened to be *blessed* with the inestimable privilege of *liberty of the press* which is guarantied by this republic to every man whether white or red."[60]

Boudinot spent much time and ink denying rumors which circulated about the Cherokees' condition and intentions. Typical of these misconceptions, in this case not entirely honest, was an Alabama senator's description of the Cherokees as "almost in a state of starvation," "compelled to subsist on roots," and recipients of "only the vices of civilization." Boudinot responded, "The above remarks by Mr. King, discover notorious ignorance of the Cherokees.—We should like to know where this honorable Senator obtained his knowledge of our wretched condition."[61] And in another issue of the *Phoenix*, he reiterated: "We repeat again that the Cherokees are not on the decline in numbers and improvement, and we hope that we shall for this once be believed, and that the advocates of Indian emigration will urge the necessity of our removal upon some other reason than that of our degraded condition."[62] An equally widespread belief was that only white residents and a few wealthy chiefs opposed removal and that the majority of Cherokees would welcome an opportunity to emigrate. Boudinot responded: "Be it known to all whom it may concern, that cunning white men and half breeds have had no influence in preventing the emigration of the Cherokees. Every person who wishes to emigrate has the perfect right to do so. The fact is, every citizen of this Nation is *cunning*."[63] If the chiefs did negotiate removal, Boudinot maintained, the people would repudiate them. "One thing however is certain—the common people are jealous of their rights, and are ready at all times, to bring their chiefs to an account. How does this accord with the assertion frequently made, that the Cherokees are but slaves to their tyrannical chiefs."[64]

The fear that a small group posing as chiefs would make a treaty constantly haunted the Cherokees. In 1829 the Council passed a law that made cession of tribal land a capital offense. Although the institution of the death penalty probably was a nineteenth-century innovation, the principle that no one could relinquish more than his own individual claim to common property, which included realty, existed in the eighteenth century.[65] The Cherokees' apprehension of a minority treaty was by no means unreasonable. Just over twenty years before they recorded the law prohibiting land cession, the unscrupulous chief Doublehead was killed for ceding land; the Cherokee executioners included Boudinot's uncle Major Ridge.[66] More recently, Cherokee chiefs in Arkansas, where emigrants had settled, exchanged their territory for land still farther west. Boudinot commented: "We are sorry that there are self-interested men in all Indian tribes, who will not scruple to sacrifice the interest of their people, and that the United States, instead of discountenancing, will enter into treaties with them, contrary to the feelings of the rest of their brethren. If such a course is pursued, there is no hope for the Indians."[67] Furthermore, the chiefs of other southern Indian nations gradually came to terms (at least on paper) with the United States—the Choctaws in 1830, the Creeks, Chickasaws, and Seminoles in 1832.

The federal government unrelentingly pressured the Cherokees to follow the example of those nations and remove. Under provisions of the Indian Removal Act of 1830, which empowered the president to negotiate Indian removal, treaty commissioners arrived in the Nation to a decidedly cold reception. Enrolling agents sent to recruit emigrants for the western territory had only limited success. Even the western Cherokees who visited the Nation to encourage removal (which would enlarge their own territory) met solid resistance. Boudinot demanded, "Why are these inter-meddling Cherokees thrust in amongst us & paid by the United States when they are unwelcomed, and possess no right in this country?"[68] The president directed the agent, Colonel Hugh Montgomery, to withhold from the National treasurer the annuity, that sum owed the Cherokees from previously ceded land, and to distribute it on a per capita basis. Since the annuity was the Cherokee government's major source of income, this order jeopardized both the publication of the *Phoenix*, which was subsidized by the Council, and the Nation's legal defense in cases pending before U. S. courts concerning the jurisdiction of Georgia over Cherokee land. Boudinot embarked on a fund-raising tour of the United States on behalf of the *Phoenix* in the fall of 1831. In his absence, Boudinot's brother, Stand Watie, supervised the publication of the *Phoenix*. The legal defense of the Cherokees also continued, with wealthy Cherokees guaranteeing payment to lawyers, and their chief counselor, William Wirt, deferring payment.[69]

In 1831 the case of the *Cherokee Nation* v. *Georgia* reached the U. S. Supreme Court. The decision in the case, which involved the arrest, conviction, and execution of George Tassel under Georgia law for murdering another Cherokee within the Nation, was inconclusive. But in the spring of 1832 the Court ruled in favor of the Cherokees in *Worcester* v. *Georgia*. The Georgia Guard had arrested the missionary Samuel Austin Worcester twice for refusal to take the oath of allegiance to the state. The first time, a Georgia judge ruled that his position as postmaster at New Echota made him a federal agent and ordered him released. Promptly relieved of his postal duties, Worcester was again arrested. This time, the Georgia court found him guilty and sentenced him and another missionary to four years in the penitentiary. The Supreme Court directed the state to free them on the grounds that Georgia laws were not valid in the Cherokee Nation. Both Georgia and President Jackson ignored the decision.[70]

Dismayed and disillusioned over the federal government's refusal to enforce a decision of the Supreme Court, Boudinot returned to the Cherokee Nation in the spring of 1832. In July his name appeared on a petition favorable to removal. When Boudinot's change of heart regarding removal became known, the Cherokee government enjoined him from publishing his views in the *Phoenix*. The editor, however, insisted that the Cherokee people had a right to read arguments for as well as against removal. Principal Chief John Ross, who led the opposition to removal, disagreed. Under pressure from Ross and in protest of censorship, Boudinot resigned in August as editor of the *Cherokee Phoenix*. Subsequently, the Council expelled members who favored removal, including John Ridge and Major Ridge.[71]

In prohibiting dissent, Ross expressed the traditional Cherokee approach to political disputes. Originally, the Cherokees arrived at decisions through consensus, and anyone who could not agree simply withdrew so that the group could present a united front. Since the Cherokees overwhelmingly opposed removal, Boudinot and other proremoval Cherokees should have withdrawn and maintained silence, according to traditional Cherokee ethics. Instead of withdrawing and individually removing as a few Cherokees had done, this minority met at New Echota in December 1835 to negotiate wholesale removal. On the twenty-ninth, the men present signed a treaty that provided for the exchange of Cherokee land in the Southeast for territory in what is today the state of Oklahoma.[72]

Those who negotiated the Treaty of New Echota considered themselves to be the "party of civilization." Certainly, they fit Boudinot's definition: most were prosperous farmers, at least nominal Christians, and literate in English or Cherokee. Their "civilized" values emphasized acquisitiveness, an acquisitiveness which, they believed, prominent Cherokee leaders had thwarted. The signers of the treaty came primarily from a rising middle class, and they resented the economic power of Principal Chief Ross, Chief Justice John Martin, and councilmen Joseph Vann and Lewis Ross, who were among the wealthiest men in the Nation. Many disgruntled Cherokees thought that this wealth derived from private reservations received under previous treaties and located beyond the limits of the Nation. The refusal of these powerful men and the reluctance of federal officials to permit reservations under new treaties frustrated the economic ambitions of the middle class. Also, political leaders awarded contracts for the operation of toll roads and ferries and issued licenses to businessmen and white employees of Cherokee entrepreneurs. Furthermore, several members of the treaty party had been unsuccessful candidates for political office, and John Ridge adamantly insisted that only the ban on elections prevented his accession as principal chief. Consequently, the signers of the removal treaty believed that they would gain politically and economically by displacing the elected leadership in treaty negotiations.[73] The benefits were immediate: Governor Wilson Lumpkin had instructed the federal enrolling officer to give protection to Cherokees favoring removal, and he exempted their property from the lottery by which Cherokee land was being distributed to whites.[74]

The political and economic ambitions that motivated most members of the treaty party do not adequately explain Boudinot's participation. While Samuel Austin Worcester condemned the treaty as a "fraudulent and wicked document," he also contended that "Mr. Boudinot was, in the ordinary sense of the term, conscientious in the part he acted."[75] Unlike the planters, businessmen, and politicians who signed the treaty, Boudinot was a journalist and missionary, a man of modest means and little personal ambition. Although he himself was not particularly well-to-do, Boudinot did equate material possessions and "civilization." Thus he sympathized with men such as his uncle and cousin who had acquired respectable estates and now looked on helplessly as whites appropriated their property. These men were the bedrock of "civilization," and their financial as well as physical destruction spelled doom for Cherokee "civilization" in general.

In acting to protect men of wealth, Boudinot believed that he took the course of a true patriot. Removal would preserve the Cherokee Nation and the promise of an expanding Indian "civilization." A young white man who was present at the signing of the Treaty of New Echota recalled years after the event that Boudinot had addressed the assembly, and the speech which he remembered certainly embodies the sentiments of a patriot:

> I know that I take my life in my hand, as our fathers have also done. We will make and sign this treaty. Our friends can then cross the great river, but Tom Foreman and his people [who violently opposed removal] will put us across the dread river of death. We can die, but the great Cherokee Nation will be saved. They will not be annihilated; they can live. Oh, what is a man worth who will not dare to die for his people? who is there here that will not perish, if this great Nation may be saved?[76]

Unfortunately for Boudinot, most Cherokees believed him to be a traitor rather than a patriot and charged that he sought to destroy rather than save the Cherokee Nation.

Boudinot justified his signing of the removal treaty as moral and humanitarian in a pamphlet, "Letters and Other Papers Relating to Cherokee Affairs: Being a Reply to Sundry Publications Authorized by John Ross," first published in 1837 in Athens, Georgia. In this work, Boudinot accused Ross of callousness and of placing political and material considerations above concern for the moral and physical condition of his people.[77] By this time Ross had abandoned his attempt to have the treaty abrogated and was trying to increase the amount of money which the Cherokees were to receive under the provisions of the treaty. But Georgians continued to prey on the Cherokees, evicting them from their homes, plying them with liquor, and defrauding them of their meager possessions. Violence, gambling, drunkenness, and prostitution were widespread in the Nation, with Cherokee authorities still powerless to prevent such vices and the Georgia Guard often party to them.

Boudinot claimed that Ross pandered to the "established habits of thinking peculiar to the aborigines," that is, to the reluctance of the majority of Cherokees to abandon their homeland even in the face of invasion. Much to Boudinot's chagrin, many Cherokees had shunned "civilization." Despite the ease with which the Sequoyah syllabary reportedly could be learned, the Cherokee census of 1835 indicates that almost 40 percent of the households in the Nation contained no literate members.[78] Less than 10 percent of the Cherokees were even nominal Christians, and the chiefs at Hightower had requested that missionaries be withdrawn from their town.[79] Local chiefs exercised considerable power, and an attempt, with which the majority of Cherokees apparently sympathized, to disrupt the constitutional convention of 1827 narrowly failed.[80] Some evidence suggests that practices such as blood vengeance, infanticide, and polygamy continued, and supposedly "indolent habits" prevailed among the majority of Cherokees, who were content with a mere subsistence.[81] These Cherokee traditionalists opposed the exchange of their ancestral homeland, which according to their belief system was located at the center of the earth, for territory to the west, the direction associated with death. For them, migration meant leaving the landforms that their mythology incorporated, the rivers and caves that were sacred, and the herbs and minerals that were essential to healing and divination.[82]

Although these objections were widespread among the Cherokees, Boudinot refused to accept the reasoning of traditionalists as valid. He countered Ross's charge that the treaty was negotiated by an unauthorized minority by insisting that a majority decision, particularly in an "Indian Community," was not always the correct one. In the Cherokee Nation, Boudinot believed, the treaty party alone understood the "true situation" and, therefore, could act legitimately on behalf of the "ignorant" masses. In becoming "civilized," members of the treaty party had acquiesced to God's plan and accepted a righteous obligation to see the plan reach fruition even if doing so meant alienation from the Cherokee people.

Boudinot objected to the proposal that Cherokees remain on their land governed by the laws of the four states in which they resided. He knew from experience that even the most "civilized" Cherokees would not be accepted by whites as equals. His arrest along with that of Ross, Martin, and other prominent Cherokees by the Georgia Guard, the Georgia law which prohibited Indians from testifying or bringing suit against whites, and other events corroborated his earlier encounter with white racism. The only hope for the continuation of Cherokee "progress" and the realization of God's plan was for the Nation to maintain political independence and territorial integrity, even if that meant transferring the body politic to the West. If the Cherokees remained in the East, Boudinot feared that they would cease to exist as a people.[83]

Proponents of Cherokee removal welcomed Boudinot's apologia as the statement of a well-educated, Christian Indian responding rationally to his people's difficulties. Wilson Lumpkin, who had been elected to the U. S. Senate, presented Boudinot's pamphlet to Congress. In 1838 the Senate published the work as Document 121, "Documents in Relation to the Validity of the Cherokee Treaty of 1835." In doing so, the United

States government effectively used Boudinot's writings as a reply to the petition signed by 15,000 Cherokees who tried in vain to prevent Senate ratification of the minority removal treaty.

The Treaty of New Echota, which the Senate ratified in 1836, allowed the Cherokees two years to move to Indian territory. During this time, Ross worked to have the treaty amended, and most Cherokees believed that their principal chief would make it possible for them to remain in their homeland. As the deadline for removal drew near, the Cherokees made few preparations for their departure; many, in fact, began planting their corn in the spring of 1838. As a result, the federal government sent in troops, who began to round up Indians and place them in stockades. The crowded conditions and summer heat began to take their toll, and Ross appealed to the government on humanitarian grounds. The Van Buren administration relented and agreed to permit the Cherokees to supervise their own removal and to wait until winter when the water supply en route would be more plentiful. In the fall of 1838 the Cherokees finally departed for their new homes in the West.

Elias Boudinot left the Cherokee Nation in the East before the mass migration of 1838–39. His wife, Harriet, had died in 1836. Within a year, he married American Board missionary Delight Sargent and took her and his six children to the new Nation in the West. He had begun building a house for his family adjacent to Samuel Worcester's mission at Park Hill when the survivors of the "trail of tears" arrived in the West. The suffering of these people had been incredible: cold, hunger, and disease had claimed the lives of four thousand of their countrymen.[84]

On the morning of June 22, 1839, near the construction site of his new house, several Cherokees approached Boudinot and requested medicine. As he led two of the men to the dispensary, at the mission, they attacked with knife and tomahawk and escaped, leaving Boudinot fatally wounded. That same day, antitreaty Cherokees also killed Major Ridge and John Ridge for their role in the removal treaty. Considering themselves executioners rather than assassins, these men based their actions on two laws: the ancient law of blood, which demanded vengeance for the deaths on the "trail of tears," and the 1829 legislation, which made cession of tribal land a capital offense.[85]

Under Cherokee law, Boudinot received the punishment he deserved. He had ceded Cherokee land without authorization and had subjected his people to a torturous relocation. As a result, Boudinot's historical reputation is, at best, tarnished. In an age of cultural pluralism, militant tribalism, and objective ethnohistory, one is tempted to condemn Elias Boudinot not only for his part in negotiating Cherokee removal but also for his narrow view of culture and society. But the issues of the twentieth century were not those of the nineteenth. In that earlier era, the physical survival of Indians, much less their cultural survival, was by no means certain. Indeed, most evidence pointed to the rapid demise of native Americans. Nevertheless, Boudinot steadfastly believed that the Cherokee people could be saved. The survival he envisioned was not individual but involved the preservation of tribal sovereignty and ethnic identity. The Cherokees, he insisted, could achieve respect and admiration as a "civilized" Indian people from the rest of mankind. No price, even removal, was too high to pay for that recognition.

In our haste to assign responsibility for the tragedy of removal, we must remember that when the treaty party met at New Echota, they did not know that four thousand would die on the "trail of tears." Georgians were invading the Cherokee country, forcing people from their homes, seizing their property, abusing them, and killing those who resisted. Georgia authorities offered little protection; federal officials, even less. Removal promised an escape from known dangers, and although other migrating tribes had experienced terrible hardships, the tragedy of Cherokee removal had yet to be enacted. The treaty party, in short, did not have the benefit of historical hindsight.

A common pastime of those who study Indian removal is speculation about what might have happened if the Cherokees had remained united in their opposition to removal. Perhaps the Georgians who took possession of Cherokee land in the lottery would have been dissatisfied with the quality of the soil, would have accepted payment for the land, and would have permitted the Cherokees to regain their farms. Perhaps the state of Georgia would have accepted a cash settlement from the United States in lieu of enforcement of the Compact of 1802. This scenario was conceivable to John Ross in 1835 and it is equally conceivable today. But a drastically different scenario must also be considered by those who play the "what if" game. Perhaps Boudinot's worst fears would have been realized. Perhaps the Cherokees would have suffered the same fate as the Apalachees or Yamasees, tribes extirpated long ago, or the Catawbas, whose constantly dwindling population barely eeked an existence out of the worthless land to which they were confined. If one is to explore what might have been, an entire spectrum of possibilities exists.

Hindsight, speculation, and condemnation are of little value in understanding Elias Boudinot. He did not know what would happen or what might have happened, but he did believe that the Cherokee Nation was in grave danger of collapse and that removal was the Cherokees' salvation. This conviction alone seems to have motivated him. Recognition of the impetus, however, makes Boudinot an only slightly less ambiguous and puzzling figure in Cherokee history, because the "Nation" he gave his life to save simply did not exist.

The Cherokee Nation was composed primarily of traditionalists who clung to the culture Boudinot dedicated his life to eradicating. Preferring a life characterized by the bonds of kinship and community, subsistence agriculture, ecological balance, and the control of events through conjury, these traditionalists resisted Christianity and "civilization." Many ignored the national government and its laws, and instead they gave their allegiance to town chiefs and councils. At the helm of the National government were Cherokees who had abandoned the traditional way of life, but they primarily governed themselves and not the masses. Cherokee society in the early nineteenth century was incredibly dynamic in part because of this cultural diversity and a general toleration of diversity. Boudinot, in seeking to create a homogeneous "civilized" nation, was going against the widespread tendency among Cherokees to accept divergent lifestyles and customs as long as they did not jeopardize the community. And because he was part of a very small minority which tried almost to compel people to undergo a cultural transformation, other Cherokees probably viewed him with some suspicion. In contrast, John Ross was personally as highly acculturated as Boudinot, but Ross represented traditionalists and did so without exerting any pressure on them to change their beliefs or their way of life. Ross sought to protect Cherokee traditionalists; Boudinot hoped to save a Nation. But his "Nation" of literate industrious farmers, nuclear family homesteads, English schools, Christian churches, and a republican government that would reach all levels of society had little basis in reality. It was a vision, a fantasy, a dream few of his people shared. Elias Boudinot was a tragic figure not just because he made a serious error in judgment or because he paid the ultimate price but because he could not accept his people, his heritage, or himself. He was the product of colonization, and his thoughts and deeds may well tell us as much about our own culture as about nineteenth-century Cherokees.

NOTES

[1]A significant study of the impact of colonization on native peoples is Albert Memmi, *The Colonizer and the Colonized*, trans. Howard Greenfeld (Boston, 1965).

[2]Thurman Wilkins, *Cherokee Tragedy: The Story of the Ridge Family and the Decimation of a People* (New York, 1970), 4–5. The best study of precontact native American cultures in the Southeast is Charles Hudson, *The Southeastern Indians* (Knoxville, 1976). For Cherokee society and kinship, see John Phillip Reid, *A Law of Blood: The Primitive Law of the Cherokee Nation* (New York, 1970), 35–48, 73–84, 113–43; William H. Gilbert, Jr., "Eastern Cherokee Social Organization" in Fred Eggan, ed., *Social Anthropology of North American Tribes* (Chicago, 1937), 285–338.

[3]William L. McDowell, ed., *Documents Relating to Indian Affairs, May 21, 1750–Aug. 7, 1754* (Columbia, S. C., 1958), 66, 69, 82–83, 504–6; McDowell, *Documents Relating to Indian Affairs* (Columbia, S. C., 1970), 45, 242, 248–49, 330, 385. Verner W. Crane, *The Southern Frontier, 1670–1732* (Durham, N. C., 1928), remains a classic. A more recent work specifically on the Cherokees is John Phillip Reid, *A Better Kind of Hatchet: Law, Trade, and Diplomacy during the Early Years of European Contact* (University Park, Pa., 1976). For the emergence of a political and economic elite in Cherokee society, see Frederick O. Gearing, *Priests and Warriors: Social Structures for Cherokee Politics in the 18th Century* (Menasha, Wis., 1962); Theda Perdue, *Slavery and the Evolution of Cherokee Society, 1540–1866* (Knoxville, 1979), 19–35.

[4]James H. O'Donnell III, *Southern Indians in the American Revolution* (Knoxville, 1973), 34–53; Gary C. Goodwin, *Cherokees in Transition: A Study of Changing Culture and Environment Prior to 1775* (Chicago, 1977), 112–24; Betty Anderson Smith, "Distribution of Eighteenth-Century Cherokee Settlements," in Duane King, ed., *The Cherokee Indian Nation: A Troubled History* (Knoxville, 1979), 46–60.

[5]In 1796 George Washington outlined the "civilization" program in a letter to the Cherokees that was reprinted in the *Cherokee Phoenix*, Mar. 20, 1828. For the program's implementation, see Henry T. Malone, *Cherokees of the Old South: A People in Transition* (Athens, Ga., 1956), 46–73. Frances Paul Prucha's masterful study of early official relations between the United States and Indians contains a section on the "civilization" program. See *American Indian Policy in the Formative Years: The Indian Trade and Intercourse Acts, 1790–1835* (Cambridge, Mass., 1962), 213–49. In *Seeds of Extinction: Jeffersonian Philanthropy and the American Indian* (Chapel Hill, N. C., 1973), Bernard W. Sheehan suggests that the belief that Indians could and should be "civilized" ultimately provided the metaphysical basis for a removal policy. Also see Ronald N. Satz, *American Indian Policy in the Jacksonian Era* (Lincoln, Neb., 1975), 246–91.

[6]Wilkins, 30; Kenny A. Franks, *Stand Watie and the Agony of the Cherokee Nation* (Memphis, 1979), 2–3; genealogical chart appended to Edward E. Dale and Gaston Litton, eds., *Cherokee Cavaliers: Forty Years of Cherokee History as Told in the Correspondence of the Ridge-Watie-Boudinot Family* (Norman, Okla., 1939).

[7]Wilkins, 103–10; Adelaide L. Fries, ed., *Records of the Moravians in North Carolina*, 7 vols. (Raleigh, N. C., 1947), 6:2640–41, 2759–7:3143; Edmund Schwarze, *History of the Moravian Missions Among Southern Indian Tribes of The United States* (Bethlehem, Pa., 1929), 107. Bishop August G. Spangenburg described the Moravian approach to Indian Christianization and "civilization" in *An Account of the Manner in which the Protestant Church of the Unitas Fratum, or United Brethren, Preach the Gospel, and Carry on their Missions Among the Heathen* (London, 1788). Robert F. Berkhofer, Jr., analyzes the mission effort in *Salvation and the Savage: Protestant Missions and American Indian Response* (Lexington, Ky., 1965).

[8]Fries, 7: 3363; Wilkins, 111–16; Ralph Henry Gabriel, *Elias Boudinot, Cherokee, and His America* (Norman, Okla., 1941), 30. Boudinot sometimes spelled his name "Boudinott" in order to distinguish himself from the elder Boudinot, who developed his ideas about the origin of American Indians in *A Star in the West; or, A Humble Attempt to Discover the Long Lost Ten Tribes of Israel, Preparatory to their Return to the Beloved City of Jerusalem* (Trenton, N. J., 1816). There is no evidence that the author's namesake embraced these ideas.

[9]Fries, 7:3363; *First Ten Annual Reports of the American Board of Commissioners for Foreign Missions, with Other Documents of the Board* (Boston, 1834), 158–59; Adam Hodgson, *Letters from North America, Written During a Tour in the United States and Canada*, 2 vols. (London, 1824), 2:293, 296.

[10]*Religious Remembrancer*, May 31, 1821.

[11]Hodgson, 2:296–98; Wilkins, 134. See pp. 43-45 below.

[12]*Report of the American Board of Commissioners for Foreign Missions* (Boston, 1823), 77; Edward C. Starr, *A History of Cornwall, Connecticut: A Typical New England Town* (New Haven, Conn., 1926), 141, 147.

[13]Wilkins, 144–52; Gabriel, 57–92; Lillian Delly, "Episode at Cornwall," *Chronicles of Oklahoma* 51 (1973): 444–50. Gabriel's biography of Boudinot focuses on the furor surrounding his marriage and places it in the context of American racial attitudes. The board closed the school in 1826 on the grounds that it was better to educate young men in their own lands so that they could not be tempted by the vices of "civilized" society. *Eighteenth Annual Report of the American Board of Commissioners for Foreign Missions* (Boston, 1827), 150–51.

[14]Jean Paul Sartre, *Anti-Semite and Jew*, trans. George J. Becker (New York, 1968), 135.

[15]Wilkins, 134.

[16]*Phoenix*, June 4, 1828.

[17]See pp. 175-180 below.

[18]See pp. 48-58 below.

[19]R. Halliburton, Jr., *Red over Black: Black Slavery Among the Cherokee Indians* (Westport, Conn., 1977), 20–31; Perdue, *Slavery*, 50–69.

[20]Malone, 134–52; E. Raymond Evans, "Highways to Progress: Nineteenth-Century Roads in the Cherokee Nation," *Journal of Cherokee Studies* 2 (1977): 394–400.

[21]The Moravians labored for nine years before making their first convert in 1809. Following a number of efforts that had to be abandoned, uninterrupted missionary work by the Presbyterians (American Board) began in 1816, by the Baptists in 1820, and by the Methodists in 1822. See Malone, 91–117. In 1830 Samuel Austin Worcester reported: "The whole number of native members of the Presbyterian churches is not far from 180. In the churches of the United Brethren are about 54. In the Baptist churches I do not know the number: probably as many as 50. The Methodists, I believe, reckon in society, more than 800; of whom I suppose the greater part are natives." *Phoenix*, May 8, 1830.

[22]*Boston Recorder*, July 29, 1825. See also pp. 45-47 below.

[23]*Laws of the Cherokee Nation: Adopted by the Council at Various Periods. Printed for the Benefit of the Nation* (Tahlequah, C. N., 1852), 3–5, 11–12: V. Richard Persico, "Early Nineteenth-Century Cherokee Political Organization" in King, 92–109.

[24]See pp. 67-79 below for this pamphlet.

[25]Samuel Blatchford, *An Address Delivered to the Oneida Indians, 23 Sept. 1810* (Albany, N. Y., 1810).

[26]Thomas Jefferson, *Notes on the State of Virginia* (Boston, 1832), 6, 63, 143, 145.

[27]Charlotte Newton, ed., "Ebenezer Newton's 1818 Diary," *Georgia Historical Quarterly* 53 (1969): 214.

[28]Jonathan Edwards, *An Account of the Life of Mr. David Brainerd* (Edinburgh, 1798), appendix, p. 52.

[29]Journal of Daniel Butrick, Sept. 6, 1826, Records of the American Board of Commissioners for Foreign Missions, Houghton Library, Harvard University, Cambridge, Mass.

[30]Sarah Tuttle, *Letters and Conversations on the Cherokee Mission* (Boston, 1830), 24.

[31]*Laws*, 84–86: Wilkins, 188.

[32]Boudinot and Worcester, trans., *Cherokee Hymns Compiled from Several Authors and Revised* (New Echota, C. N., 1829), *The Gospel According to Matthew* (New Echota, C. N., 1829), *The Acts of the Apostles* (New Echota, C. N., 1833), *The Gospel of Jesus Christ According to John* (Park Hill, C. N., 1838), *The Gospel According to Luke* (Park Hill, 1840), *The Epistles of John* (Park Hill, C. N., 1840), *The Epistles of Paul to Timothy* (Park Hill, C. N., 1844), *The Epistles of Peter* (Park Hill, C. N., 1848); Boudinot, trans., *Poor Sarah or the Indian Woman* (New Echota, C. N., 1833).

[33]Boudinot's editorial policy appeared in the first issue. For selected editorials, see pp. 89-145.

[34]*Phoenix*, July 9, 1828, June 24, 1829; Benjamin Gold to Hezekiah Gold, Dec. 8, 1829, Cherokee Letters Collection, Georgia Department of Archives, Atlanta, Ga. Because the *Phoenix* was consciously employed for propaganda purposes, it must be used with care. See Perdue, "Rising From the Ashes: The *Cherokee Phoenix* as an Ethnohistorical Source," *Ethnohistory* 24 (1977): 207–17.

[35]*Phoenix*, June 18, 1828.

[36]Ibid., July 30, 1828.

[37]Ibid., Oct. 8, 1830.

[38]*Phoenix*, May 28, 1828.

[39]Ibid., July 30, 1828.

[40]Ibid., Jan. 6, 1830.

[41]*Phoenix*, July 21, 1828.

[42]Ibid., Jan. 6, 1830.

[43]Ibid., Sept. 30, 1829.

[44]Ibid., June 10, 1829.

[45]Ibid., Sept. 10, 1828.

[46]*Phoenix*, Jan. 14, 1829.

[47]Ibid., Nov. 12, 1828. One source of rumors that Boudinot was only nominal editor turned out to be the white printer of the *Phoenix*, Isaac Harris. Harris refused to give up his job gracefully and had to be forcibly ejected from the printing office. See Althea Bass, *Cherokee Manager: A Life of Samuel Austin Worcester* (Norman, Okla., 1936), 129.

[48]*Phoenix*, July 30, 1828.

[49]Ibid., Apr. 21, 1828.

[50]*Phoenix*, May 28, 1828. On Sept. 4, 1829, Boudinot published the constitution of the Cherokee Temperance Society, on whose executive board he served.

[51]Ibid., July 9, 1828.

[52]*Phoenix*, May 21, 1828.

[53]Ibid., Aug. 12, 1829.

[54]*Phoenix*, Nov. 26, 1828.

[55]Carl J. Vipperman, "'Forcibly if We Must': The Georgia Case for Cherokee Removal, 1802–1832" *Journal of Cherokee Studies* 3 (1978): 103–10.

[56]*Phoenix*, May 29, 1830.

[57]Ibid., Mar. 5, 1831.

[58]*Phoenix*, Aug. 12, 1831.
[59]Ibid.
[60]*Phoenix*, Aug. 12, 1831.
[61]Ibid., May 6, 1828.
[62]Ibid., July 21, 1828.
[63]*Phoenix*, Dec. 31, 1828.
[64]Ibid., July 29, 1829.
[65]*Laws*, 136–37; Alexander Hewatt, *An Historical Account of the Rise and Progress of the Colonies of South Carolina and Georgia, 1779*, 2 vols. (London, 1779), 2:4.
[66]Wilkins, 34–40; William G. McLoughlin, "Thomas Jefferson and the Beginning of Cherokee Nationalism, 1806–1809," *William and Mary Quarterly* 3d ser., 32 (1975): 547–80.
[67]*Phoenix*, Aug. 20, 1828.
[68]Ibid., Aug. 27, 1828.
[69]Ibid., Dec. 3, 1831, Feb. 18, 1832; Grace Steele Woodward, *The Cherokees* (Norman, Okla., 1963), 167.
[70]John Hutchins, "The Trial of Samuel Austin Worcester," *Journal of Cherokee Studies* 2 (1977): 356–74.
[71]Wilkins, p. 253. See also pp. 159-75 below.
[72]Charles Kappler, ed., *Indian Affairs: Laws, and Treaties*, 2 vols. (Washington, D. C., 1904), 2:239–47.
[73]The Treaty Party's claim to be the "party of civilization" can be found in pp. 160-61 below; George W. Paschal, "To the Public," n.d., Cherokee Nation papers, Univ. of Oklahoma Archives, Norman, Okla.; and John Rollin Ridge to the editor, *New York Tribune*, May 28, 1866.
[74]Georgia Governor's Letterbook, 1833, Georgia Department of Archives, Atlanta, Ga.
[75]Worcester to D. Greene, June 28, 1838, Andover Theological Seminary Archives, Andover, Mass.
[76]This is a recollection of Boudinot's speech by J. W. H., Underwood, who attended the signing of the Treaty of New Echota and made the official copies of the document. Underwood's father was the Cherokee Nation's local lawyer. *Cartersville Courant*, Mar. 26, 1885.
[77]See pp. 159-225 below.
[78]Census of 1835 (Henderson Roll), Record Group 75: Indian Affairs, National Archives, Washington, D.C.
[79]McLoughlin, "Cherokee Anti-Mission Sentiment, 1824–1828," *Ethnohistory* 21 (1974): 361–70; Berkhofer, *Salvation and the Savage*, 155–56.
[80]J. P. Evans, "Sketches of Cherokee Characteristics," n.d., John Howard Payne Papers, Newberry Library, Chicago, Ill.; Samuel Worcester to Jeremiah Evarts (Mar. 29, 1827), Isaac Proctor to Evarts (May 10, 1827), William Chamberlain to Evarts (May 3, 1827), Records of the American Board; John Cocke to the Secretary of War (July 1, 1827), Journal of the Commissioners (July 3, 1827), Letters Received, 1824–1881, U.S. Office of Indian Affairs, Record Group 75, National Archives, Washington, D.C.
[81]*Laws*, 79, 133. Many well-to-do Cherokees, including Chief Justice John Martin, had more than one wife despite the law prohibiting polygamy. James F. Corn, *Red Clay and Rattlesnake Springs* (Cleveland, Tenn., 1972), 48–51.

That many Cherokees lived at the subsistence level has been demonstrated by McLoughlin and Walter H. Conser, Jr., in "The Cherokees in Transition: A Statistical Analysis of the Federal Cherokee Census of 1835," *Journal of American History* 64 (1977): 678–703.

[82]The importance of the land to the Cherokee belief system is clear in James Mooney, *Myths of the Cherokee and Sacred Formulas of the Cherokees* (19th and 7th Annual Reports of the Bureau of American Ethnology; reprinted, Nashville, Tenn., 1972). See esp. 15, 239, 246–47.

[83]For Ross's side of the issue, see Gary E. Moulton, *John Ross, Cherokee Chief* (Athens, Ga., 1978).

[84]Woodward, 192–218.

[85]Grant Foreman, "The Murder of Elias Boudinot," *Chronicles of Oklahoma* 12 (1934): 19–24.

Selected Contributions
to Periodicals
in the United States

« « « Elias Boudinot had an unusually public life. He was among the first generation of English-educated Cherokees, and this alone created something of a sensation in nineteenth-century America. His marriage to a white woman engendered a heated debate over interracial marriage in supposedly liberal New England. He edited the first Indian newspaper, which created considerable controversy particularly in Georgia, and he signed the highly publicized Treaty of New Echota. In short, Boudinot had a life filled with excitement and drama, a life in which the reading public was intensely interested. Boudinot whetted their appetite for information about himself and the Cherokees by contributing to white periodicals. Furthermore, as the most articulate of his countrymen, he often acted as their spokesman, but he always phrased general concerns in very personal terms. As a result, many whites, especially those who read the major reform journals of the day, became almost as intimately acquainted with Boudinot's thoughts as with his deeds. Missionaries and philanthropists encouraged Boudinot in his correspondence not only because he revealed the hopes and fears of the Cherokees but because he also was living proof of the feasibility of converting and "civilizing" the American Indians.

Boudinot's first letters were written while he was a student at the American Board's Foreign Mission School in Cornwall, Connecticut. The school provided a secondary education for the most promising graduates of mission schools among various native American tribes and in foreign countries. Supported by donations, the Foreign Mission School employed its students in publicizing the institution's work. Students corresponded with benefactors, missionary societies, and churchmen throughout the world, and these letters appeared in religious periodicals. The concerns of students centered on their own salvation and on the Christianization of the entire world. Like the American Board, the students considered universal conversion to be imminent; their enthusiasm had not yet been tempered by the harsh realities of the mission field. Boudinot was caught up in the religious fervor that permeated the Foreign Mission School, and he filled his letters with personal soul-searching.

After Boudinot returned to the Cherokee Nation, he became less obsessed with his own spiritual state and more interested in the moral and intellectual condition (and he tended to equate the two) of his people. He appealed to benefactors, in the same way the American Board did, to support the Cherokees' Moral and Literary Society, their efforts toward universal literacy, and their struggle against encroachments by whites. Whatever the purpose or theme of his letters and articles, Boudinot imbued them with a missionary zeal; his writings, he believed, were the fulfillment of a divine imperative. Although this sense of mission, which is evident even in his earliest letters, made Boudinot a forceful spokesman for the Cherokees, it also contributed to the elitism, rigidity, and intolerance which he later exhibited.

There is surprisingly little biographical scholarship on Boudinot. In *Elias Boudinot, Cherokee, and His America* (Norman, Okla., 1941), Ralph Henry Gabriel focused on his subject's private life (which was not very private) and on the racial attitudes of white America. Articles dealing with specific incidents include Lillian Delly, "Episode at Cornwall," *Chronicles of Oklahoma* 52 (1973): 444–50; and Grant Foreman, ed., "The Murder of Elias Boudinot," *Chronicles of Oklahoma* 12 (1934): 19–24. The first four chapters of Kenny A. Franks' biography of Boudinot's brother, *Stand Watie and the Agony of the Cherokee Nation* (Memphis, 1979), contain pertinent information. The correspondence of Boudinot and his relatives has been published in Edward E. Dale and Gaston Litton, eds., *Cherokee Cavaliers: Forty Years of Cherokee History as Told in the Correspondence of the Ridge-Watie-Boudinot Family* (Norman, Okla., 1939). By far the best treatment of Boudinot and the Ridges can be found in Thurman Wilkins, *Cherokee Tragedy: The Story of the Ridge Family and the Decimation of a People* (New York, 1970).

Elias Boudinot lived in a rapidly changing society. Works which provide insight into that society include Duane King, ed., *The Cherokee Indian Nation: A Troubled History* (Knoxville, 1979); William G. McLoughlin and Walter H. Conser, Jr., "The Cherokees in Transition: A Statistical Analysis of the Federal Cherokee Census of

1835," *Journal of American History* 64 (1977): 678–703; Henry T. Malone, *Cherokees of the Old South: A People in Transition* (Athens, Ga., 1956); Theda Perdue, *Slavery and the Evolution of Cherokee Society, 1540–1866* (Knoxville, 1979); Marion L. Starkey, *The Cherokee Nation* (New York, 1946); Rennard Strickland, *Fire and the Spirits: Cherokee Law from Clan to Courts* (Norman, Okla., 1975); and Grace Steele Woodward, *The Cherokees* (Norman, Okla., 1963).

LETTERS TO PERIODICALS

Missionary Herald,[1] August 1821
[To the Baron de Compagne][2]

Foreign Mission School, Cornwall, (Con.)
Jan. 8, 1821[3]

Honored and Respected Sir,

Having been requested by my beloved teacher, Mr. Daggett,[4] I have the pleasure of writing to you; and, in the name of my fellow students, to thank you for your benevolent donation of 100 ducats. We feel thankful to the Giver of every good and perfect gift, that we are not destitute of Christian friends, who are willing to give their property for our sustenance, while receiving an education in this charitable institution. We are here, far from our native countries, brought here by the kind providence of God; and blessed be his name, that he has given us friends to support us, and to instruct us in human knowledge, but especially in that science, which treats about the immortal soul, and the only way to everlasting felicity. While we are looking with grateful hearts, to the Christian people of the U. S. we are grateful to think, that we have a kind benefactor in Switzerland.

My honored Sir, we have nothing in this world with which we can reward you, for your act of benevolence. Only we return you our grateful thanks. But I hope the Lord will reward you, and make you the instrument of good to many souls. May he yet grant you prosperous, peaceful, and useful days of your remaining life, and a crown of glory in the life to come. May your prayers be answered for this school; that numbers here may be trained up, who shall go into the vineyard of the Lord, and be faithful laborers to bringing many unto Christ, who are now sitting in darkness. Our school promises extensive good. Here are numbers, we hope, who are willing to be employed in the work of the Lord.

We need the prayers of all Christian people, and we are truly encouraged to think, that we are remembered by the Christians of Europe as well as of America. You will likely, Sir, wish to know from what nation I came. I am a Cherokee, from a nation of Indians living in the southern part of the United States. There are eight of us here from that nation. Six out of eight profess to be the followers of the meek and lowly Jesus. I came to this school more than two years ago; and, if it is the will of God, I expect to leave it in about one or two years. I sometimes feel an ardent desire to return to my countrymen and to teach them the way of salvation. Pray for me that my faith fail not, and that I may not finally prove insincere. That we may meet in the kingdom, which is eternal in the heavens, is the wish of your unworthy and unknown young friend,

ELIAS BOUDINOT

Religious Remembrancer,[5] October 13, 1821

Cornwall, Conn.

Brother P.[6]—As Brother Brown[7] is writing to you, it may not be improper for me to fill the vacant part of this sheet. Considering the correspondence which we agreed to support, and the friendship we formed, I doubt not but these few and imperfect lines will be received by you. I am happy to say that I have again commenced my studies under better circumstances than when you was here.[8] The journey which I performed (to Burlington, N. J.) has greatly benefited me.[9] I feel myself relieved from the many complaints to which I was subject, which hindered me from my daily pursuits; I can now study without being molested by headache, weakness, dizziness, &c. But what shall I say concerning my spiritual interest? I cannot but blush, whenever I turn my pen to write upon this subject. There is great leanness in my soul. Perhaps I must at last be cast away and dashed to pieces, when the storm shall arise which will sweep away the wicked from the earth. You know that many are called, but that few are chosen. Those who only say "Lord, Lord," will not be saved, but they, and they only, who do the commandments of Christ. We cannot tell who is a Christian and who is not. For true religion is planted in the heart of the subject. We are liable to mistake respecting the foundation on which we place our eternal interests. "The heart is deceitful above all things, and desperately wicked."[10] Perhaps my profession is unsound; for the evidences of true piety do not consist in the outward performances of the duties required. I have been lately doubting what course to take when I leave this institution. When you was here, you know that I proposed studying Theology.[11] But it is not certain whether I shall. I feel myself deficient in those important Christian graces which constitute a true preacher of the gospel. But let the earth rejoice, the hearts of the children of men are in the hands of God, and he can turn them withersoever he pleases. I have now opened my heart to you, that you may pray for me, that I may not be shaken by every wind. I hope we shall have the pleasure of seeing you again in Cornwall.— With much respect, and wishes for your success in your ministerial work,

I am, dear sir, your's affectionately,

ELIAS BOUDINOT

Boston Recorder and Telegraph,[12] July 29, 1825

FROM THE CHEROKEE NATION

Messrs. Editors,[13]— As you are known to be the friends of Indian improvement, and favorable to whatever concerns them, I hope you will not think it a disgrace to insert the following circular in your valuable paper, and oblige the Subscriber.

To the Benevolent,— You will notice, in a late number of the Boston Recorder and Telegraph, the Constitution and Minutes of the "Moral and Literary Society of the Cherokee Nation." In them you will perceive the ultimate objects, and imagine the prospects, of this infant association. Though the degree of good which would result from it, is at present hid from human conception, yet it is no part of an extravagant feeling, to hope for the greatest good for the Indian name. Though the efficient means and exertions lie in the body which composes it, yet its existence is much depending of the good will and aid of our American brethren. It is the object of this, therefore, benevolent friends, respectfully to invite you, and all those who pray for our prosperity, to give the mite of assistance, by supporting the *Library* intended to be established. Do you wish well to the Indian character?— evince that wish by deed. Do you pray for Indian improvement?— support your prayers to the God of nature, by assisting the needy, feeding the hungry, and enlightening the benighted. Are you a philanthropist, and do you desire your Aboriginal friends to be respected and honored?— spread knowledge and religion in their slippery path, and obstruct their way to oblivion, by the charms of education. What true lover of his country is there, who is not also a patriot of his neighbors? What true Christian is there, who does not drink the sweet draughts of benevolence?

Notwithstanding the current opinion, as respects Indian condition, is not very favorable, it is nevertheless an acknowledged fact, that among the Cherokees, great and rapid improvement has been made, both in information and industry. Many who a short time since, bore the appellation of Savage, have bid a final adieu to the course and practices of their fathers.

Imagine, my friends, the change there would be in this nation, if ye but act nobly and justly with them. Few moons would come and go,— then the traces of vice and ignorance would fly with the wind; and only here and there would be one who could say, "here stood my father's wigwam, and there was the place of his warlike weapon." The Cherokees have improved much by the efforts of the public, and by their own exertions. They have done considerable in regulating their national affairs, and improving their moral condition. The Society in question has the main objects of cultivating morality, discountenancing vice, and supporting and protecting every thing calculated to enlighten the nation. A Library of good books, will, of course, be attached to it. Books on Travels, Histories, both ancient and modern, Maps, and in fine, books of all descriptions tending to the objects of the Society, will be gratefully received and acknowledged.

We have now, my friends, whoever you are, wherever you live, opened a door for your benevolence—our hearts are ready to receive your aid and support, and we will bless you for them.

Suppose not the Indians entirely devoid of gratitude and respect —they glory in friendship—for like yourself they are God's workmanship;— and what is he but love.

Perhaps here and there lives one, who might lay claim against Indian ravages, or mourn an ancient father or mother expiring beneath the slow consuming fire, and would still cry for Indian extermination. If there be, and whoever you be, dignify human nature by forgetting the injury, and forgiving the transgression. We do not wish to palliate any act of injustice—but those deeds are past—with the wind they are gone. Our fathers, too true, did you the injury,—but where are they? Their bones now moulder beneath some lonely shed, and the scanty earth which covers them is now all they can claim; and perhaps even that is cleft in twain by the plough that procures you nourishment. Their possessions once were great—a boundless country, supplying them with game—and the multitude of the watery elements were theirs. You now live on their ruins! Can you still harbor revenge? It is highly necessary that the Indians should become moral. For where is the nation that can exist without morality? And think ye a nation can be respected without knowledge?

Consider your privileges, and the condition of the Indians, your fellow beings; moreover, remember that they have a lasting claim on your benevolence.

Communications relating to the Society may be addressed to the Subscriber, Spring Place, Cherokee Nation.[14]

ELIAS BOUDINOT,
Corresponding Sec'y.

May 28, 1825

Journal of Humanity; and Herald of the American Temperance Society,[15] July 1, 1829

CHEROKEE AFFAIRS

Extract of a letter to Rev. E. Cornelius,—[16]
dated New Echota, March 11, 1829

Dear Sir,— I take the liberty of addressing a line to you. I do it from the knowledge I have of your friendly feelings toward the Indians. It is an interesting time with the Cherokees, and I tell you, my friend, I tremble for them. There is not, in my opinion, a sufficient degree of interest for the welfare of the Aborigines in the United States, even in the *Christian Community*, to save them from oppression, and from the evil consequences of disorganization. This is what I dread. As long as we continue as a people in a body, with our internal regulations, we can continue to improve in civilization and respectability. Now the efforts of the General Government and the State of Georgia are directly opposed to our interests. The General Government is engaged in effecting emigration to the west, thereby dividing us;[17] and the State of Georgia is attempting oppressive laws over us, and encouraging her outcast citizens to intrude upon our lands, and to behave with impudence towards our inoffensive citizens.[18] How far these efforts will be carried I know not. Perhaps I need faith. I know God is almighty; and he is very merciful—perhaps he will still remember us and save us. We need the prayers of all God's people. Cannot you interest the Christian people within the circle of your acquaintance? I am afraid the Indians are not sufficiently remembered in the prayers of all good people.

ELIAS BOUDINOT

American Annals of Education,[19] April 1, 1832

INVENTION OF A NEW ALPHABET

[The man who invents a valuable machine to diminish labor, or increase wealth, is deemed worthy of public honors and rewards. If it facilitates the intercourse of men, and the means of improvement, he is ranked still higher; and he who produces something original, whether it be an instrument, or a book, or a plan, or even a single truth, which contributes directly and in a high degree to the promotion of intellectual light, is placed upon the calendar of public benefactors, to whom we pay a never ceasing tribute of gratitude and respect. Watt, and Whitney, and Fulton, and Arkwright, and Franklin, and Harvey, are claimed as an honor to their country on such grounds; and the birthday of Robert Raikes, is a jubilee on both sides of the ocean.

But a *Cadmus* is so rarely seen, and the invention of a written language is an effort of genius and perseverance so unlike any combination of wheels and levers and moving powers, —so distinct from any new arrangement of words and ideas, or any of those plans and systems which genius has devised or benevolence executed, to employ written language as a means of improving mankind —that we have no standard by which to estimate at once, the value of the original discovery of the *instrument*, by means of which all these operations of beneficence are performed.

Let us, however, imagine every book in our language to be blotted out, let us suppose ourselves unable to communicate our thoughts to the absent, or to keep a record of the past, or to preserve our knowledge for the future, with no other evidence of our rights and property but beads, and wampum, and landmarks, and oral testimony, and we may approximate the value which should be placed upon the labors of *Sequoyah*, the inventor of the alphabet which serves as the medium of intercourse to the Cherokee nation.[20] Let us examine the multitude of efforts which have been made to devise a perfect alphabet for our own language, by the most learned men, and we can better estimate the honor due to an untutored Indian, who has produced an alphabet by which a Cherokee boy may learn to read his native language in two or three days, as readily as we could read our own, after months of instruction. We are persuaded that we shall gratify our readers in presenting them the following account of this remarkable invention, which we requested from Mr. Elias Boudinot, himself a Cherokee, and the editor of the national paper the Cherokee Phenix, as *prepared* and *corrected* by himself.][21]

TO THE EDITOR OF THE ANNALS OF EDUCATION.

Many of your readers are aware of the existence of the Cherokee Alphabet; but few, perhaps, have had access to a history of its invention, and hardly any have any idea of the nature of the Alphabet itself. It is to be regretted that this remarkable display of genius has not been more generally noticed in the periodicals of the day, and a proper tribute paid to the untutored inventor. It is not yet too late to do justice to this great benefactor of the Cherokees, who, by his inventive powers, has raised them to an elevation unattained by any other Indian nation, and made them a reading and intellectual people.

In compliance with your request, I have therefore thought proper to present to the readers of the 'Annals of Education,' a short account of this invention, and some particulars relating to the nature of the Alphabet. In giving the former, I shall take occasion to use the account given by Mr. Knapp, in his first lecture on 'American Literature.'[22] The facts stated by him can be relied upon, as they were derived from Sequoyah himself, through the interpretation of intelligent Cherokees. Mr. Knapp prefaces his account thus:

> 'The Indians themselves are becoming philologists and grammarians, and exciting the wonder of the world, by the invention of letters. The invention of the Cherokee alphabet, has excited the astonishment of the philosopher in this country and in Europe; but as I have not as yet seen any satisfactory account of the progress and history of this greatest effort of genius of the present day, I will state what I know of it, from the lips of the inventor himself.'

Mr. Knapp then relates the manner in which his interview with Sequoyah was conducted.

> 'In the winter of 1828, a delegation of the Cherokees visited the city of Washington, in order to make a treaty with the United States, and among them was Se-quo-yah',* the inventor of the Cherokee alphabet. His English name was George Guess;[23] he was a half-blood; but had never, from his own account, spoken a single word of English up to the time of his invention, nor since. Prompted by my own curiosity, and urged by several literary friends, I applied to Sequoyah, through the medium of two interpreters, one a half-blood, Capt. Rogers,[24] and the other a full-blood chief, whose assumed English name was John Maw, to relate to me, as minutely as possible, the mental operations and all the facts in his discovery. He cheerfully complied with my request, and gave very deliberate and satisfactory answers to every question; and was at the same time careful to know from the interpreters if I distinctly understood his answers. No stoick could have been more grave in his demeanor than was Sequoyah; he pondered, according to the Indian custom, for a considerable time after each question was put, before he made his reply, and often took a whiff of his calumet, while reflecting on an answer.'

*The spelling of the name is conformed to the Cherokee standard.

The appearance and habits of Sequoyah are those of a full-blooded Cherokee, though his grandfather, on the father's side, was a white man.[25] He was educated in all the customs of his nation, and, as Mr K. says, was and is to this day ignorant of any language but his own.

> 'The details of the examination are too long for the closing paragraph of this lecture; but the substance of it was this: That he, Sequoyah, was now about sixty-five years old, but could not precisely say; that in early life he was gay and talkative; and although he never attempted to speak in Council but once, yet was often, from the strength of his memory, his easy colloquial powers, and ready command of his vernacular, story-teller of the convivial party. His reputation for talents of every kind gave him some distinction when he was quite young, so long ago as St. Clair's defeat.[26] In this campaign, or some one that soon followed it, a letter was found on the person of a prisoner, which was wrongly read by him to the Indians. In some of their deliberations on this subject, the question arose among them, whether this mysterious power of *the talking leaf*, was the gift of the Great Spirit to the white man, or the discovery of the white man himself? Most of his companions were of the former opinion, while he as strenuously maintained the latter. This frequently became a subject of contemplation with him afterwards, as well as many other things which he knew, or had heard, that the white man could do; but he never sat down seriously to reflect on the subject, until a swelling on his knee confined him to his cabin, and which at length made him a cripple for life, by shortening the diseased leg.[27] Deprived of the excitements of war, and the pleasures of the chase, in the long nights of his confinement, his mind was again directed to the mystery of the power of *speaking by letters*; the very name of which, of course, was not to be found in his language.'

The *immediate* circumstances which induced him to the great undertaking, are not stated by Mr Knapp. It appears that he was led to think on the subject of writing the Cherokee language by a conversation which took place at a certain town called Sauta.[28] Some young men were remarking on the wonderful and superior talents of the white people. One of the company said that white men could put a talk upon a piece of paper and send it at any distance, and it would be perfectly understood by those who would receive it. All admitted that this was indeed an art far beyond the reach of the Indian, and they were utterly at a loss to conceive in what way it was done. Sequoyah, after listening for a while in silence to the conversation, raised himself, and putting on an air of great importance, observed, 'You are all fools; why the thing is very easy; I can do it myself.' And taking up a flat stone which lay near him, he commenced making words on it with a pin. After a few minutes he told them what he had written, by making a mark for each word. This produced a laugh and the conversation on that subject ended. The inventive powers of Sequoyah were however now put in active operation, although it would seem from the narrative of Mr K. that he had thought on the subject long before,[29] and had to contend with the prejudices of some of his nation, who believed that the knowledge of letters belonged only to the white man. Some of this portion of his countrymen attempted to convince him that God had made that great distinction between the white and red man, by relating to him the following tradition:

In the beginning God created Yv* we yah e, a term applied to an Indian, signifying a *real* or *genuine man*; and the yv we na gv, or *white man*. The Indian was the elder, and in his hands the Creator placed a *book*; in the hands of the other he placed a *bow* and *arrow*, with a command that they should both make a good use of them. The Indian was very slow in receiving the book, and appeared so indifferent about it that the white man came and stole it from him when his attention was directed another way. He was then compelled to take the bow and arrow, and gain his subsistence by pursuing the chase. He had thus forfeited the book which his Creator had placed in his hands, and which now of right belonged to his white brother.

The narration of such a story was not, however, sufficient to convince Sequoyah, and to divert him from his great purpose. After the interview at Sauta alluded to above, he went home, purchased materials, and in earnest began to paint the Cherokee language on paper. The process of his labors is properly detailed by Mr. Knapp in the following paragraph.

*The character denoting the Cherokee nasal sound of *u* in *under*.

'From the cries of wild beasts, from the talents of the mocking-bird, from the voices of his children and his companions, he knew that feelings and passions were conveyed by different sounds, from one intelligent being to another. The thought struck him to try to ascertain all the sounds in the Cherokee language. His own ear was not remarkably discriminating, and he called to his aid, the more acute ears of his wife and children. He found great assistance from them. When he thought that he had distinguished all the different sounds in their language, he attempted to use pictorial signs, images of birds and beasts, to convey these sounds to others, or to mark them in his own mind. He soon dropped this method, as difficult or impossible, and tried arbitrary signs, without any regard to appearances, except such as might assist him in recollecting them, and distinguishing them from each other.'

Sequoyah, at first, thought of no way but to make a character for each word. He pursued this plan for about a year, in which time he had put down several thousand characters. He was then convinced that the object was not to be attained in that way. But he was not to be discouraged. He firmly believed there was some way in which the Cherokee language could be expressed on paper, and after trying several other methods, he at length hit upon the idea of *dividing the words into parts or syllables*. He had not proceeded far on this plan, when he found to his great satisfaction, that the same characters would apply in different words, and that the number would be comparatively few. After putting down and learning all the syllables that he could think of, he would listen to speeches, and the conversation of strangers, and whenever a word occurred which had a part or syllable in it, which he had not before thought of, he would recollect it until he had made a character for it. In this way he soon discovered all the syllables in the language. After commencing upon the last plan, it is believed he completed his system in about a month.[30] He adopted a number of English letters which he took from a spelling book then in his possession. Mr. Knapp then goes on to state:

'At first, these signs were very numerous; and when he got so far as to think his invention was nearly accomplished, he had

> about two hundred characters in his Alphabet. By the aid of his daughter, who seemed to enter in the genius of his labors, he reduced them, at last to eighty-six, the number he now uses. He then set to work to make these characters more comely to the eye, and succeeded. As yet, he had not the knowledge of the pen as an instrument, but made his characters on a piece of bark, with a knife or nail. At this time he sent to the Indian agent, or some trader in the nation, for paper and pen. His ink was easily made from some of the bark of the forest trees, whose coloring properties he had previously known; and after seeing the construction of the pen, he soon learned to make one; but at first he made it without a slit; this inconvenience was, however, quickly removed by his sagacity.'

During the time he was occupied in inventing the alphabet, he was strenuously opposed by all his friends and neighbors. He was frequently told that he was throwing away his time and labor, and that none but a delirious person, or an idiot, would do as he did. But this did not discourage him. He would listen to the expostulations of his friends, and then deliberately light his pipe, pull his spectacles over his eyes, and sit down to his work, without attempting to vindicate his conduct. After completing his system, he found much difficulty in persuading the people to learn it. Nor could he succeed until he went to the Arkansas and taught a few persons there, one of whom wrote a letter to some of his friends in the Cherokee nation, east of the Mississippi, and sent it by Sequoyah, who read it to the people.[31]

So contemptible were his efforts considered by the Cherokees generally, that he was laughed at as a 'fool.' I recollect very well, the first intimation I had of the attempt of Sequoyah to invent an alphabet for the Cherokee language. In the winter of 1822,'23, I was travelling with an intelligent Cherokee, who is now the principal Chief of the nation,[32] on a road leading by the residence of Sequoyah. I had never heard of him until my companion pointed to a certain cabin on the way-side, and observed, 'there, in that house resides George Guess, who has been for the last year attempting to invent an alphabet. He has been so intensely engaged in this foolish undertaking, that he has neglected to do other labor, and permitted his farm to be overrun with weeds and briars.' We rode on, and I thought no more of

Sequoyah and his alphabet, until a portion of the Cherokees had *actually* become a reading people. The first evidence I received of the existence of the alphabet, was at a General Council held in New Echota in 1824, when I saw a number of the Cherokees reading and writing in their own language, and in the new characters invented by one of their untutored citizens.[33]

The mode by which Sequoyah introduced his alphabet to the notice of his Arkansas brethren, is minutely described by Mr. Knapp.

> 'His next difficulty was to make his invention known to his countrymen; for by this time he had become so abstracted from his tribe and their usual pursuits, that he was viewed with an eye of suspicion.[34] His former companions passed his wigwam without entering it, and mentioned his name as one who was practising improper spells, for notoriety or mischievous purposes; and he seems to think that he should have been hardly dealt with, if his docile and unambitious disposition had not been so generally acknowledged by his tribe. At length he summoned some of the most distinguished of his nation, in order to make his communication to them—and after giving them the best explanation of his discovery that he could, stripping it of all supernatural influence, he proceeded to demonstrate to them, in good earnest, that he had made a discovery. His daughter, who was now his only pupil, was ordered to go out of hearing, while he requested his friends to name a word or sentiment which he put down, and then she was called in and read it to them; then the father retired, and the daughter wrote; the Indians were wonder struck; but not entirely satisfied. Sequoyah then proposed, that the tribe should select several youths from among their brightest young men, that he might communicate the mystery to them. This was at length agreed to, although there was some lurking suspicion of necromancy in the whole business. John Maw, (his Indian name I have forgotten.) a full-blood, with several others, were selected for this purpose. The tribe watched the youths for several months with anxiety; and when they offered themselves for examination, the feelings of all were wrought up to the highest pitch. The youths were separated from their master, and from each other, and watched with great care. The uninitiated directed what the master and pupil should write to each other, and these tests were varied in such a manner, as not only to destroy their infidelity, but most

firmly to fix their faith. The Indians, on this, ordered a great feast, and made Sequoyah conspicuous at it. How nearly is man alike in every age! Pythagoras did the same on the discovery of an important principle in geometry. Sequoyah became at once school-master, professor, philosopher, and a chief. His countrymen were proud of his talents, and held him in reverence as one favored by the Great Spirit.'

Mr. Knapp then goes on to describe his efforts as to numbers, of which I have no knowledge than what is contained in this account.

'He did not stop here, but carried his discoveries to numbers. He of course knew nothing of the Arabick digits, nor of the power of Roman letters in the science. The Cherokees had mental numerals to one hundred, and had words for all numbers up to that; but they had no signs or characters to assist them in enumerating, adding, subtracting, multiplying, or dividing. He reflected upon this until he had created their elementary principle in his mind; but he was at first obliged to make words to express his meaning, and then signs to explain it. By this process he soon had a clear conception of numbers up to a million. His great difficulty was at the threshold, to fix the powers of his signs according to their places. When this was overcome, his next step was in adding up his different numbers in order to put down the fraction of the decimal, and give the whole numbers to his next place. But when I knew him, he had overcome all these difficulties, and was quite a ready arithmetician in the fundamental rules.

I ought to add, that the figures in use among the Cherokee, are the Arabic figures.

After having narrated the result of his interview with Sequoyah, Mr. Knapp states further particulars relating to the genius and talents of this 'American Cadmus.'

'This was the result of my interview; and I can safely say, that I have seldom met a man of more shrewdness than Sequoyah. He adhered to all the customs of his country; and when his associate chiefs on the mission assumed our costume, he was dressed in all respects like an Indian. Sequoyah is a man of diversified talents; he passes from metaphysical and philosophical investigation to mechanical occupations, with the greatest of ease. The only practical mechanics he was acquainted with, were a few bungling blacksmiths, who could make a rough tomahawk, or tinker the lock of a rifle; yet he became a white and silver smith, without any instruction, and made spurs and silver spoons with neatness and skill, to the great admiration of people of the Cherokee nation. Sequoyah has also a great taste for painting. He mixes his colors with skill; taking all the art and science of his tribe upon the subject, he added to it many chemical experiments of his own, and some of them were very successful, and would be worth being known to our painters. For his drawings he had no model but what nature furnished, and he often copied them with astonishing faithfulness. His resemblances of the human form, it is true, are coarse, but often spirited and correct; and he gave action, and sometimes grace, to his representations of animals. He had never seen a camel hair pencil, when he made use of the hair of wild animals for his brushes. Some of his productions discover a considerable practical knowledge of perspective; but he could not have formed rules for this. The painters in the early ages were many years coming to a knowledge of this part of their art; and even now they are more successful in the art than perfect in the rules of it. The manners of the American Cadmus are the most easy, and his habits those of the most assiduous scholar, and his disposition is more lively than that of any Indian I ever saw. He understood and felt the advantages the white man had long enjoyed, of having the accumulations of every branch of knowledge, from generation to generation, by means of a written language, while the red man could only commit his thoughts to uncertain tradition. He reasoned correctly, when he urged this to his friends as the cause why the red man had made so few advances in knowledge in comparison with us; and to remedy this was one of his great aims, and one which he has accomplished beyond that of any other man living, or perhaps, any other who ever existed in a rude state of nature.'

Mr. Knapp closes by observing that 'the Government of the United States had a fount of types cast for his alphabet,' &c. which, however, is a mistake. The types now used at New Echota in printing the Cherokee Phenix, were paid for by the Cherokee Government and the voluntary subscriptions of their friends in the United States, and procured through the kind agency of the Treasurer of the American Board of Commissioners for foreign missions.[35]

As to the nature and characteristics of the Alphabet, I cannot do better than refer you to a very satisfactory and correct account furnished by the Rev. Samuel A. Worcester, a missionary among the Cherokees, and inserted in the first number of the Cherokee Phenix.[36]

When the usefulness of the Cherokee Alphabet became fully developed, it spread through the nation in a manner unprecedented. Reading and writing very soon became common, for within a few months after its introduction, there were Cherokees in various parts of the nation who could use the '*talking leaf*.' It is worthy of remark, that it was at first confined to the more obscure individuals of the Cherokees, nor did the most intelligent portion consider it of any importance until their senses gave evidence of the existence and utility of this remarkable invention, when they saw them read and write in their own language.[37]

To increase its utility, the Council of the Cherokee nation had a fount of types cast, as has been already observed, and a newspaper established, printed in the English and Cherokee languages. About 200 copies of this newspaper are circulated weekly, in the nation, and read by hundreds in every section of the country. At the same press have also been published in Cherokee, the Gospel of Matthew, and a Hymn book; and a tract containing portions of Scripture. It is found that these publications are read with great interest, and weekly meetings are held in some neighborhoods, to read the Cherokee Phenix.

It is perhaps difficult to say what proportion of the Cherokee may be called a reading people.[38] At a convention of gentlemen, well capable of forming a correct judgment, held at New Echota in 1830, six years after the invention of the Cherokee alphabet, it was calculated that upwards of one half of the adult males could read and write in their own language. I am convinced there is nothing exaggerated in this calculation. And if they are suffered to go on as they have done, it will be but a few years before reading and writing will be universal among them.

E. Boudinot.

NOTES

[1]The *Missionary Herald* was published in Boston by the American Board of Commissioners for Foreign Missions. Founded by Jedidiah Morse to counteract Unitarianism, the periodical appeared under several titles, including *The Panoplist*, from 1805 until 1951.

[2]The Baron de Compagne, who lived near Zurich, Switzerland, contributed $212 in 1820 and $664 in 1821 to the Foreign Mission School. He learned about the school from acquaintances at the Basle Missionary Seminary, which had been founded in 1816 "for the purpose of furnishing the various evangelical Missionary Societies with pious and educated German and Swiss youths, as ministers of the Gospel among the heathen." *Missionary Herald*, Mar. 1820, Dec. 1821, May 1822.

[3]Boudinot was seventeen years old.

[4]Rev. Herman Daggett was principal of the Foreign Mission School from 1818 to 1824.

[5]The *Religious Remembrancer* was a Presbyterian weekly published in Philadelphia that printed articles on theology as well as revivals and missionary work.

[6]Rev. Nicholas Patterson was the minister of the Third Presbyterian Church in Baltimore, Md.

[7]David Brown was a Cherokee student at Cornwall who went on to study at Andover. The *Religious Remembrancer* not only printed his letter, which was similar to Boudinot's, but also correspondence from David's sister Catherine, who taught in an American Board mission at Creek Path. The Browns were great favorites of the missionaries. The American Board employed David to translate the New Testament from Greek, but his knowledge of Cherokee was so limited that Boudinot and Samuel Austin Worcester had to do another translation. Catherine died in 1822, and the poignant story of her brief life was told in Rufus Anderson, *Memoir of Catherine Brown, A Christian Indian of the Cherokee Nation* (Philadelphia, 1831). David died in 1829. Information about the Brown family can be found in Mary Alves Higginbotham, "The Creek Path Mission," *Journal of Cherokee Studies* 1 (1976): 72–86.

[8]Rev. Patterson visited Cornwall in May 1821 and became acquainted with Elias Boudinot and David Brown, whom he listed in an earlier issue of the *Religious Remembrancer* (June 9, 1821) as "professors of religion."

[9]Boudinot had been to New Jersey to visit the ailing president of the American Bible Society, whose name he had adopted. He spent two or three weeks with the octogenerian, "who always took particular delight in every attempt to meliorate the condition of the American Indians." The elder Boudinot died in Oct. 1821. *Missionary Herald*, Dec. 1821.

[10]Jeremiah 17:9.

[11]The Foreign Mission School provided the equivalent of a secondary education. In order to study theology and become an ordained minister, Boudinot needed to enroll in a seminary. After this letter was written, he decided to attend Andover Theological Seminary, an institution founded in 1808 by Trinitarian Congregationalists and Presbyterians as a "bulwark against Unitarianism." See John A. Andrew III, *Rebuilding the Christian*

Commonwealth: New England Congregationalists and Foreign Missions, 1800–1830 (Lexington, Ky., 1976), 15–18, for the origin of Andover and its relationship to the American Board. Before Boudinot could begin his training, however, he suffered a recurrence of his old illness and returned to the Cherokee Nation. *Report of the American Board*, 77.

[12]The *Boston Recorder* was a Congregationalist magazine published by two Boston businessmen, Nathaniel Willis and Sidney E. Morse. It carried religious news in addition to articles on foreign and domestic politics, education, agriculture, temperance, and other secular subjects.

[13]Willis and Morse.

[14]The fate of this particular society is uncertain, but the Cherokees established a number of other similar organizations. As editor of the *Cherokee Phoenix*, Boudinot published constitutions of the Brainerd Cherokee Book Society, the Cherokee Temperance Society, and the Missionary Society. An editorial note mentioned "several societies for the spread of religion and morality." *Phoenix*, Sept. 4, 1829; Sept. 30, 1829; Oct. 8, 1830. The female students at Brainerd mission established a missionary society and sent the proceeds from their sewing to the American Board in order to aid the spread of Christianity. Nancy Reece to Rev. David Green, n.d. (probably 1828), John Howard Payne Papers, Newberry Library, Chicago, Ill. Black slaves owned by Cherokees organized the Wills Valley Benevolent Society, which made contributions to the American Colonization Society. William Chamberlain to R. R. Gurley, Mar. 19, 1830, June 7, 1831, Records of the American Colonization Society, Library of Congress, Washington, D. C.

[15]The *Journal of Humanity; and Herald of the American Temperance Society*, published in Andover, Mass., focused on temperance but included other material intended to encourage morality.

[16]Elias Cornelius was an agent of the American Board of Commissioners for Foreign Missions. He recruited Elias Boudinot for the Foreign Mission School and escorted him to Cornwall. He later became corresponding secretary of the board.

[17]In 1802 the state of Georgia agreed to relinquish western lands included in the colonial charter in exchange for a promise by the United States to extinguish Indian land titles within the state at some unspecified future time. In the 1820s Georgia began agitating for immediate execution of the agreement. Attention focused first on the Creeks, who lived in the western part of the state, and in 1827 the Creeks ceded land within Georgia's boundaries. The Creek cession occurred in the same year the Cherokees established a constitutional republic, and the state of Georgia was free to devote its time to this presumed violation of sovereignty. The state called on the federal government to act, but the first move by the United States was rather indirect. In 1828 the United States negotiated a treaty with the Arkansas Cherokees, who had moved west in 1808–10 and 1817–19 following land cessions, whereby they would move still farther west to a "permanent home." Article eight of the treaty provided that the federal government would furnish each Cherokee head of household who resided in one of the states east of the Mississippi a rifle, blanket, kettle, five pounds of tobacco, and compensation for his property if he enrolled for emigration to this new Cherokee homeland. The

government also promised to pay the cost of transportation to the west and upkeep for one year after arrival. If a person took four others with him, he was to be paid $50 "provided he and they shall have emigrated from within the Chartered limits of the State of Georgia." Kappler, 2: 288–92. In an editorial in the *Phoenix*, Boudinot noted that the language guaranteeing Cherokee title to this territory was almost identical to that in a 1792 treaty. Since a number of cessions had followed that particular treaty, Boudinot wondered: "What is then the security of this *new, last,* and *permanent* home of our brethren?" He also predicted that few Cherokees would enroll. *Phoenix*, July 9, 1828.

[18]In the fall of 1827 the Georgia legislature passed a series of resolutions that charged that the federal government had violated the compact of 1802 and asserted sole jurisdiction over Cherokees within the state. *Acts of Georgia* (1827), 236–49. In Dec. 1828, Georgia annexed Cherokee territory, extended Georgia law over whites (effective immediately) and Cherokees (effective June 1, 1830) living in that territory, and prohibited Cherokees from testifying in cases involving whites. *Acts of Georgia* (1828), 88–89. See Carl Jackson Vipperman, "Wilson Lumpkin and Cherokee Removal" (M.A. thesis, Univ. of Georgia, 1961), and "'Forcibly if We Must.'"

[19]The *American Annals of Education*, published in Boston, championed such unorthodox programs as physical education, normal schools, and the lyceum movement and printed articles on foreign educational methods and systems. Founded in 1826 by William Russell, it was the first important education journal in America.

[20]Sequoyah was born about 1770 in a village on the Litte Tennessee River. He later moved to Willstown in present-day Alabama. He apparently began his work on an alphabet about 1809. His efforts were interrupted by the Creek War of 1813–14, in which he served, and treaty negotiations in 1816, which culminated in the cession of land in Alabama. In 1818 Sequoyah moved to Arkansas and resumed his work. In 1821 he abandoned earlier attempts to design a character for each word and instead devised a symbol for each syllable. These symbols could be combined to make various words. After he adopted this method, Sequoyah reportedly completed the 86-symbol syllabary in about one month. He introduced this method of writing to Cherokees in Arkansas and then traveled east to teach it to citizens of the Cherokee Nation in 1822 or 1823. In 1824 the eastern Council honored Sequoyah with a medal, and he returned to his home in Arkansas. In 1828 Sequoyah, using his English name, George Guess, signed the treaty that ceded Cherokee land in Arkansas, and he moved with those Cherokees into what is today northeastern Oklahoma. He helped reconcile these Old Settlers and the Cherokees who arrived in 1839 after the final cession of Cherokee land in the east. In 1842 Sequoyah left the Cherokee Nation to search for still another group of Cherokees who reportedly were living in Mexico, and he died while on this quest. The earliest written account of Sequoyah's work appeared in the *Phoenix*, Aug. 13, 1828. Jack Frederick Kilpatrick has reprinted this article along with material from the Wahnenauhi manuscript, which was written in the Sequoyah syllabary by Lucy Keys about 1889, and other sources in *Sequoyah of Earth and Intellect* (Austin, 1965). Biographies of Sequoyah

include George E. Foster, *Sequoyah, The American Cadmus and Modern Moses* (Philadelphia, 1885), and Grant Foreman, *Sequoyah* (Norman, Okla., 1938).

[21]This introduction presumably was written by the editor, William C. Woolbridge, who had requested information about Sequoyah from Boudinot.

[22]Samuel Lorenzo Knapp, author of *Lectures on American Literature, With Remarks on Some Passages of American History* (New York, 1827), had met Sequoyah while he was in Washington negotiating cession of the Arkansas territory. Boudinot reprinted Knapp's lecture on Sequoyah in the *Phoenix*, July 29, 1829. It is interesting and revealing that Boudinot relied on the account of a white man for information about Sequoyah and that he does not mention the sketch written specifically for the *Phoenix* by a correspondent identified only as "G. C."

[23]"Sequoyah" may not be a Cherokee name but rather a name derived from some other language. Kilpatrick, 5. His English name is sometimes spelled Gist or Guist.

[24]John Rogers was also an Arkansas Cherokee and a signer of the Treaty of 1828.

[25]Scholars have long speculated about Sequoyah's lineage. His father may have been George Gist, an itinerant German peddler (see Foster, 12–23) or Col. Nathaniel Gist of the Continental Army (see Foremam, *Sequoyah*, 75–6). His paternity has been of less concern to Cherokees, whose kinship system is matrilineal (see Kilpatrick, 6).

[26]In 1791, combined force of Delawares, Miamis, and Shawnees defeated Gen. Arthur St. Clair in the Ohio valley. The implication that Sequoyah participated is probably apocryphal.

[27]The origin of Sequoyah's lameness is uncertain. He may, in fact, have been crippled from birth.

[28]Echota.

[29]He supposedly began work on a method of writing Cherokee about 1809.

[30]This occurred in 1821.

[31]Sequoyah actually developed the syllabary in Arkansas and then returned to the Cherokee Nation to teach it to his eastern tribesmen.

[32]John Ross was principal chief of the Cherokee Nation from 1827 until his death in 1866. See Rachel Caroline Eaton, *John Ross and the Cherokee Indians* (Chicago, 1921); and Moulton, *John Ross*.

[33]The fact that many Cherokees had mastered the Sequoyah syllabary before Boudinot knew of its existence indicates how very far removed he was from most of his countrymen.

[34]Sequoyah may have been "viewed with an eye of suspicion" because of his previous involvement in land cession. If so, the suspicion was well founded because in 1828 he signed another cession which promised him $500.

[35]The primary purpose of "An Address to the Whites" (1826), reprinted below, and the lecture tour during which it was delivered was to raise money for the press and types.

[36]Samuel Austin Worcester, a missionary of the American Board, served the Cherokees from 1825 until his death in 1859. He became Boudinot's friend and collaborator. They worked together on the Cherokee language

and on translations of the New Testament, hymnals, and religious tracts. Worcester often contributed to the *Cherokee Phoenix*, and his letters have been annotated and published in Jack Frederick Kilpatrick and Anna Gritts Kilpatrick, *New Echota Letters: Contributions of Samuel A. Worcester to the Cherokee Phoenix* (Dallas, 1968). For a biography, see Althea Bass.

[37]Most missionaries and some of the more highly acculturated Cherokees had difficulty accepting a system of writing devised by an illiterate native speaker. They tended to favor the orthography developed by John Pickering, a noted philologist whom the American Board had employed. The vast majority of Cherokees, however, would have nothing to do with Pickering's grammar. Consequently, Worcester and others began to urge acceptance of the Sequoyah syllabary. Worcester wrote: "Whether or not the impression of the Cherokees is correct, in regard to the superiority of their own alphabet for their own use, that impression they have, and it is not easy to be eradicated. It would be a vain attempt to persuade them to relinquish their own method of writing." *Missionary Herald*, July 1827.

[38]According to the census of 1835 (Henderson Roll), 18 percent of the households in the Cherokee Nation contained people who read English, 43 percent had Cherokee readers, and 39 percent claimed no literate members in either language. Record Group 75, National Archives, Washington, D. C.

An Address
to the
Whites
Delivered in the First Presbyterian Church,
on the 26th of May, 1826,

by Elias Boudinott,
A Cherokee Indian

PHILADELPHIA:
Printed by William F. Geddes
1826

« « « In October 1825 the Cherokee Council appointed Elias Boudinot as an agent "to solicit and receive donations in money from individuals, or societies throughout the United States, for the object of establishing and supporting a national academy, and for procuring two sets of types to fit one press, to establish a printing office at New Town, (C. N.) one set of types to be composed of English letters, the other of Cherokee characters, the invention of George Guist, a Cherokee." As remuneration, the agent received 8 percent of the amount collected.

Boudinot embarked on his journey early in 1826. He made his appeal for funds in many American cities, including Charleston, Philadelphia, and Boston, and his appearances were widely publicized and well attended. The *Boston Recorder* (April 21, 1826) commented, "This young man was about four years in the Foreign Mission School at Cornwall, where he made commendable progress in knowledge," and reported that in one week Boudinot spoke in Salem on Sunday, and at two different Boston churches on Monday and Wednesday. While he was in Philadelphia, Boudinot published the text of his speech as a pamphlet entitled "An Address to the Whites." The pamphlet, he hoped, would reach more people than he could personally and would encourage them to support the "civilization" of the Cherokees. Financially, Boudinot's tour was successful enough to permit the purchase of a press for $1,500, but the national academy did not materialize until after removal.

In "An Address to the Whites," Boudinot chronicled his people's progress along the road to "civilization," a course that had been charted for them when the U. S. government was in its infancy. For the development of this policy, see Francis Paul Prucha, *American Indian Policy in the Formative Years: The Indian Trade and Intercourse Acts, 1790–1834* (Cambridge, Mass., 1962). Two important works which analyze the white attitudes toward Indians that helped shape the "civilization" program are Roy Harvey Pearce, *The Savages of America: A Study of the Indian and the Idea of Civilization* (Baltimore, 1953), and Robert F. Berkhofer, Jr., *The White Man's Indian: Images of the American Indian from Columbus to the Present* (New York, 1979). Philanthropists and missionaries played a major role in the "civilization" of the Indians. In *Seeds of Extinction: Jeffersonian Philanthropy and the American Indian* (Chapel Hill, N. C., 1973), Bernard W. Sheehan examined the early nineteenth-century belief that the Indian could and should be "civilized" and related that belief to the removal policy. Robert F. Berkhofer, Jr., demonstrated that Protestant missions involved the "civilization" of Indians who, in order to be accepted into church membership, had to abandon aboriginal customs in *Salvation and the Savages: An Analysis of Protestant Missions and American Indian Response, 1787-1862* (Lexington, Ky., 1965).

For histories of denominational work among the Cherokees, see related chapters in Edmund Schwarze, *History of the Moravian Missions among Southern Indian Tribes of the United States* (Bethlehem, Pa., 1923); John A. Andrew III, *Rebuilding the Christian Commonwealth: New England Congregationalists and Foreign Missions, 1800-1830* (Lexington, Ky., 1976); and William Ellsworth Strong, *The Story of the American Board* (New York, 1969). The most successful American Board mission is the subject of Robert Sparks Walker, *Torchlights to the Cherokees: The Brainerd Mission* (New York, 1931), and Theda Perdue, "Letters from Brainerd," *Journal of Cherokee Studies* 4 (1979): 4–9. Althea Bass has written a biography of the missionary who was Boudinot's friend and collaborator, *Cherokee Messenger: A Life of Samuel Austin Worcester* (Norman, Okla., 1936).

ADDRESS, &c.

To those who are unacquainted with the manners, habits, and improvements of the Aborigines of this country, the term *Indian* is pregnant with ideas the most repelling and degrading. But such impressions, originating as they frequently do, from infant prejudices, although they hold too true when applied to some, do great injustice to many of this race of beings.

Some there are, perhaps even in this enlightened assembly,

who at the bare sight of an Indian, or at the mention of the name, would throw back their imaginations to ancient times, to the ravages of savage warfare, to the yells pronounced over the mangled bodies of women and children, thus creating an opinion, inapplicable and highly injurious to those for whose temporal interest and eternal welfare, I come to plead.

What is an Indian? Is he not formed of the same materials with yourself? For "of one blood God created all the nations that dwell on the face of the earth."[1] Though it be true that he is ignorant, that he is a heathen, that he is a savage; yet he is no more than all others have been under similar circumstances. Eighteen centuries ago what were the inhabitants of Great Britain?

You here behold an *Indian*, my kindred are *Indians*, and my fathers sleeping in the wilderness grave—they too were *Indians*. But I am not as my fathers were—broader means and nobler influences have fallen upon me. Yet I was not born as thousands are, in a stately dome and amid the congratulations of the great, for on a little hill, in a lonely cabin, overspread by the forest oak, I first drew my breath; and in a language unknown to learned and polished nations, I learnt to lisp my fond mother's name. In after days, I have had greater advantages than most of my race; and I now stand before you delegated by my native country to seek her interest, to labour for her respectability, and by my public efforts to assist in raising her to an equal standing with other nations of the earth.

The time has arrived when speculations and conjectures as to the practicability of civilizing the Indians must forever cease. A period is fast approaching when the stale remark—"Do what you will, an Indian will still be an Indian," must be placed no more in speech. With whatever plausibility this popular objection may have heretofore been made, every candid mind must now be sensible that it can no longer be uttered, except by those who are uninformed with respect to us, who are strongly prejudiced against us, or who are filled with vindictive feelings towards us; for the present history of the Indians, particularly of that nation to which I belong, most incontrovertibly establishes the fallacy of this remark. I am aware of the difficulties which have ever existed to Indian civilization, I do not deny the almost insurmountable obstacles which we ourselves have thrown in the way of this improvement, nor do I say that difficulties no longer remain; but facts will permit me to declare that there are none which may not easily be overcome, by strong and continued exertions. It needs not abstract reasoning to prove this position. It needs not the display of language to prove to the minds of good men, that Indians are susceptible of attainments necessary to the formation of polished society. It needs not the power of argument on the nature of man, to silence forever the remark that "it is the purpose of the Almighty that the Indians should be exterminated." It needs only that the world should know what we have done in the few last years, to foresee what yet we may do with the assistance of our white brethren, and that of the common Parent of us all.

It is not necessary to present to you a detailed account of the various aboriginal tribes, who have been known to you only on the pages of history, and there but obscurely known. They have gone; and to revert back to their days would be only to disturb their oblivious sleep; to darken these walls with deeds at which humanity must shudder; to place before your eyes the scenes of Muskingum Sahta-goo[2] and the plains of Mexico, to call up the crimes of the bloody Cortes and his infernal host; and to describe the animosity and vengeance which have overthrown, and hurried into the shades of death those numerous tribes. But here let me say, that however guilty these unhappy nations may have been, yet many and unreasonable were the wrongs they suffered, many the hardships they endured, and many their wanderings through the trackless wilderness. Yes, "notwithstanding the obloquy with which the early historians of the colonies have overshadowed the character of the ignorant and unfortunate natives, some bright gleams will occasionally break through, that throw a melancholy lustre on their memories. Facts are occasionally to be met with in their rude annals, which, though recorded with all the colouring of prejudice and bigotry, yet speak for themselves, and will be dwelt upon with applause and sympathy when prejudice shall have passed away."[3]

Nor is it my purpose to enter largely into the consideration of the remnants, of those who have fled with time and are no more—. They stand as monuments of the Indian's fate. And should they ever become extinct, they must move off the earth, as did their fathers. My design is to offer a few disconnected facts relative to the present improved state, and to the ultimate prospects of that particular tribe called Cherokees to which I belong.

The Cherokee nation lies within the charted limits of the states of Georgia, Tennessee, and Alabama.[4] Its extent as defined by treaties is about 200 miles in length from East to West, and about 120 in breadth. This country which is supposed to contain about 10,000,000 of acres exhibits great varieties of surface, the most part being hilly and mountaneous, affording soil of no value. The vallies, however, are well watered and afford excellent land, in many parts particularly on the large streams, that of the first quality. The climate is temperate and healthy, indeed I would not be guilty of exaggeration were I to say, that the advantages which this country possesses to render it salubrious, are many and superior. Those lofty and barren mountains, defying the labour and ingenuity of man, and supposed by some as placed there only to exhibit omnipotence, contribute to the healthiness and beauty of the surrounding plains, and give to us that free air and pure water which distinguish our country. These advantages, calculated to make the inhabitants healthy, vigorous, and intelligent, cannot fail to cause this country to become interesting. And there can be no doubt that the Cherokee Nation, however obscure and trifling it may now appear, will finally become, if not under its present occupants, one of the Garden spots of America. And here, let me be indulged in the fond wish, that she may thus become under those who now possess her; and ever be fostered, regulated and protected by the generous government of the United States.

The population of the Cherokee Nation increased from the year 1810 to that of 1824, 2000 exclusive of those who emigrated in 1818 and 19 to the west of the Mississippi—of those who reside on the Arkansas the number is supposed to be about 5000.[5]

The rise of these people in their movement towards civilization, may be traced as far back as the relinquishment of their towns; when game became incompetent to their support, by reason of the surrounding white population.[6] They then betook themselves to the woods, commenced the opening of small clearings, and the raising of stock; still however following the chase. Game has since become so scarce that little dependence for subsistence can be placed upon it. They have gradually and I could almost say universally forsaken their ancient employment.[7] In fact, there is not a single family in the nation, that can be said to subsist on the slender support which the wilderness would afford. The love and the practice of hunting are not now carried to a higher degree, than among all frontier people whether white or red. It cannot be doubted, however, that there are many who have commenced a life of agricultural labour from mere necessity, and if they could, would gladly resume their former course of living. But these are individual failings and ought to be passed over.

On the other hand it cannot be doubted that the nation is improving, rapidly improving in all those particulars which must finally constitute the inhabitants an industrious and intelligent people.

It is a matter of surprise to me, and must be to all those who are properly acquainted with the condition of the Aborigines of this country, that the Cherokees have advanced so far and so rapidly in civilization. But there are yet powerful obstacles, both within and without, to be surmounted in the march of improvement. The prejudices in regard to them in the general community are strong and lasting. The evil effects of their intercourse with their immediate white neighbours, who differ from them chiefly in name, are easily to be seen, and it is evident that from this intercourse proceed those demoralizing practices which in order to surmount, peculiar and unremitting efforts are necessary. In defiance, however, of these obstacles the Cherokees have improved and are still rapidly improving. To give you a futher view of their condition, I will here repeat some of the articles of the two statistical tables taken at different periods.

In 1810 there were 19,500 cattle; 6,100 horses; 19,600 swine; 1,037 sheep; 467 looms; 1,600 spinning wheels; 30 waggons; 500 ploughs; 3 saw-mills; 13 grist-mills &c. At this time there are 22,000 cattle; 7,600 horses; 46,000 swine; 2,500 sheep; 762 looms; 2,488 spinning wheels; 172 waggons; 2,943 ploughs; 10 saw-mills; 31 grist-mills; 62 Blacksmith-shops; 8 cotton machines; 18 schools; 18 ferries; and a number of public roads. In one district there were, last winter, upwards of 0000 volumes of good books; and 11 different periodical papers both religious and political, which were taken and read. On the public roads there are many decent Inns, and few houses for convenience, &c., would disgrace any country. Most of the schools are under the care and tuition of christian missionaries, of different denominations,[8] who have been of great service to the nation, by inculcating moral and religious principles into the minds of the rising generation. In many places the word of God is regularly preached and explained, both by missionaries and natives; and there are numbers who have publicly professed their belief and interest in the merits of the great Saviour of the world.[9] It is worthy of remark, that in no ignorant country have the missionaries undergone less trouble and difficulty, in spreading a knowledge of the Bible, than in this. Here, they have been welcomed and encouraged by the proper authorities of the nation,[10] their persons have been protected, and in very few instances have some individual vagabonds threatened violence to them.[11] Indeed it may be said with truth, that among no heathen people has the faithful minister of God experienced greater success, greater reward for his labour, than in this. He is surrounded by attentive hearers, the words which flow from his lips are not spent in vain. The Cherokees have had no established religion of their own,[12] and perhaps to this circumstance we may attribute, in part, the facilities with which missionaries have pursued their ends.[13] They cannot be called idolators; for they never worshipped Images. They believed in a Supreme Being, the Creator of all, the God of the white, the red, and the black man. They also believed in the existence of an evil spirit who resided, as thought, in the setting sun, the future place of all who in their life time had done iniquitously. Their prayers were addressed alone to the Supreme Being, and which if written would fill a large volume, and display much sincerity, beauty and sublimity.[14] When the ancient customs of the Cherokees were in their full force, no warrior thought himself secure, unless he had addressed his guardian angel; no hunter could hope for success, unless before the rising sun he had asked the assistance of his God, and on his return at eve he had offered his sacrifice to him.[15]

There are three things of late occurance, which must certainly place the Cherokee Nation in a fair light, and act as a powerful argument in favor of Indian improvement.

First. The invention of letters.

Second. The translation of the New Testament into Cherokee.

And third. The organization of a Government.

The Cherokee mode of writing lately invented by George Guest, who could not read any language nor speak any other than his own, consists of eighty-six characters, principally syllabic, the combinations of which form all the words of the language. Their terms may be greatly simplified, yet they answer all the purpose of writing, and already many natives use them.[16]

The translation of the New Testament, together with Guest's mode of writing, has swept away that barrier which has long existed, and opened a spacious channel for the instruction of adult Cherokees.[17] Persons of all ages and classes may now read the precepts of the Almighty in their own language. Before it is long, there will scarcely be an individual in the nation who can say, "I know not God neither understand I what thou sayest," for all shall know him from the greatest to the least. The aged warrior over whom has rolled three score and ten years of savage life, will grace the temple of God with his hoary head; and the little child yet on the breast of its pious mother shall learn to lisp its Maker's name.

The shrill sound of the Savage yell shall die away as the roaring of far distant thunder; and the Heaven wrought music will gladden the affrighted wilderness. "The solitary places will be glad for them, and the desert shall rejoice and blossom as a rose."[18] Already do we see the morning star, forerunner of approaching dawn, rising over the tops of those deep forests in which for ages have echoed the warrior's whoop. But has not God said it, and will he not do it? The Almighty decrees his purposes, and man cannot with all his ingenuity and device countervail them. They are more fixed in their course than the rolling sun—more durable than the everlasting mountains.

The Government, though defective in many respects, is well suited to the condition of the inhabitants. As they rise in information and refinement, changes in it must follow, until they arrive at that state of advancement, when I trust they will be admitted into all the privileges of the American family.[19]

The Cherokee Nation is divided into eight districts, in each of which are established courts of justice, where all disputed cases are decided by a Jury, under the direction of a circuit Judge, who has jurisdiction over two districts. Sheriffs and other publice officers are appointed to execute the decisions of the courts, collect debts, and arrest thieves and other criminals.[20] Appeals may be taken to the Superior Court, held annually at the seat of Government.[21] The Legislative authority is vested in a General Court, which consists of the National Committee and Council. The National Committee consists of thirteen members, who are generally men of sound sense and fine talents. The National Council consists of thirty-two members, beside the speaker, who act as the representatives of the people.[22] Every bill passing these two bodies, becomes the law of the land.[23] Clerks are appointed to do the writings, and record the proceedings of the Council. The executive power is vested in two principal chiefs, who hold their office during good behaviour, and sanction all the decisions of the legislative council. Many of the laws display some degree of civilization, and establish the respectability of the nation.

Polygamy is abolished.[24] Female chastity and honor are protected by law.[25] The Sabbath is respected by the Council during session. Mechanics are encouraged by law.[26] The practice of putting aged persons to death for witchcraft is abolished[27] and murder has now become a governmental crime.[28]

From what I have said, you will form but a faint opinion of the true state and prospects of the Cherokees. You will, however, be convinced of three important truths.

First, that the means which have been employed for the christianization and civilization of this tribe, have been greatly blessed. Second, that the increase of these means will meet with final success. Third, that it has now become necessary, that efficient and more than ordinary means should be employed.

Sensible of this last point, and wishing to do something for themselves, the Cherokees have thought it advisable that there should be established, a Printing Press and a Seminary of respectable character; and for these purposes your aid and patronage are now solicited. They wish the types, as expressed in their resolution, to be composed of English letters and Cherokee characters. Those characters have now become extensively used in the nation; their religious songs are written in them; there is an astonishing eagerness in people of all classes and ages to acquire a knowledge of them; and the New Testament has been translated into their language. All this impresses on them the immediate necessity of procuring types. The most informed and judicious of our nation, believe that such a press would go further to remove ignorance, and her offspring superstition and prejudice, than all other means. The adult part of the nation will probably grovel on in ignorance and die in ignorance, without any fair trial upon them, unless the proposed means are carried into effect. The simplicity of this method of writing, and the eagerness to obtain a knowledge of it, are evinced by the astonishing rapidity with which it is acquired, and by the number who do so. It is about two years since its introduction, and already there are a great many who can read it. In the neighborhood in which I live, I do not recollect a male Cherokee, between the ages of fifteen and twenty five, who is ignorant of this mode of writing. But in connexion with those for Cherokee characters, it is necessary to have types for English letters. There are many who already speak and read the English language, and can appreciate the advantages which would result from the publication of their laws and transactions in a well conducted newspaper. Such a paper, comprising a summary of religious and political events, &c. on the one hand; and on the other, exhibiting the feelings, disposition, improvements, and prospects of the Indians; their traditions, their true character, as it once was and as it now is; the ways and means most likely to throw the mantle of civilization over all tribes; and such other matter as will tend to diffuse proper and correct impressions in regard to their condition—such a paper could not fail to create much interest in the American community, favourable to the aborigines, and to have a powerful influence on the advancement of the Indians themselves. How can the patriot or the philanthropist devise efficient means, without full and correct information as to the subjects of his labour. And I am inclined to think, after all that has been said of the aborigines, after all that has been written in narratives, professedly to elucidate the leading traits of their character, that the public knows little of that character. To obtain a correct and complete knowledge of these people, there must exist a vehicle of Indian intelligence, altogether different from those which have heretofore been employed. Will not a paper published in an Indian country, under proper and judicious regulations, have the desired effect? I do not say that Indians will produce learned and elaborate dissertations in explanation and vindication of their own character; but they may exhibit specimens of their intellectual efforts, of their eloquence, of their moral, civil and physical advancement, which will do quite as much to remove prejudice and to give profitable information.

The Cherokees wish to establish their Seminary, upon a footing which will insure to it all the advantages, that belong to such institutions in the states.[29] Need I spend one moment in arguments, in favour of such an institution; need I speak one word of the utility, of the necessity, of an institution of learning; need I do more than simply to ask the patronage of benevolent hearts, to obtain that patronage.

When before did a nation of Indians step forward and ask for the means of civilization? The Cherokee authorities have adopted the measures already stated, with a sincere desire to make their nation an intelligent and virtuous people,[30] and with a full hope that those who have already pointed out to them the road of happiness, will now assist them to pursue it. With that assistance, what are the prospects of the Cherokees? Are they not indeed glorious, compared to that deep darkness in which the nobler qualities of their souls have slept. Yes, methinks I can view my native country, rising from the ashes of her degradation, wearing her purified and beautiful garments, and taking her seat with the nations of the earth. I can behold her sons bursting the fetters of ignorance and unshackling her from the vices of heathenism. She is at this instant, risen like the first morning sun, which grows brighter and brighter, until it reaches its fulness of glory.

She will become not a great, but a faithful ally of the United States.[31] In times of peace she will plead the common liberties of

America. In times of war her intrepid sons will sacrifice their lives in your defence. And because she will be useful to you in coming time, she asks you to assist her in her present struggles. She asks not for greatness; she seeks not wealth; she pleads only for assistance to become respectable as a nation, to enlighten and ennoble her sons, and to ornament her daughters with modesty and virtue. She pleads for this assistance, too, because on her destiny hangs that of many nations. If she complete her civilization—then may we hope that all our nations will—then, indeed, may true patriots be encouraged in their efforts to make this world of the West, one continuous abode of enlightened, free and happy people.

But if the Cherokee Nation fail in her struggle, if she die away, then all hopes are blasted, and falls the fabric of Indian civilization. Their fathers were born in darkness, and have fled in darkness; without your assistance so will their sons. You see, however, where the probability rests. Is there a soul whose narrowness will not permit the exercise of charity on such an occasion? Where is he that can withhold his mite from an object so noble? Who can prefer a little of his silver and gold, to the welfare of nations of his fellow beings? Human wealth perishes with our clay, but that wealth gained in charity still remains on earth, to enrich our names, when we are gone, and will be remembered in Heaven, when the miser and his coffers have mouldered together in their kindred earth. The works of a generous mind sweeten the cup of affiction; they enlighten the dreary way to the cold tomb; they blunt the sting of death, and smooth his passage to the unknown world. When all the kingdoms of this earth shall die away and their beauty and power shall perish, his name shall live and shine as a twinkling star; those for whose benefit he done his deeds of charity shall call him blessed, and they shall add honor to his immortal head.

There are, with regard to the Cherokees and other tribes, two alternatives; they must either become civilized and happy, or sharing the fate of many kindred nations, become extinct. If the General Government continue its protection, and the American people assist them in their humble efforts, they will, they must rise. Yes, under such protection, and with such assistance, the Indian must rise like the Phoenix, after having wallowed for ages in ignorance and barbarity. But should this Government withdraw its care, and the American people their aid, then, to use the words of a writer,[32] "they will go the way that so many tribes have gone before them; for the hordes that still linger about the shores of Huron, and the tributary streams of the Mississippi, will share the fate of those tribes that once lorded it along the proud banks of the Hudson; of that gigantic race that are said to have existed on the borders of the Susquehanna; of those various nations that flourished about the Potomac and the Rhappahannoc, and that peopled the forests of the vast valley of Shenandoah. They will vanish like a vapour from the face of the earth, their very history will be lost in forgetfulness, and the places that now know them will know them no more."

There is, in Indian history, something very melancholy, and which seems to establish a mournful precedent for the future events of the few sons of the forest, now scattered over this vast continent. We have seen every where the poor aborigines melt away before the white population. I merely speak of the fact, without at all referring to the cause. We have seen, I say, one family after another, one tribe after another, nation after nation, pass away; until only a few solitary creatures are left to tell the sad story of extinction.

Shall this precedent be followed? I ask you, shall red men live, or shall they be swept from the earth? With you and this public at large, the decision chiefly rests. Must they perish? Must they all, like the unfortunate Creeks, (victims of the unchristian policy of certain persons,) go down in sorrow to their grave?[33]

They hang upon your mercy as to a garment. Will you push them from you, or will you save them? Let humanity answer.

NOTES

[1]Acts 17:26.

[2]In 1782 about 100 Christian Delawares who had settled on the Muskingum River in eastern Ohio were massacred by whites.

[3]This quotation is from Washington Irving, "Traits of Indian Character," *The Analectic Magazine*, Feb. 1814, pp. 145–56.

[4]Territory west of the Little Tennessee River in North Carolina was also a part of the Cherokee Nation. Boudinot may have omitted this section accidentally because it was remote and constituted only a small fraction of the

Nation's land and people. On the other hand, this particular part of the Cherokee Nation was inhabited by the most conservative Cherokees, of whom Boudinot strongly disapproved.

[5]Return J. Meigs, the U.S. Agent for the Cherokees, conducted a census in 1810. The manuscript is located in the Moravian Archives, Winston-Salem, N. C. In 1824 the Cherokee Council authorized a census. *Laws*, 43–44; *Cherokee Phoenix*, June 18, 1828. No census was available for the Arkansas Cherokees.

[6]During the 18th century, wars involving Cherokees forced many people to leave their traditional towns, which no longer afforded protection. Invasions by the British in the French and Indian War and the colonists in the American Revolution destroyed scores of towns, many of which were either relocated or abandoned. Early U.S. Indian policy encouraged the Cherokees to disband their traditional towns and build isolated homesteads. McDowell, 246–47, 249, 256–57; John Howard Payne Papers, 9:53, Newberry Library, Chicago, Ill. Also see Smith, 46–60; Douglas C. Wilms, "Cherokee Settlement Patterns in Nineteenth-Century Georgia," *Southeastern Geographer* 14 (1974): 46–53.

[7]Boudinot may be referring to the decline of the deerskin trade in the late 18th century or he may have believed that the Cherokees had been nomadic hunters before European contact. In reality, agriculture was at least as important as hunting in the aboriginal Cherokee economy and dictated a relatively stationary existence. For aboriginal agriculture, see Hudson, 289–300; and G. Melvin Herndon, "Indian Agriculture in the Southern Colonies," *North Carolina Historical Review* 44 (1967): 283–97. For 19th-century agriculture, see Douglas C. Wilms, "Cherokee Land Use in the State of Georgia, 1800–1838" (Ph.D. diss., Univ. of Georgia, 1972).

[8]Moravians, Presbyterians (American Board missionaries, many of whom were Congregationalists, affiliated with the Tennessee synod), Baptists, and Methodists ministered to the Cherokees.

[9]When Boudinot delivered his address, probably fewer than 5 percent of the Cherokees were Christians. By 1830 over 7 percent had converted, and in 1835 the proportion of Christians stood at about 9 percent. *Phoenix*, May 8, 1830; McLoughlin and Conser, 702.

[10]The promise of English schools and not Christian churches prompted the Cherokees to welcome missionaries. When the Moravians delayed the opening of their school, the chiefs threatened expulsion. Fries, 6:2721–22.

[11]The most serious incident of antimission sentiment occurred at Etowah (Hightower) in 1824. The local chiefs requested the recall of a blacksmith and a minister/teacher supported by the American Board. The chiefs charged that the blacksmith asked exhorbitant prices for inferior work, that a Christian slaveholder could not control his non-Christian slaves, that converts cast spells with hymns about damnation, and that the minister forbade Christians to gather in the townhouse. The Cherokee national government refused to withdraw the missionaries and organized opposition to Christianity subsided. McLoughlin, "Cherokee Anti-Mission Sentiment." Isolated incidents, both direct and indirect, continued to threaten mission work. Isaac Proctor to Jeremiah Evarts, July 28, 1827, Journal of Daniel Butrick, Sept. 8,

1830, Records of the American Board of Commissioners for Foreign Missions, Houghton Library, Harvard University, Cambridge, Mass.

[12]This statement is simply not true. See Charles Hudson, "The Cherokee Concept of Natural Balance," *Indian Historian* 3 (1970): 51–54; Mooney, *Myths*; Rennard Strickland, *Fire and the Spirits: Cherokee Law From Clan to Court* (Norman, Okla., 1975).

[13]Missionaries actually experienced great difficulty in converting the Cherokees. The Moravians had worked among the Cherokees for nine years before gaining their first convert. In four years of intensive missionary effort, the American Board counted only 14 Indian church members. Other denominations had similar results. The most successful were the Methodists, who recruited hundreds of members at camp meetings in the summer of 1830. It may be coincidental, but this wave of revivalism occurred at the same time that the state of Georgia began enforcing her oppressive laws over the Cherokees. Malone, 91-117.

[14]Boudinot was so thoroughly Christianized that he did not understand the religion of his own people. The Cherokees did not believe in a "Supreme Being" or an "evil spirit." In his introduction to *Sacred Formulas*, the 19th-century anthropologist James Mooney wrote: "It is evident from a study of these formulas that the Cherokee Indian was a polytheist and that the spirit world was to him only a shadowy counterpart of this. All his prayers were for temporal and tangible blessings—for health, for long life, for success in the chase, in fishing, in war and in love, for good crops, for protection and for revenge. He had no great spirit, no happy hunting ground, no heaven, no hell, and consequently death had for him no terrors and he awaited the inevitable end with no anxiety as to the future" (319). The Cherokees invoked a number of spirits in their formulas, including "the apportioner" or the sun, "Long Man" or the river, and "Red Man" who was associated with thunder (340–42).

[15]The warrior invoked red spirits who lived in the east and governed power, triumph, and success. The hunter appealed to fire and water as well as to Tsu'l'kalû', a mythical giant who owned all the game. A hunter always cast bloodstained leaves into the river and a piece of meat into the fire. Mooney, *Sacred Formulas*, 369–75, 388–91.

[16]See pp. 48-58.

[17]Boudinot is referring to the translation by David Brown and George Lowrey, which the Council commissioned in 1826. Since the Council authorized only one copy, the manuscript had to be passed from person to person. This made it unlikely that "persons of all ages may now read the precepts of the Almighty in their own language." Furthermore, the translation was so poor that Boudinot and Worcester soon undertook the task of producing a second Cherokee New Testament. *Laws*, 81.

[18]Isaiah 35:1.

[19]Boudinot did not mean assimilation. He believed that when the Cherokee government had reached a certain level of sophistication, the Cherokee people as a distinct political entity could enjoy the rights and privileges of other Americans.

[20]On Oct. 20, 1820, the National Committee and Council voted to divide

the Nation into districts and to establish a council house in each district "for the purpose of holding councils to administer justice in all causes and complaints that may be brought forward for trial." *Laws*, 11.

[21]In 1822 the legislature established a superior court composed of the district court judges "to determine all causes which may be appealed from the District Courts." Ibid., 28.

[22]In 1817 a Council composed of representatives of 54 towns delegated power to a Standing Committee of 13. The committee was supposed to manage the Nation's affairs when the Council was not in session and to submit its decisions to the Council for ratification. The Council continued to be an amorphous body composed of representatives of the towns until 1820, when the committee and Council apportioned four delegates to each judicial district. Frequently, the term "Council" is used to refer to both houses collectively. Ibid., 4–5, 14–15. The Constitution of 1827, which superceded the articles of government of 1817, provided for the election of two committeemen and three councilmen from each district. Ibid., 120.

[23]Bills also had to be approved by the two principal chiefs.

[24]In 1819 the committee and Council prohibited white men from taking more than one Indian wife and "recommended that all others should also have but one wife hereafter." Ibid., 10. In 1825, they amended this law "so that it should not be lawful hereafter, for any person or persons whatsoever, to have more than one wife." Ibid., 57.

[25]The law against rape and attempted rape was passed in 1825. A person convicted "for the first offence, shall be punished with fifty lashes upon the bare back, and the left ear cropped off close to the head; for the second offence, one hundred lashes and the other ear cut off; for the third offence, death." Ibid., 54.

[26]In 1819 the National Committee "unanimously agreed, that schoolmasters, blacksmiths, salt petre and gun powder manufacturers, ferrymen and turnpike keepers, and mechanics, are privileged to reside in the Cherokee Nation" if their employers procured a permit and accepted responsibility for their behavior. The committee also decided to allow blacksmiths, millers, ferrymen, and turnpike keepers "to improve and cultivate twelve acres of ground for the support of themselves and their families." Ibid., 5–6.

[27]Elderly people often were accused of witchcraft because the Cherokees believed that witches lived extraordinarily long lives by killing others, particularly children, and adding the years left in a normal lifespan to their own. Raymond D. Fogelson, "An Analysis of Cherokee Sorcery and Witchcraft" in *Four Centuries of Southern Indians*, ed. Charles M. Hudson (Athens, Ga., 1975), 119–20.

[28]Murderers traditionally had been punished by the relatives of their victims. See Reid, *A Law of Blood*; and Strickland, *Fire and the Spirits*.

[29]Boudinot is using the term "seminary" to mean public high school; the Cherokees had no intention of establishing a theological seminary. The Nation did not realize its goal of establishing a high school before removal. In their new nation in the west, however, they built two "seminaries," one for men and one for women, which opened in 1851.

[30]By "intelligent" and "virtuous," Boudinot means educated and Christian.

[31]He implies that the Cherokee Nation should be independent of the United States, which is consistent with his opposition to assimilation.

[32]Washington Irving. See n. 3.

[33]On Feb. 12, 1825, William McIntosh, a Creek chief, signed an unauthorized treaty that provided for land cession and removal of his tribe. The Creeks executed McIntosh and employed two Cherokees, John Ridge and David Vann, as secretaries and translators for a delegation that went to Washington to seek abrogation of the treaty. In 1826 the federal government renegotiated the land cession, which included all Creek land in Georgia except a small tract on the Alabama border. Gov. George M. Troup insisted that the original treaty was valid and ordered a survey of all Creek land in Georgia before the Creeks could vacate. In the spring of 1826, when Boudinot wrote these words, the Creeks were in severe straits and war seemed to be a distinct possibility. Furthermore, an attempt was underway to discredit the two Cherokees, who had proven to be shrewd negotiators, in order to deprive the Creeks, few of whom spoke English, of spokesmen of their choice. The next year, Col. Thomas L. McKenney, superintendent of Indian Affairs, refused to recognize the Cherokees as agents of the Creeks, and the Creeks gave up their remaining lands in Georgia. Ulrich B. Phillips, *Georgia and State Rights* (Washington, D. C., 1902), 61–65; Kenneth Coleman, ed., *A History of Georgia* (Athens, Ga., 1977), 130–31; Angie Debo, *The Road to Disappearance* (Norman, Okla., 1941), pp. 89–94: Wilkins, *Cherokee Tragedy*, 153–80.

Selections from the *Cherokee Phoenix*

« « « Boudinot's journey generated sufficient funds for the Cherokees to purchase a press. The General Council commissioned the Prudential Committee of the American Board to have types in the Sequoyah syllabary cast at a Boston foundry. The governing board of the missionary society also purchased with funds forwarded by the Cherokee government English types and a printing press, which originally were scheduled to arrive in the Nation in 1827. In anticipation of that event, the General Council at its meeting in the fall of 1826 appropriated $250 for the construction of a printing office in New Echota, the Nation's capital, and named the newspaper the *Cherokee Phoenix*. The Council appointed Isaac Harris, a white man, printer at a salary of $400 per year. An appropriation of $300 per year was made for the salary of an editor who would "translate matter in the Cherokee language," purchase supplies, manage the paper's finances, and apprentice a Cherokee youth to the printer in addition to fulfilling his normal editorial duties. When first offered the position, Boudinot declined because the Cherokee editor earned less than the white printer. The American Board agreed to supplement Boudinot's salary, however, and he accepted.

The Prudential Committee shipped the press and type by steamboat to Augusta, Georgia, in November 1827. From Augusta, they had to be transported by wagon over two hundred miles. Considering that the press, types, and furniture for the printing office weighed over a ton, it is not surprising that the shipment did not arrive at New Echota until early in 1828. Then the printer and his journeyman, John F. Wheeler, discovered that no paper had been sent, so Harris departed for Knoxville, Tennessee, to purchase a supply. His journey took about two weeks. In the meantime, Wheeler made cases for the type and with the assistance of John Candy, the Cherokee apprentice, began to familiarize himself with the Cherokee syllabary.

The prospectus for the *Cherokee Phoenix* had appeared in October 1827, and the first issue was published on February 21, 1828. Almost a year later, on February 11, 1829, the newspaper became the *Cherokee Phoenix and Indians' Advocate*. Boudinot borrowed heavily from other periodicals, a practice common among white newspapers of the day, in order to fill the columns of the *Phoenix* with articles on foreign affairs, U. S. news, and human interest stories. Cherokee material generally was limited to laws, documents, correspondence, and whatever local news Boudinot happened to hear. His editorials dealt primarily with Cherokee domestic matters or Indian-white relations; he rarely ventured comment on issues in which Indians were not involved.

The Council, which subsidized the paper, expected the editor of the *Phoenix* to express the dominant sentiments in the Nation. For this reason, Boudinot's growing support of Cherokee removal in the summer of 1832 led to his resignation on August 1. The paper continued until 1834, when the federal government's failure to pay annuities into the National treasury forced suspension of publication. In 1835, the Georgia Guard accompanied by Boudinot's brother, Stand Watie, seized the press and types in order to prevent Ross from using them to publicize his opposition to removal.

The *Cherokee Phoenix* occupies a special place in the history of both journalism and native Americans, as Robert G. Martin, Jr., pointed out in "*Cherokee Phoenix*: Pioneer of Indian Journalism," *Chronicles of Oklahoma* 25 (1947): 102–18. Barbara F. Luebke examined the journalistic career of its first editor in "Elias Boudinot, Cherokee Editor: The Father of American Indian Journalism" (Ph.D. diss. University of Missouri, 1981), and his editorials in "Elias Boudinott, Indian Editor: Editorial Columns from the *Cherokee Phoenix*," *Journalism History* 6 (1979): 48–53. Henry T. Malone discussed the political implications of the newspaper in "The *Cherokee Phoenix:* Supreme Expression of Cherokee Nationalism," *Georgia Historical Quarterly* 34 (1950): 163–88, while Theda Perdue questioned the accuracy of much of the material about the Cherokees in "Rising from the Ashes: The *Cherokee Phoenix* as an Ethnohistorical Source," *Ethnohistory* 24 (1977): 207–18. Jack Frederick Kilpatrick and Anna Gritts Kilpatrick edited the articles and letters of the American Board missionary who collaborated with Boudinot on the translation of religious matter in *New Echota Letters: Contributions of Samuel A. Worcester to the Cherokee Phoenix* (Dallas, 1978). Other Cherokee newspapers continued the tradition of the *Phoenix*, as Cullen Joe Holland demonstrated in "The Cherokee Indian Newspapers, 1828–1906" (Ph.D. diss., University of Minnesota, 1956). In *Let My People Know: American Indian Journalism, 1828–1978* (Norman, Okla., 1981), James E. Murphy and Sharon M. Murphy placed the *Phoenix* in the context of native American journalism as a whole.

The following selections from the *Cherokee Phoenix* constitute approximately one-fourth of Boudinot's editorials, and they should be viewed merely as representative of his contributions to the *Phoenix*. All editorials that dealt with traditional Cherokee culture (and there were relatively few) have been reprinted, as have most comments on social, religious, and intellectual life in the Cherokee Nation. Factual reports of events and lightly annotated public documents have been omitted. Finally, if several editorials focused on the same issue, such as Boudinot's arrest by the Georgia Guard, only the most comprehensive has been included.

October, 1827

PROSPECTUS

For publishing at New Echota, in the Cherokee Nation,
A WEEKLY NEWSPAPER
TO BE CALLED THE
Cherokee Phoenix

It has long been the opinion of judicious friends to the civilization of the Aborigines of America, that a paper published exclusively for their benefit, and under their direction, would add great force to the charitable means employed by the public for their melioration. In accordance with that opinion, the legislative authorities of the Cherokees have thought fit to patronize a weekly paper, bearing the above title;[1] and have appointed the subscriber to take charge of it as Editor. In issuing this PROSPECTUS the Editor would, by no means, be too sanguine, for he is aware that he will tread upon *untried ground*: Nor does he make any pretensions to learning, for it must be known that the great and sole motive in establishing this paper, is the benefit of the *Cherokees*. This will be the great aim of the Editor, which he intends to pursue with undeviating steps. Many reasons might be given in support of the utility of such a paper as that which is now offered to the public, but it is deemed useless. There are many true friends to the Indians in different parts of the Union, who will rejoice to see this feeble effort of the Cherokees to rise from their ashes, like the fabled PHOENIX. On such friends must principally depend the support of our paper.

The Alphabet lately invented by a native Cherokee, of which the public have already been apprized, forms an interesting medium of information to those Cherokees who are unacquainted with the English language. For their benefit Cherokee types have been procured.[2]

The columns of the Cherokee Phoenix will be filled, partly with English, and partly with Cherokee print; and all matter which is of common interest will be given in both languages in parallel columns.[3]

As the great object of the Phoenix will be the benefit of the Cherokees, the following subjects will occupy its columns.

1. The laws and public documents of the Nation.
2. Account of the manners and customs of the Cherokees, and their progress in Education, Religion and the arts of civilized life; with such notices of other Indian tribes as our limited means of information will allow.
3. The principal interesting news of the day.
4. Miscellaneous articles, calculated to promote Literature, Civilization, and Religion among the Cherokees.[4]

In closing this short Prospectus, The Editor would appeal to the friends of Indians, and respectfully ask their patronage. Those who have heretofore manifested a christian zeal in promoting our welfare and happiness, will no doubt lend their helping hand.

ELIAS BOUDINOTT

February 21, 1828

TO THE PUBLIC

We are happy in being able, at length, to issue the first number of our paper, although after a longer delay than we anticipated.[5] This delay has been owing to unavoidable circumstances, which, we think, will be sufficient to acquit us, and though our readers and patrons may be wearied in the expectation of gratifying their eyes on this paper of no ordinary novelty, yet we hope their patience will not be so exhausted, but that they will give it a calm perusal and pass upon it a candid judgment. It is far from our expectation that it will meet with entire and universal approbation, particularly from those who consider learning and science necessary to the merits of newspapers. Such must not expect to be gratified here, for the merits, (if merits they can be called,) on which our paper is expected to exist, are not alike with those which keep alive the political and religious papers of the day. We lay no claim to extensive information; and we sincerely hope, this public disclosure will save us from the severe criticisms, to which our ignorance of many things, will frequently expose us, in the future of our editorial labors.— Let the public but consider our motives, and the design of this paper, which is, the benefit of the Cherokees, and we are sure, those who wish well to the Indian race, will keep out of view all failings and deficiencies of the Editor, and give a prompt support to the first paper ever published in an Indian country, and under the direction of some remnants of those, who by the most mysterious course of providence, have dwindled into oblivion. To prevent us from the like destiny, is certainly a laudable undertaking, which the Christian, the Patriot, and the Philanthropist will not be ashamed to aid. Many are now engaged, by various means and with various success, in attempting to rescue, not only us, but all our kindred tribes, from the impending danger which has been so fatal to our forefathers; and we are happy to be in a situation to tender them our public acknowledgments for their unwearied efforts. Our present undertaking is intended to be nothing more than a feeble auxiliary to these efforts. Those therefore, who are engaged for the good of the Indians of every tribe, and who pray that salvation, peace, and the comforts of civilized life may be extended to every Indian fire side on this continent, will consider us as co-workers together in their benevolent labors. To them we make our appeal for patronage, and pledge ourselves to encourage and assist them, in whatever appears to be for the benefit of the Aborigines.

In the commencement of our labours, it is due to our readers that we should acquaint them with the general principles, which we have prescribed to ourselves as rules in conducting this paper. These principles we shall accordingly state briefly. It may, however, be proper to observe that the establishment which has been lately purchased, principally with the charities of our white brethren, is the property of the Nation, and that the paper, which is now offered to the public, is patronized by, and under the direction of, the Cherokee Legislature, as will be seen in the Prospectus already before the public.[6] As servants, we are bound to that body, from which, however, we have not received any instructions, but are left at liberty to form such regulations for our conduct as will appear to us most conducive to the interests of the people, for whose benefit, this paper has been established.

As the Phoenix is a national newspaper, we shall feel ourselves bound to devote it to national purposes. "The laws and public documents of the Nation," and matters relating to the welfare and condition of the Cherokees as a people, will be faithfully published in English and Cherokee.

As the liberty of the press is so essential to the improvement of the mind, we shall consider our paper, a *free paper*, with, however, proper and usual restrictions.[7] We shall reserve to ourselves the liberty of rejecting such communications as tend to evil, and such as are too intemperate and too personal. But the columns of this paper shall always be open to free and temperate discussions on matters of politics, religion, &c.

We shall avoid as much as possible, controversy on disputed doctrinal points in religion.[8] Though we have our particular belief on this important subject, and perhaps are as strenuous upon it, as some of our brethren of a different faith, yet we consciencіously think, & in this thought we are supported by men of judgment that it would be injudicious, perhaps highly pernicious, to introduce to this people, the various minor differences of Christians. Our object is not sectarian, and if we had a wish to support, in our paper, the denomination with which we have the honor and privilege of being connected, yet we know our incompetency for the task.[9]

We will not unnecessarily intermeddle with the politics and affairs of our neighbors. As we have no particular interest in the concerns of the surrounding states, we shall only expose ourselves to contempt and ridicule by improper intrusion. And though at times, we should do ourselves injustice, to be silent, on matters of great interest to the Cherokees, yet we will not return railing for railing, but consult mildness, for we have been taught to believe, that "A soft answer turneth away wrath; but grievous words stir up anger."[10] The unpleasant controversy existing with the state of Georgia, of which, many of our readers are aware, will frequently make our situation trying, by having hard sayings and threatenings thrown out against us, a specimen of which will be found in our next.[11] We pray God that we may be delivered from such spirit.

In regard to the controversy with Georgia, and the present policy of the General Government, in removing, and concentrating the Indians, out of the limits of any state, which, by the way, appears to be gaining strength, we will invariably and faithfully state the feelings of the majority of our people. Our views, as a people, on this subject, have been sadly misrepresented.[12] These views we do not wish to conceal, but are willing that the public should know what we think of this policy, which, in our opinion, if carried into effect, will prove pernicious to us.

We have been asked which side of the Presidential question we should take. Our answer is, we think best to take a neutral stand, and we know that such a course is most prudent, as we have no vote on the question, and although we have our individual choice, yet it would be folly for us to spend words and time on a subject, which has engrossed very much, the attention of the public already.[13]

In fine, we shall pay a sacred regard to truth, and avoid, as much as possible, that partiality to which we shall be exposed. In relating facts of a local nature, whether political, moral, or religious, we shall take care that exaggeration shall not be our crime. We shall also feel ourselves bound to correct all mistatements, relating to the present condition of the Cherokees.

How far we shall be successful in advancing the improvement of our people, is not now for us to decide. We hope, however, our efforts will not be altogether in vain.— Now is the moment when mere speculation on the practicability of civilizing us is out of the question. Sufficient and repeated evidence has been given, that Indians can be reclaimed from a savage state, and that with proper advantages, they are as capable of improvement in mind as any other people; and let it be remembered, notwithstanding the assertions of those who talk to the contrary, that this improvement can be made, not only by the Cherokees, but by all the Indians, *in their present locations*. We are rendered bold in making this assertion, by considering the history of our people within the last fifteen years. There was a time within our remembrance, when darkness was sadly prevalent, and ignorance abounded amongst us—when strong and deep rooted prejudices were directed against many things relating to civilized life—and when it was thought a disgrace, for a Cherokee to appear in the costume of a white man. We mention these things not by way of boasting, but to shew our readers that it is not a visionary thing to attempt to civilize and christianize all the Indians, but highly practicable.

It is necessary for our white patrons to know that this paper is not intended to be a source of profit, and that its continuance must depend, in a great measure, on the liberal support which they may be pleased to grant us. Though our object is not gain, yet we wish as much patronage, as will enable us to support the establishment without subjecting it to pecuniary difficulties. Those of our friends, who have done so much already for us by instructing us in the arts of civilized life, and enabling us to enjoy the blessings of education, and the comforts of religion, and to whose exertions may be attributed the present means of improvement in this Nation, will not think it a hard matter that their aid should now be respectfully requested. In order that our paper may have an extensive circulation in this Nation and out of it, we have fixed upon the most liberal terms possible; such, in our opinion, as will render it as cheap as most of the Southern papers; and in order that our subscribers may be prompt in their remittances, we have made considerable difference between the first and the last payments. Those who have any experience in the management of periodicals will be sensible how important it is, that the payments of subscribers should be prompt and regular, particularly where the existence of a paper depends upon its own income. We sincerely hope that we shall never have any occasion to complain of the delinquency of any of our patrons.[14]

We would now commit our feeble efforts to the good will and indulgence of the public, praying that God will attend them with his blessings, and hoping for that happy period, when all the Indian tribes of America shall arise, Phoenix like, from their ashes, and when the terms, "Indian depredation," "war-whoop," "scalping knife" and the like, shall become obsolete, and for ever be "buried deep under ground."

March 13, 1828

CONGRESS.—Our last Washington papers contain a debate which took place in the house of representatives, on the resolution, recommended by the Committee on Indian Affairs, published in the second Number of our paper.[15] It appears that the advocates of this new system of civilizing the Indians are very strenuous in maintaining the novel opinion, that it is impossible to enlighten the Indians, surrounded as they are by the white population, and that they assuredly will become extinct, unless they are removed. It is a fact which we would not deny, that many tribes have perished away in consequence of white population, but we are yet to be convinced that this will always be the case, in spite of every measure taken to civilize them. We contend that suitable measures to a sufficient extent have never been employed. And how dare these men make an assertion without sufficient evidence? What proof have they that the system which they are now recommending, will succeed. Where have we an example in the whole history of man, of a Nation or tribe, removing in a body, from a land of civil and religious means, to a perfect wilderness, *in order to be civilized*. We are fearful these men are building castles in the air, whose fall will crush those poor Indians who may be so blinded as to make the experiment. We are sorry to see that some of the advocates of this system speak so disrespectfully, if not contemptuously, of the present measures of improvement, now in successful operation among most of the Indians in the United States—the only measures too, which have been crowned with success, and bid fair to meliorate the condition of the Aborigines.

March 20, 1828

We were not a little diverted, in noticing lately, in a paper, to which we are not now able to recur, a motion made in the House of Representatives, by Mr. Wilde,[16] a member from Georgia, to take measures to ascertain, what white persons have assisted the Cherokees in forming the late constitution; and in what way, and to what extent, such assistance has been afforded. It is a little surprising that in almost every instance, wherein the Indians have undertaken to imitate their white brethren, and have succeeded, (to be sure not in a remarkable degree,) it is currently noised about, that all is imposition, as though Indians were incapable of performing the deeds of their white neighbours.—This evidences an extreme prejudice. We cannot conceive to ourselves, what benefit Mr. Wilde expected to receive in offering such a motion, or who are the persons that are suspected of having interfered in this affair? We believe that the Cherokees are as scrupulous, in avoiding such interference, as Mr. W. if not more so.

It has been customary of late to charge the Missionaries with the crime of assisting the Indians, and unbecomingly interfering in political affairs; and as some of these are the only white persons (with few exceptions) in this Nation, who are capable of affording any substantial assistance, it is probable Mr. W. had a distant reference to them. We can, however, assure him, that he need not be under any apprehension from this class of our population, for the Cherokees will not, by any means, permit them to have any thing to do with their public affairs, and we believe, that as their sole object is to afford religious instruction, the societies under which they labour particularly forbid their interference in political matters. We know this is the case with the Presbyterian Missionaries,[17] and we doubt not that it is equally true with respect to the others, and as far as our acquaintance extends, we are prepared, and would not hesitate, to express our belief, that they have conformed to the rules of their Societies. They have our hearty approbation for what they have done amongst us, and we hope those at a distance will reward them by their kind wishes and sympathies, instead of affixing to them the term of "*mercenary missionaries*." They certainly deserve better treatment. Perhaps this short article will be considered an imposition by such persons as are wont to judge at a distance and without evidence, and as nothing more than a Missionary's own defence.

Our object, when we commenced to pen this article, was to correct the mistake, under which some may labour, and to declare once and for all, that no white man has had any thing to do in framing our constitution, and all the public acts of the Nation. The Cherokees only are accountable for them, and they certainly do not wish to have any innocent person implicated wrongfully.—We hope this practice of imputing the acts of Indians to white men will be done away.

April 3, 1828

We have reason to think that the complaint of our correspondent "Oakfuskie," is too well founded, at least as as it respects the Officers of this District.[18]—We have heard of thefts around us, and unless this abominable practice is in time vigorously restrained by enforcing the laws of this Nation, the citizens will not be secure in their property. If the officers of this district are not more vigilant than they are at present, we should not be much surprised if the old game should be played over—the existence of a league between White and Cherokee thieves. This is the worst of all confederacies; for as soon as a stolen property passes the boundary line, the owner need not flatter himself to see it. It is incumbent on the civil officers of this nation to secure those vagabonds who carry with them wherever they go, the deep stain of the guilt of stealing: and now is the time to arrest this practice, by inflicting an exemplary punishment on those, who are now acknowledged by all to be really guilty. Yet nothing is done with them—they are permitted to go at large, running stolen horses to Sand Town and other places on the frontiers of Georgia, where there are not wanting men whose professed business is to receive such stolen property.

We are likewise informed that Bear's Paw, who committed Murder not long since at Sumach, is permitted to run unmolested. We doubt whether any effort has been made to bring him to justice. The indifference of our officers to this Murderer has emboldened others, as will appear from the following facts, which we have received from a credible source.

A man by the name of Gunnowsoske, who was lately tried at Coosewattee court for stealing, convicted and punished, was a short time since, caught and bound for the same offense, by Bear's Paw (another Bear's Paw) from whom it appears, Gunnowsoske stole a side saddle and some other articles, which is said to have constituted half the property of this poor man. In the presence of three others, Bear's Paw told the prisoner that it was an unpleasant duty which now devolved upon them, to be under the necessity of bringing him to deserved punishment. They did not wish to do it, and that if he promised never to steal again as long as he lived, and to be a good man in the future, they would release him.—The prisoner replied that he would promise no such thing, but would steal as long as he lived, and that they might punish him as often as they pleased. These words were hardly uttered, when Bear's Paw struck him dead with an axe. Thus it appears as another person has been killed at Sumach.— It is to be wished that the officers of this District were more vigilant and more attentive to their duties. Unless they do speedily go to work, they will make themselves liable to public reprehension; and these frequent thefts and murders will go to confirm the world in the opinion that we are still savages.

May 14, 1828

INDIAN EMIGRATION

Col. Thomas L. McKenney, late special Agent to the Southern Indians, in a letter to the Secretary of war, dated Choctaw Country, Oct. 10th, 1828, makes an estimate of the probable expense of removing the Chickasaw Indians.[19] The utmost extent of cost is estimated at 494,750 dollars, including the cost of a visit to examine the country, the cost of their houses, mills, work shops, orchards, fences, and their stock of all kinds, all of which are to be replaced by the United States. According to the foundation which Col. McKenney has laid down, we make the following estimate of the probable cost of the removal of the Cherokees, (if that were to be the case.)

The population of the Cherokee Nation, we will put down at 13,000, (which is below the actual number.)[20] We will suppose (following Col. McKenney's suppositions) the families to average five souls, which will give 2,600 houses. These houses, we do not suppose can be built for less than an average cost of 200 dollars, which in our opinion is quite moderate. Most of these houses it is true, are poor, and may be built for a small amount, yet there are many which will require the double and trible of what we put down as an average cost.— Few of the best houses cannot be built for less sums than two, three, and four thousand dollars, including barns, cribs, &c.— This part of the expense will then be $520,000.

The number of mills, grist, and saw, is fifty, which may be replaced for the sum of $25,000, supposing each mill to cost $500.

Their shops are sixtytwo in number, and these estimated at $50 each will cost $3,000.

Their orchards perhaps may be replaced for $8,000.

The fences of the Chickasaws are estimated by Col. McKenney at $50,000. $250,000 will then be but a moderate estimate for this item of the expense attending the removal of the Cherokees.

There are in this Nation 7,685 horses, these at $40 per head, will cost $307,320.

22,531 black cattle at $10 per head will cost $225,310.

46,700 hogs owned by the Cherokees, at $3 per head, will cost $140,100.

The probable cost of a visit to examine the country, may be the same as estimated by Col. McKenney, $10,000, and of their removal to it, $350,000. This is by no means an extravagant estimate, for Col. McKenney puts down the cost of the removal of the Chickasaws, who are but four thousand in number, at $100,000.

The total amount of cost, then, for the foregoing items, will be $1,783,730. And supposing we add a fourth for the expense of the Government, the Schools, the military, and other items not enumerated, the whole amount of expense in removing the Cherokees become the limits of any State or Territory will be $2,229,662.

If this project is intended, as we are told by its advocates, for the good and civilization of the Cherokees and other Indians, cannot this sum be put to a better use?— Supposing with this money, the United States begin to establish Schools in every part of this Nation? With this money let their be a college founded, where every advantage of instruction may be enjoyed. Let books, tracts, &c. be published in Cherokee and English, and distributed throughout the Nation and every possible effort be made to civilize us, let us at the same time be protected in our rights. What would be the consequences? If we fail to improve under such efforts, we will then agree to remove.

October 1, 1828

INTEMPERANCE

Intemperance[21] is the curse of mankind. It spreads desolation in societies and families. It is the parent of strife, the cause of diseases, and almost every species of misery. To the Indians, intemperance occasioned by the use of ardent spirits has been pernicious. It has been our shame in the eyes of other people, and has planted the common opinion, that the love of whiskey is a necessary trait of the Indian's character. Though this opinion is erroneous, yet the fact that intemperance is sadly prevalent and its effects awfully great among the Indians, we cannot deny. Among us, it has been a wide spreading evil. It has cost us lives, and a train of troubles. It has been an enemy to our national prosperity, industry, and intellectual improvement.— Even at this day, when it is generally conceded that we are the most civilized of all the Aboriginal tribes, we see this enemy of all good stalking fourth in triumph, carrying desolation and misery into families and neighborhoods. The murders committed in this Nation, with very few exceptions, are occasioned by intoxication. The only two public executions by hanging originated from the same cause. And what but whiskey produces all our accidents, all our strifes, fightings and stabbings?

It is to be lamented that ardent spirits should have ever been introduced among the Indians by the white man, but more so that, at this enlightened age, our intelligent citizens and the intelligent citizens of the neighboring states should encourage this worst of all poisons, by making it a subject of trafic. But is it not ten times more to be regreted, that professors of religion should engage in this trade of death? How is such conduct to be reconciled with Christian principles, and with the doctrine of universal benevolence?— Some of those who send whiskey here from Ten. we are credibly informed are professors of religion. How can they pray, "thy kingdom come," and desire the universal spread of the Gospel in heathen countries, particularly among their neighbors, the Indians, when they are sending death and destruction in our ranks? If this paper should ever meet the eyes of such persons, we would solemnly warn them of the mischief they are doing. Are you not aware that you are making a nation of drunkards? Are you not aware that you are causing deaths, murders, and a host of evils? To our fellow citizens, particularly professors of religion, who make it a business of traficing in whiskey, we would say, what availeth all our professions of patriotism when we are encouraging an enemy of such notoriety? What availeth our feeble exertions to enlighten our more ignorant brethren, when we are feeding them with coals of fire, and strewing their path with deadly poison? To our Legislators and civil leaders who have not scrupled to deal in ardent spirits, we would say, what availeth all legislative acts to prevent intemperance, when some of our law givers are encouraging it by retailing whiskey.[22]

Our Cherokee readers will bear with us when we speak so plain upon this important subject. It is a subject which ought to occupy the attention of every citizen who sincerely desire that we may become a happy and intelligent people. Intemperance forms the great obstacle, and it is the hope that the public sentiment of this Nation may be aroused to the removal of this obstacle, that we freely bring this subject before our readers. Something far more efficient must be done than has hitherto been attempted. The public mind must bear upon this evil. Legislative resolutions will effect but little, unless they are sustained by the united opinion of the intelligent and virtuous portion of the nation.

We would sincerely hope, while so much is doing abroad to arrest the progress of intemperance, the citizens of this nation will not be inattentive to the call of their country—the call is imperious—it cannot be misunderstood. The call is to the Christian, and to the patriot. If an enemy were to come among us in a warlike attitude, and commence, unprovoked, a work of destruction with our women and children, our property, and with our most sacred rights, what patriot is there who would countenance the enemy, and remain an idle spectator? But fellow citizens, we have an enemy among us, a far more dangerous enemy, because its progress is unobserved, and because it insinuates itself as a friend, but mark ye, deaths by violence, deaths by diseases and deaths by accidents, sickness and famine, profanity and indecencies, and a host of other evils, are its trophies and triumphs.

January 21, 1829

"Vigil"[23] might reasonably entertain one cheering consideration, and that is, the gradual diminution of such practices as described by him in his communication.— If he had visited this Nation *thirty years* ago, and witnessed the practices of the inhabitants in their full extent, his tears would have flowed more freely, and the consideration of their wretchedness would have been without a redeeming thought.— At that period the Cherokees resided in villages, in each of which was a "Townhouse," the head quarter of frivolity. Here were assembled almost every night (we are told, we speak from hearsay for we were born under an era of reformation,) men and women, old and young, to dance their *bear dance*, *buffalo dance*, *eagle dance*, *green-corn dance* &c. &c. &c.[24] and when the day appeared, instead of going to their farms, and labouring for the support of their families, the young and middle aged of the males were seen to leave their houses, their faces fantastically painted, and their heads decorated with feathers, and step off with a merry whoop, which indicated that they were *real men*, to a ball play, or a meeting of a similar nature.[25] Such in a word was the life of a Cherokee in those days during spring & summer seasons. In the fall and winter seasons they were gone to follow the chase, which occupation enabled them to purchase of the traders a few items of clothing, sufficient to last perhaps until the next hunting time. From the soil they derived a scanty supply of corn, barely enough to furnish them with gah-no-ha-nah[26] and this was obtained by the labor of women and grey headed men, for custom would have it that it was disgraceful for a young man to be seen with a hoe in his hand, except on particular occasions.[27]

In those days of ignorance and heathenism, prejudices against the customs of the whites were inveterate, so much so that white men, who came along the Cherokees, had to throw away their costume and adopt the *leggings*. In a moral and intellectual point of view the scenery was dark & gloomy, nevertheless it has not been impenetrable. The introduction of light and intelligence has struck a mortal blow to the superstitious practices of the Cherokees, and by the aid of that light, a new order of things is introduced, and it is to be hoped will now eradicate the vestiges of older days.

January 28, 1829

It is frequently said that the Indians are given up to destruction, that it is the will of heaven, that they should become extinct and give way to the white man. Those who assert this doctrine seem to act towards these unfortunate people in a consistent manner, either in neglecting them entirely, or endeavoring to hasten the period of their extinction. For our part, we dare not scrutinize the designs of God's providence towards the Cherokees. It may suffice to say that, his dealings have been merciful and very kind. He inclined the heart of GEORGE WASHINGTON, when we were in a savage state, to place us under the protection of the United States, by entering into a treaty of peace and friendship with our forefathers, on the second day of July, in the year of our Lord one thousand seven hundred and ninety one;[28] in which treaty is the following provision:

> That the Cherokee Nation may be led to a greater degree of civilization, and to become herdsmen and cultivators, instead of remaining hunters, the United States will, from time to time, furnish gratuitously, the said nation with useful implements of husbandry.

He furthermore inclined that illustrious man, and his successors in office, and the Agents of the United States, to carry the foregoing provision into execution. By his overruling providence, a door was opened for the introduction of those implements of husbandry; and at this day, were Washington living, he would find that his expectations and wishes were realized. He would rejoice, and those who compassionated the Indians with him would rejoice to see that the Cherokees have in great measure become herdsmen and cultivators—they are no more hunters and warriors.[29] Where they were accustomed to hunt the deer, the bear and the beaver, are seen their farms, & they labor peaceably, for the troubles of warfare do not now molest them.

We cannot enumerate all the dealings of God towards us in a temporal point of view. They are gracious, and in our minds would convey the belief that he has mercy still in store for us. But what are his dealings in a spiritual point of view? "If the Lord were pleased to destroy us he would not have shewed us all these things nor would, as at this time, have told us such things as these." We have heard great things indeed, salvation by Jesus Christ. To what purpose has God opened the hearts of Christians of different denominations to commiserate, not only the

Cherokees, but all the other tribes? To what purpose are contributions freely made to support missionaries and Schools? To what purpose is it that these missionaries meet with such remarkable success, and that preachers are rising from among the Cherokees themselves? To what purpose is it that hundreds have made a public profession of religion,[30] and that the number is rapidly increasing? To what purpose is it that, that the knowledge of letters has been disseminated with a rapidity unknown heretofore, and that eight hundred copies of a Cherokee HYMN BOOK is now issuing from our press?[31] What do all these indicate? Do they indicate the displeasure of God against us, and the certainty of our extinction? It is not for man to pry into the designs of God where he has not expressly revealed them, but from past blessings we may hope for future mercies.

The causes which have operated to exterminate the Indian tribes that are produced as instances of the certain doom of the whole Aboriginal family appear plain to us. These causes did not exist in the Indians themselves, nor in the will of heaven, nor simply in the intercourse of Indians with civilized man, but they were precisely such causes as are now attempted by the state of Georgia—by infringing upon their rights—by disorganizing them, and circumscribing their limits. While he possesses a national character, there is hope for the Indian.[32] But take his rights away, divest him of the last spark of national pride, and introduce him to a new order of things, invest him with oppressive laws,[33] grevious to be borne, he droops like the fading flower before the noon day sun. Most of the Northern tribes have fallen a prey to such causes, & the Catawbas of South Carolina, are a striking instance of the truth of what we we say.[34] There is hope for the Cherokee as long as they continue in their present situation, but disorganize them, either by removing them beyond the Mississippi, or by imposing on them "heavy burdens," you cut a vital string in their national existence.

Things will no doubt come to a final issue before long in regard to the Indians, and for our part, we care not how soon. The State of Georgia has taken a strong stand against us, and the United States must either defend us in our rights, or leave us to our foe. In the former case, the General Government will redeem her pledge solemnly given in treaties.— In the latter, she will violate her promise of protection, and we cannot, in future, depend consistently, upon any guarantee made by her to us, either here or beyond the Mississippi.

February 18, 1829

NATIONAL ACADEMY

Sometime ago we inserted a short notice as an advertisement, headed NEW ECHOTA ACADEMY. From this circumstance some of our friends have fallen into an error, in supposing that the NATIONAL ACADEMY had commenced its operation.[35] The notice above referred to, was calculated to deceive those who knew that it had been the intention of the authorities of the nation to establish such an institution.

A Seminary of a respectable grade, such an one as was contemplated to be established in this place, is very much needed among us. We still hope that something will be done towards it. If the interest of the avails of the reservation expressly devoted to the support of education among the Cherokees,[36] and which will probably be sold next fall, was laid out in the establishment and support of the contemplated Academy, we believe it would meet the wish of the nation. The nation has not otherwise any means of supporting it.— The power of applying the school fund in question, we believe is left, according to a treaty stipulation, with the President of the United States. He will no doubt be willing to gratify the wishes of his Cherokee *children*, more so as the funds properly belong to them.

We consider it high time for this nation to do something for themselves in encouraging and supporting education. We are glad, however, to testify to the public, that there is a commendable disposition in this respect in a large portion of our citizens.— The Cherokees as a nation have had sufficient time to learn and appreciate the advantages of knowledge: for what else distinguishes them from their brethren? What but a larger share of information makes them more respected? It becomes every citizen then, particularly every ruler, as a guardian of the nation's welfare, to do his utmost endeavor to forward education. It is this which will ensure respect. It is this which will preserve us from the common burial place of Indians—oblivion in which many tribes are forgotten, & to which many would suppose us to be hastening.

INDIAN CLANS

Most of our readers probably know what is meant by Indian clans.[37] It is no more than a division of an Indian tribe into large families. We believe this custom is universal with the North American Indians. Among the Cherokees are seven clans such as Wolf, Deer, Paint, &c. This simple division of the Cherokees formed the grand work by which marriages were regulated, and murder punished. A Cherokee could marry into any of the clans except two, that to which his father belongs, for all of that clan are his fathers and aunts and that to which his mother belongs, for all of that clan are his brothers and sisters, a child invariably inheriting the clan of his mother. This custom which originated from time immemorial was observed with the greatest strictness. No law could be guarded and enforced with equal caution. In times past, the penalty annexed to it was not less than death. But it has scarcely perhaps never been violated, except within a few years. Now it is invaded with impunity, though not to an equal extent with other customs of the Cherokees.

But it was the mutual law of clans as connected with murder, which rendered this custom savage and barbarous. We speak of what it was once, not as it is now, for the Cherokees, after experiencing sad effects from it, determined to, and did about twenty years ago in a solemn council, abolish it. From that time, murder has been considered a governmental crime.— Previous to that, the following were too palpably true, viz:

The Cherokees as a nation, had nothing to do with murder.

Murder was punished upon the principle of retaliation.

It belonged to the clan of the murdered to revenge his death.

If the murderer fled, his brother or nearest relative was liable to suffer in his stead.

If a man killed his brother, he was answerable to no law or clan.

If the murderer (this however is known only by tradition) was not as respectable as the murdered, his relative, or a man of his clan of a more respectable standing was liable to suffer.

To kill, under any circumstance whatever, was considered murder, and punished accordingly.

Our readers will say, "those were savage laws indeed." They were, and the Cherokees were then to be pitied, for the above were not mere inoperative laws, but were rigorously executed. But we can now say with pleasure, that they are all repealed, and are remembered only as vestiges of ignorance and barbarism.[38]

June 17, 1829

From the documents which we this day lay before our readers, there is not a doubt of the kind of policy, which the present administration of the General Government intends to pursue relative to the Indians.[39] President Jackson has, as a neighboring editor remarks, "recognized the doctrine contended for by Georgia in its full extent." It is to be regretted that we were not undeceived long ago, while we were hunters and in our savage state. It appears now from the communication of the Secretary of War to the Cherokee Delegation, that the illustrious Washington, Jefferson, Madison and Monroe[40] were only tantalizing us, when they encouraged us in the pursuit of agriculture and Government, and when they afforded us the protection of the United States, by which we have been preserved to this present time as a nation. Why were we not told long ago, that we could not be permitted to establish a government within the limits of any state? Then we could have borne disappointment much easier than now. The pretext for Georgia to extend her jurisdiction over the Cherokees has always existed. The Cherokees have always had a government of their own. Nothing, however, was said when we were governed by savage laws, when the abominable law of retaliation carried death in our midst, when it was a lawful act to shed the blood of a person charged with witchcraft, when a brother could kill a brother with impunity, or an innocent man suffer for an offending relative.[41] At that time it might have been a matter of charity to have extended over us the mantle of Christian laws & regulations. But how happens it now, after being fostered by the U. States, and advised by great and good men to establish a government of regular law; when the aid and protection of the General Government have been pledged to us; when we, as dutiful "children" of the President, have followed his instructions and advice, and have established for ourselves a government of regular law;[42] when everything looks so promising around us, that a storm is raised by the extension of tyrannical and unchristian laws, which threatens to blast all our rising hopes and expectations?

There is, as would naturally be supposed, a great rejoicing in Georgia. It is a time of "important news"—"gratifying intelligence" —"The Cherokee lands are to be obtained speedily." It is even reported that the Cherokees have come to the conclusion to sell, and move off to the west of the Mississippi—not so fast. We are yet at our homes, at our peaceful firesides, (except those contiguous to Sandtown, Carroll, &c.)[43] attending to our farms and useful occupations.

We had concluded to give our readers fully our thoughts on the subject, which we, in the above remarks, have merely introduced, but upon reflection & remembering our promise, that we will be moderate, we have suppressed ourselves, and have withheld what we had intended should occupy our editorial column. We do not wish, by any means, unnecesarily to excite the minds of the Cherokees. To our home readers we submit the subject without any special comment. They will judge for themselves. To our distant readers, who may wish to know how we feel under present circumstances, we recommend the memorial,[44] the leading article in our present number. We believe it justly contains the views of the nation.

July 15, 1829

The eagerness which is manifested in Geo. to obtain the lands of the Cherokees has frequently led the journals of that state to deceive the people, by stating, that we are "making extensive preparations to remove to the west." So desirable it is to get rid of these troublesome Cherokees, that every flying report is grasped at as an undoubted fact, & spread abroad to the rejoicing of thousands. The late statement of the *Georgia Journal*,[45] to which we have already referred, is a very good example. No sooner does this statement make its appearance, before we had time to take breath, & certainly before we had the opportunity of contradicting it, it is copied into many papers, and now there is hardly a paper with which we have the honor of exchanging, but what has informed its readers that "the Cherokees are making extensive preparations to remove." We happen to know this to be an assertion without the least foundation. We hope the same papers will say on what they may consider "good authority," that the Cherokees are *not* making any preparation to remove, but on the contrary, that they continue to make improvements as heretofore. We see houses erecting wherever we go—they are enlarging their farms—the progress of education is encouraging, and the improvement in morals has never been so flattering.—These are facts on which the public may depend, until we shall inform them otherwise. We know not what course the Cherokees may finally determine to pursue, but we have no hesitation in stating the above as being most correct in regard to them at present. We do not undertake to say that they will remain here at all hazards, for "persecution—what will it not accomplish?" as the *Journal of Commerce* remarks. We know, however, the feelings of many individuals—in regard to them, we speak with confidence when we say, coercion alone will remove them to the western country alloted for the Indians.

July 1, 1829

The Editor of the Milledgeville Recorder, elated by the "certainty of obtaining at an early day" the lands now in the occupance of the Cherokees, directs the attention of Georgians to the growing importance of the State. If he is not deceived in regard to the certainty of obtaining the lands, he is most egregiously mistaken in his calculations. He supposes the population of the State will, in ten years, be doubled, and in twenty years tripled. The Cherokee country is indeed "picturesque, beautiful and healthy," yet it is by no means calculated to support dense population, only about one sixth part being fit for cultivation. If this territory was added to the State, Georgia would not yet become the rival of New York, Pennsylvania, or even of Ohio. She will have to overcome one great obstacle before she becomes a great state—slavery.[46]

September 9, 1829

The intruders,[47] who to say the least have acted more like savages towards the Cherokees, than the Cherokees towards them, are still permitted to continue in their unlawful proceedings, notwithstanding the frequent complaints made to the agent, Col. Montgomery.[48] We were in hopes the executive of the United States would respect the laws entrusted to their administration, although they may be inclined to question many of our rights. One right, however, the United States cannot possibly deny us—the right of calling upon her to execute her own laws. It will be remembered by our readers, that Mr. Eaton, in his letter to the Cherokee delegation, stated that orders had been forwarded to the Agent for the removal of Intruders. This was as long ago as last spring. Since then nothing effective has been done or attempted.— Whether this tardiness is designed or not we are not able to say—we have our fears. We shall, however, know how to appreciate the "straight & good talk" of our father the President, & understands what he means when he says, "your father loves his redchildren." Have we not occasion to question his fatherly professions, when he has been ordering the military against us, merely because a malicious white child of his has told a falsehood, but will not raise his hand to protect us from encroachments and insults, under which we have been laboring for months? Is he not dealing out a "forked" justice to us?

February 10, 1830

FIRST BLOOD SHED BY THE GEORGIANS!!

Since writing the above, we have been told by a gentleman who passed this place as an express to the agent, from the principal chief, that a Cherokee has, at last, been *killed* by the intruders, and three more taken bound into Georgia! We are not prepared this week to give the public any particulars respecting this unpleasant affair. The general facts are, however, these, the particulars of which will be given in our next. A company of Cherokees, among whom were some of our most respectable citizens, constrained by the repeated aggressions and insults of a number of intruders, who had settled themselves far in the country, & likewise by the frequent losses sustained by many of our citizens in cattle and horses from their own countrymen, who are leagued in wickedness with our civilized brothers, started the other day, under the authority of the Principal Chief to correct, at least part of the evil. They were out two days in which time they arrested four Cherokee horse-thieves. These received exemplary punishment. They found also 17 families of intruders, living, *we believe*, in Cherokee houses.[49] These they ordered out and after safely taking out their beddings, chairs, &c. the houses were set on fire. In no instance was the least violence used on the part of the Cherokees. When the company returned home, five of them tarried on the way, who, we are sorry to say, had become intoxicated. In this situation, they were found by a company of intruders, twenty five in number—One was killed, & three taken into Georgia. Thus a circumstance, which we have for a long time dreaded, and which has been brought about by the neglect of this executive to remove the great nuisance to the Cherokees, has happened. We are nevertheless, glad, that the injury received is on the side of this nation. It has been the desire of our enemies that the Cherokees may be urged to some desperate act—thus far this desire has never been realized, and we hope, notwithstanding the great injury now sustained, their wonted forbearance will be continued. If our word will have any weight with our countrymen in this very trying time, we would say, *forbear, forbear*—revenge not, but leave vengeance to him "to whom vengeance belongeth."

P. S. On last Saturday, it was reported, that a large company of Georgians were on their way to arrest Mr. Ross and Major Ridge.[50] We think it not improbable that an attempt of that kind will be made. If so, self defence, on the part of the Cherokees, many of whom, we understand, were at Ross's and Ridge's, would undoubtedly be justifiable.

April 7, 1830

INTRUDERS

We stated week before last that the intruders collected at the gold mines[51] had been warned off by the Agent, and that many of them had agreed to leave the country. It appears that almost all had departed, until it was ascertained that the agent had procured no warrants in Georgia,[52] as it was supposed he would—they have now returned with redoubled force, and unless a speedy check is put to their ingressions, there will be in a very short time four times as many as there are now. It cannot be questioned but that they are encouraged by some of the leading men of the neighboring counties, by the lawyers especially, who will stand "between them and all danger." This is no great matter of surprise when it is known that some of the *officers of the United States* have been clandestinely encouraging intruders into the nation—we do not mean the United States' agent, but the *appraisers*.[53] A number of the intruders with whom the late difficulties existed, have lately certified that they came into the nation through the encouragement given to them by these appraisers, who told them that it was perfectly safe to take possession of all the improvements abandoned by the emigrants, and that this encouragement was given, as they understood from the appraisers, upon authority of a letter from the President of the United States,—and furthermore, some of these certifiers heard the letter read! That such a letter has emanated from the executive of the United States we are not yet disposed to believe, but that such an encouragement has been given by authorized officers of the Government, we have no manner of doubt. On these officers then, and on the government whose servants they are, must rest the responsibility arising from difficulties with the intruders introduced by them into the nation. And what is the design of this underhanded management? Is there any thing good in it. No, but abundance of evil—one Cherokee has already been barbarously murdered! The design is the same with that kept in view, if not avowed, by the proceedings of the State of Georgia, and the Gen. Government: the forced removal of the Cherokees—They will not effect this by *open force*, but they will *wear them out* by *permitting*, yea, *encourging* intruders to come in their midst, and by harrassing them in other innumerable ways. This is what *we* call *force*—this is what *we* call *oppression, systematic oppression.*

April 21, 1830

The Committee of Indian Affairs in the House of Representatives, in page 21 of their report[54] say:

> That the greatest portion, even of the poorest class of the Southern Indians, may, for some years yet, find the means of sustaining life, is probable; but, when the game is all gone, as it soon must be, and their physical as well as moral energies shall have undergone the farther decline, which the entire failure of the resources of the chase has never failed to mark in their downward career, the hideous features in their prospects will become more manifest.

Whoever really believes that the Cherokees subsist on game, is most wretchedly deceived, and is grossly ignorant of existing facts. *The Cherokees do not live upon the chase*, but upon the fruits of the earth produced by their labour. We should like to see any person point to a single family in this nation who obtain their clothing and provisions by hunting. *We* know of no one. We do not wish to be understood as saying that they do not hunt—they do hunt some, probably, about as much as white people do in new counties, but they no more depend upon this occupation for living than new settlers do. Game has been nearly extinct for the last thirty years, and even previous to that, when the Cherokees depended upon the chase for subsistence, they were obliged to obtain their full supply of meat and skins out of what is now the limits of this nation.[55] Cut off the last vestige of game in these woods, and you cannot starve the Cherokees—they have plenty of corn, and domestic animals, and they raise their own cotton, and manufacture their own clothing.[56]

> The committee do not mean to exaggerate, either in the statement of facts, as they are believed to exist, or in the deductions which they make from them, as to the future prospects of the Indians.

The Committee have, nevertheless, greatly exaggerated—all their statements, of what they call *facts*, are nothing but unfounded assertions.

> The intelligent observer of their character will confirm all that is predicted of their future condition, when he learns that the maxim, so well established in other places, "that an Indian cannot work," has lost none of its universality in the practice of the Indians of the South; that there, too, the same improvidence and thirst for spirituous liquors attend them, that have been the foes of their happiness elsewhere; that the condition of the common Indian is perceptibly declining, both in the means of subsistence and the habits necessary to procure them; and that upon the whole, the mass of the population of the Southern Indian tribes are a less respectable order of human beings now, than they were ten years ago.

The maxim of our enemies, "that an Indian cannot work," the committee suppose "well established," and it would most certainly be well established if they could but prove their naked assertions. We know of many Indians who not only *work*, but work *hard*. Who labors for the Cherokee and builds his house, clears his farm, makes his fences, attends to his hogs, cattle and horses; who raises his corn, his cotton and manufactures his clothing? Can the committee tell? Yes, they have an answer at hand. He has no house, no farm, no hogs, cattle, no corn to save him from starvation, and clothing to cover him from nakedness.

We know not what to say to such assertions. The above maxim has been received by many as truth, but not by the intelligent observers of their character, but by their enemies and such as have not had the means of knowing facts. But suppose it was once well founded and correctly applied, it has long since lost its universality. We invite any person who may be hesitating on this point to come and see and judge for himself—we are not afraid that the truth, the whole truth, should be known—we desire it—we invite "the most rigid scrutiny."

"That an Indian has an inherent thirst for spirituous liquor," is another maxim which the committee think is well applied to the Cherokees. On the charge of intemperance, we are very far from pleading *not guilty*—we have ourselves raised our voice against this crying sin.[57] But if the charge is, that the Cherokees have greater thirst for spirits than whitemen, we unhesitatingly deny it. It is not so—we speak from personal observation. Facts form the only proper criterion in this case, and what is the actual state of things? We know, most certainly know, that among the whites of the surrounding counties intemperance and brutal intoxication (at which humanity may well shudder,) may be witnessed in every neighborhood. Go to their elections and courts and number those who are under the influence of inebriating drink, and then come into the nation, and visit the Indian elections, courts and the General Council and make a disinterested comparison, and we pledge ourselves that there is less intemperance here on these occasions than among the whites. It is an incontrovertible fact, for the truth of which we appeal to all honest eye-witnesses, that on those public occasions, particularly at the General Council, which continues four weeks, a drunken Indian is seldom to be seen. We are sorry that intemperance does exist, but is it not universal? There has been of late considerable reformation among the Cherokees in common with other parts of the country.

Against the statement of the committee that "the condition of the common Indian is perceptibly declining," we must give our unbiased testimony, and appeal to facts repeatedly made public—*the common Indian among the Cherokees is not declining, but rising.*

> The Cherokees are generally understood to have made further advances in civilization than the neighboring tribes, and a description of their real situation may make it of less importance to notice, in detail, the condition of the others. Upon this point the committee feel sensibly the want of that statistical and accurate information, without which, they are aware that they cannot expect their representations to be received with entire confidence. To supply this deficiency, however, they have sought information from every proper source within their reach and do not fear that the general correctness of their statements will be confirmed by the most rigid scrutiny.

Here then, is the great mystery—*the committee feel sensibly the want of* STATISTICAL *and* ACCURATE *information!* This accounts for their misrepresentations.— But was it impossible to obtain correct statistical information? They thought so we presume, for they sought it "from every *proper source*." If they had only applied for testimonies which disinterested persons would not consider *improper*, the information would most easily have been obtained. *We* could have furnished them with a true copy of a statistical table taken in 1824, & by inquiring at the Agency, we doubt not they could have found another taken in 1810.[58] By comparing these they would have formed a true foundation for facts and accurate deductions. But no, such a course would not possibly answer—they seek information from somewhere else, not from documents, and resident whitemen, but from the enemies of the Indians, who are looking with eager expectation to their removal, that they may take possession of the spoil, obtained by means the most unmanly and iniquitous.

May 15, 1830

Our readers will perceive, from the proceedings of the Senate, that the bill reported by Mr. White[59] has *passed* that body and the amendments proposed by Mr. Frelinghuysen[60] *rejected*! So we feared it would be the case. It has been a matter of doubt with us for some time, whether there were sufficient virtue and independence in the two houses of Congress, to sustain the plighted fate of the Republic, which has been most palpably sacrificed by the convenience of the Executive. Our doubts are now at an end—the *August Senate* of the United States of America, (tell it not in Gath, publish it not in the streets of Askelon,) has followed the heels of the President, and deliberately laid aside their treaties. They have declared that they will not be governed by these solemn instruments, made and ratified by their advice and consent. When it comes to this, we have indeed fallen upon evil times. Very soon the House of Representatives will decide, if it has not already decided, on this important question. It is much to be feared the Representatives of the people will not respond to the views and feelings of their constituents, but deliver their weak allies to their enemies. Be that as it may—let both Houses of Congress decide as they may, we confidently think justice will be done, even if the Cherokees are not in the land of the living to receive it—posterity will give a correct verdict. But we are not now making such an appeal—we hope we are not yet at the end of our row—we hope there is yet a *tribunal*[61] where our injured rights may be defended and protected, and where self interest, party and sectional feelings have nothing to do.— Let then the Cherokees be *firm* and *united*—Fellow citizens, we have asserted our rights, we have defended them thus far, and we will defend them yet by all lawful and peaceable means.— We will no more beg, pray and implore; but we will *demand* justice, and before we give up and allow ourselves to despondency we will, if we can, have the solemn adjudication of a tribunal, whose province is to interpret the treaties, *the supreme law of the land.* Let us then be *firm* and *united.*

June 19, 1830

In our last was given the proceedings of the House of Representatives on the Indian bill, to the time when it was ordered to a third reading. In this day's paper will be found the final proceedings, and the adoption of the amendment by the Senate. We stated last week that if the amendment was adopted, or the bill failed, by the refusal of the Senate to adopt it, our fears would not be realized in their full extent. But since, upon mature reflection, and after reading the doings of the Senate which the reader can see for himself, we are constrained to say, the formal acknowledgment of the validity of treaties is but a mock show of justice. This is evident from the fact that the very men who have all along contended for the unconstitutionality of treaties with the Indians, were the first to agree to the amendment of the House, & to reject the amendments offered by Messrs. Frelinghuysen, Sprague and Clayton.[62] The bearing of the bill then on the interests of the Indians will be the same as if it had passed in its original shape.

We confess our ignorance, our utter ignorance, of the views of the majority of the members of Congress, so far as they have been developed, on the rights of the Indians, and the relation in which they stand to the United States, on the score of treaties; nor can we discern the consistency of contending for the unconstitutionality of these treaties, and yet at the same time, declaring that *they shall not be violated*, which a man of common sense would take to be the meaning of the amendment. If a treaty is unconstitutional, it is of course null and void, and cannot be violated. If a treaty may *not be violated*, it is taken for granted that it is binding; and if it is binding, the parties to it have a right to demand its enforcement. How are we then to understand the decision of the Senate on this important subject? What do they mean by adopting the proviso, and at the same breath deliberately refusing to enforce the provisions of the existing treaties? We can find no suitable answer but this, *palpable injustice is meditated against the poor Indians*!

It is somewhat surprising that many well meaning persons, who would never in other circumstances, lend their aid and influence to do injustice to the Indians should be perfectly blinded by this bill. They believe, as its advocates represent to them, that it is harmless, and that its operation cannot be otherwise than highly beneficial. But they are greatly deceived —the bill is not harmless, nor was it ever intended to be harmless. For the truth of this assertion, look at the decision of the Senate, rejecting the several amendments for the protection of the Indians? This 500,000 dollars is intended to co-operate with any other expedient, which will play at our backs like a flaming sword, while this sum will address itself to our fears & avarice.[63]

Compulsion behind, while the means of escape are placed before. Go or perish. And this is said when treaties are declared to be binding, and in them ample provisions are made for the protection of the Indians. Who would trust his life and fortune to such a faithless nation? No Cherokee *voluntarily* would.

At this time of much distress and darkness, the Cherokees can have some consoling thoughts—they have been ably and most manfully defended to the last, and although self-interest and party and sectional feelings have triumphed over justice, yet it has been only by a pitiful majority, and against the known will and feelings of the good people of these United States. Those worthy advocates of Indian rights in the Senate and House of Representatives will be remembered while there is a living Cherokee—and notwithstanding oppression and power may crush us and utterly destroy us, yet their laudable efforts to save us, will be estimated in their proper light, and held in pleasing recollection by the Christian and Philanthropist of future ages, and of all countries.

January 8, 1831

During last summer, a Cherokee, by the name of George Tassel, was arrested within the limits of this nation by the Sheriff of Hall County,[64] for murder committed upon the body of another Cherokee, likewise within the limits of the nation. Tassel was taken over the line, and committed to jail. At the last term of Superior Court of Hall County, he was brought out for trial, but the Judge postponed the trial until a convention of Judges at Milledgeville[65] should pronounce upon the constitutionality of the act extending the jurisdiction of the State over the Cherokees. As was to be expected, the convention decided in favor of the jurisdiction of the State. Judge Clayton[66] therefore called a court for the purpose of trying Tassel, who was accordingly tried on the 22d of November, and found *guilty*. It appears that Judge Clayton refused to grant an appeal by a writ of error, to the Supreme Court of the United States, and even refused to certify that Tassel was tried. Tassel was therefore sentenced to be hung on the 24th of last month, on which day he was executed, in defiance of a writ of error sanctioned by the Chief Justice of the United States,[67] and served upon Governor Gilmer,[68] on the 22d, two days previous to the execution. We invite the readers' attention to the following interesting information which we copy from the Milledgeville Recorder. The conduct of the Georgia Legislature is indeed surprising—one day they discountenance the proceedings of the nullifiers of South Carolina—[69] at another, they even out-do the people of South Carolina, and authorize their Governor to hoist the flag of rebellion against the United States! If such proceedings are sanctioned by the majority of the people of the U. States, the Union is but a tottering fabric, which will soon fall and crumble into atoms.

February 19, 1831

We have already noticed the late law of Georgia, making a high misdemeanor, punishable with four years imprisonment at hard labour in the penitentiary, for any white man to reside, after the 1st of March, *within the limits of the Cherokee nation*, (so the copy of the laws we received reads—let the people of Alabama, Tennessee and North Carolina look out—the Georgia legislature is carrying its sovereignty too far,) unless he takes the oath of allegiance, and obtains from the Governor's agent a permit to continue his residence *until further orders*.[70] We cannot help alluding again to that law as being extremely unjust, without saying any thing of its oppressive tendency, both to the whites and Cherokees. It is certainly oppressive on the whites, even admitting that the state of Georgia has an undoubted jurisdiction over the Cherokee territory. Why is it that it is required of *them* to take the oath, when by extension of that jurisdiction, they were admitted as citizens of the state? Is such a requirement made of other citizens? Do the constitution and the laws recognize such a distinction? But what becomes of the liberty of conscience in this case?— Here a white man cannot enjoy that liberty without going to the penitentiary.

What are the effects of this law on the Cherokees? Disastrous. Just such effects as were intended the law should produce. The design appears to be to bring them back to their old station—

carry them back twenty years hence. Deprive them of all their means of improvement, and remove all the whites, and it is thought by some, the great obstacle is taken out of the way, and there will be no difficulty to bring the Cherokees to terms. If this is not the *design* it may possibly be the *tendency* of the law. Now let the reader just consider. If we introduce a minister of the Gospel to preach to us the way of life and salvation, here is a law of Georgia, a Christian law too it is said, ready to seize him and send him to the Penitentiary, in violation of the constitution of the state itself.[71] (See Constitution of Georgia, Art. 4–Sec. 10,) If we bring in a white man to teach our children, he is also arrested and suffers a similar punishment. If we wish a decent house built, and invite a carpenter into the nation to do the work, here is a law which forces him from our employ and soon numbers him with culprits. If we introduce a Blacksmith, or any other mechanic, it is the same. Is it not natural to suppose that the tendency of such a law on the Cherokees would be disastrous? It forces from them the very means of their improvement in religion and morals, and in the arts of civilized life.

March 26, 1831

The Georgia Guard[72] who arrested Mr. Worcester[73] and others went by way of Hightower and arrested the Rev. John Thompson—They also took Mr. William Thompson. The latter had resided for the last few years at that place as a blacksmith, but had removed on the first of March, and was at the time of his arrest a citizen of Carroll County.[74] The prisoners, six in number, were now conducted to the place of encampment, five miles further. Next morning the Guard, instead of going directly into Georgia, turned the course towards their headquarters, where they arrived the day following, in true military stile, under the sound of fife and drum. Here Col. Nelson[75] delivered the prisoners into the hands of the Governor's agent, Col. Sanford,[76] who took them under his special charge. Perceiving that Mr. William Thompson was one of the number, he immediately ordered to have him put in jail. However, by means of the intercession of his companions and the officiers who arrested him, Mr. Thompson was discharged and permitted to return home, after being in jail but a short time. Four of the others, viz: Messrs. Worcester, Thompson, Wheeler[77] and Gann were, on Thursday morning, marched towards Laurenceville with a sufficient Guard under the command of Sanford himself.— They arrived there on the same evening, the court being in session. On the next day they were brought before his honor Judge Clayton by a writ of Habeas Corpus for examination. The case was continued to Saturday, on which day his honor discharged Messrs. Worcester and Thompson, because the first was a *Postmaster* and the other a *missionary*, considering both in the light of *Agents of the Government*.[78] It is proper to observe that the counsel for the prisoners did not make a plea to that effect, but studiously refrained from it. The other two, Gann & Wheeler, together with Messrs. J. A. Thompson & B. F. Thompson, who were arrested on the same charge in Laurenceville on Thursday evening, were bound, in the sum of $250 each, to appear in Court in September. It is thought there is very little hope of their escaping the penitentiary, for the Judge decided that the law is constitutional, and there is no clause in it which can except them from its operation, as in the case of the missionaries. We are yet unwilling to believe that such an unrighteous law can be executed in a Christian land.

The foregoing is the history, told in a few words, of this affair, as far as it has proceeded. We were very much surprised to hear that the missionaries were discharged on the ground of their being agents of the government. Who ever thought of such a thing before? It shows that a Judge may twist a law into what shape he pleases, if policy makes it necessary, for we are confident the greatest hostility was directed against the missionaries, and that the law was intended particularly to embrace them. We know it was so understood in Milledgeville and elsewhere. If the missionaries are agents of the Government, as Judge Clayton has decided, then the public may rest assured Gen. Jackson will *reform* them out. If he could, he would like to do it very well; but it is a matter of thankfulness that they are not his agents, and are still out of his hands.

Among many *honorable acts* of the President towards the Cherokees is his giving leave to Georgia, against an express provision of the intercourse law of 1802,[79] to survey the Cherokee territory.[80] Several companies of Georgia surveyors are now busily engaged in their work, no one to make afraid or molest. They have already run three sectional lines, and they will soon cut the company up into districts of nine miles square. We suppose the President looks upon these proceedings with approbation, & this is, among others, what his admirers call an *honorable act*.

PONEY CLUB

This is the name given to an association of thieves scattered along the frontier in Carroll and other new counties in Georgia —It is this club which Brooks, Commanding the Georgia Guard, said in a circular he would root out of the nation, and not permit to live within the limits of the Cherokee territory. This promise was very good, but like all other promises of the white man lately, it meant exactly the reverse of what it was supposed to mean. The club, instead of being expelled, has been introduced by authority. Some of the leaders and the most abandoned members, and a few who were accesary in the murder of Chuwoyee[81] are authorized to settle in this nation, and are permitted by Georgia to occupy some of the improvements abandoned by emigrants.[82] We understand all the Philpots and others of their connections are thus snugly brought into the nation. It is certainly mortifying to see such people receiving encouragement & protection from laws, when at the same time men of undoubted virtue—and fit for any Society in the civilized world are dragged about as felons. In what a humiliating position are placed the honor and virtue of a state when such things are permitted.

This poney club has been a great pest to those Cherokees living near the frontier. They have stolen property to large amount from them, we presume not less than five hundred head of cattle and horses. It is said there are now very few left for them to steal. But when they have nothing to steal, they easily find other methods to harrass the Cherokees. The following is but an instance among many.

A few days since two of these white men came to a Cherokee house, for the purpose, they pretended, of buying some provisions. There was no person about the house but one woman of whom they inquired for some corn, beans, &c. The woman told them she had nothing to sell. They then went off in the direction of the field belonging to this Cherokee family. They had not been gone but a few minutes when the woman of the house saw a heavy smoke rising from that direction. She immediately hastened to the field and found the villains had set the woods on fire but a few rods from the fences, which she found already in a full blaze. There being a very heavy wind that day, the fire spread so fast, that her efforts to extinguish it proved utterly useless. The entire fence was therefore consumed in a short time. It is said that during her efforts to save the fence the men who had done the mischief were within sight, and were laughing heartily at her! To permit all this we are told is *honorable*.

April 16, 1831

CHEROKEE NATION
VS.
THE STATE OF GEORGIA

Under this head we copied into our paper the views of intelligent editors and correspondents respecting the opinion of the Supreme Court on the Cherokee case.[83] For our own part we think we understand the nature of the decision, and it is just as we supposed it would be if the motion for an injunction could not be sustained. But we perceive that an effort is insuing to mislead the public—to produce the impression that the case has not only been dismissed, but the pretensions of Georgia & the views of the Executive have been sustained by the Court. It is said by some that the case is "settled," forever put to rest, and a hope is entertained, that nothing more will be said on the subject. Now we apprehend this is doing injustice to the Supreme Court. The case is not settled for the great question at issue between the

State of Georgia and the Cherokees was not before that tribunal. The only question before it was, whether it had original jurisdiction— whether the Cherokee nation was a foreign state in the sense of the constitution, & the decision went no further than to say, as we understand it, that the Court has *not* original jurisdiction, and that the Cherokee nation was *not* a foreign state in the sense of the constitution. How such a decision can be understood and construed as sustaining the pretensions of Georgia and the views of the President of the United States, we are not able to say. Every body knows what the pretensions of Georgia and the views of Gen. Jackson are—Now let these be carefully compared with the views, expressed by the Court in their opinion—we say let them be diligently compared, and the public will see if there is any thing in the latter which supports the former. For our part we can discover no similarity between them, but on the contrary a *wide* difference.

It is true the Court says that it cannot protect the Cherokees *as a nation*, but does it say that they are not entitled to the protection of the Gen. Government? The opinion plainly intimates that it is the duty of the Executive and Congress of the United States to redress the wrongs, and to guard the rights of the Cherokees if they are oppressed. The whole responsibility is thus thrown, by a judicial decision, upon those branches of the Government. The rights of the Cherokees are as plain, as sacred, as they have been, and the duty of the Government to secure those rights is as binding as ever. What will the Cherokees do under such circumstances? What else can they do but remain peaceably where they are and continue to call upon the *people* of the United States to fulfill their engagements, their solemn promises which have been repeatedly made and which have always been regarded until the commencement of Mr. Eaton's "new era." We see nothing to alter their determination to remain and to maintain their rights by all suitable measures. The land is theirs—their right to it is "unquestionable," and it cannot be taken away from them without great injustice to them and everlasting infamy to the United States. They stand upon a perfectly safe ground as regards themselves—if they suffer, they will suffer unrighteously—if their rights and their property are forceably taken away from them the responsibility will not be upon them, but upon their treacherous "guardians."

We hope the fears of the Editor of the National Gazette will never be realized. The Cherokees are for peace—they have been in amity with the United States for the last forty years—they have been her faithful allies in time of war—they have buried the hatchet long since, and given their word that the blood of the white man shall not stain their hands.— Why should they now fly to rash and unavoidable measures to vindicate their injured rights? They will not, at least we think they will not; and such is our advice. It is more blessed to suffer than to be the oppressors.— It is more blessed than to gain by unrighteous means. If the white man must oppress us—if he must have the lead, and throw us penniless upon the wild world, and if our cries and expostulations will avail nothing at the door of those who have promised to be our guardians and protectors, *let it be so*. We are in the path of duty, and the Judge of all the earth will vindicate our cause in his own way and in his own good time.

May 28, 1831

POST OFFICE REFORM

Who would have thought?—but so it is—The *searching operation* of the Government has penetrated into the wilderness? New Echota has fall under the proscription of Major Barry,[84] the Post Master General. On last Monday our worthy P. Master, Rev. S. A. Worcester, who has given general satisfaction for the faithful and able manner in which he has discharged the duties of his office, was turned out, to make way for Wm. J. Tarvin, a trader who came into the nation under a license from the United States' Agent, according to the law of 1802, regulating trade and intercourse with the Indian tribes,[85] but who has since taken the oath of allegiance to Georgia, and is now selling spirituous liquor to the Indians, against the express injunction of the law referred to above. The present administration must be Lynx-eyed if they can see from Washington "public interest" suffering in these woods, and if they can "promote" it in this manner. If the Post Master General had inquired of those who are interested in the management of the Post Office in this place, he would have learnt that they had a perfect confidence in the Gentleman whom he has turned out, and that the present incumbent would not have been recommended by them to that station. But no; it is the "public interest" he is promoting, and he is doing it in a fine way.

July 16, 1831

GEORGIA & THE MISSIONARIES

The persecution now progressing against the missionaries seems to be unrelenting, which proves to our mind that the law of Georgia against white men was particularly intended for them. The object of the Legislature was to get them out of the country; but as it would have been too courageous to effect this without some pretext, the act requiring an oath of allegiance was passed, with which it must have been known, the missionaries, as conscientious men, could not comply. This being the case, it was supposed the only alternative left them to avoid the penalty of the law was to remove and to leave their Churches and Schools. But as some of them have thought proper not to do even that, they are dragged about as felons, and are to be shut up in the Penitentiary for a term not less than four years. "*Law enforced to strictness sometimes becomes the severest injustice.*"[86] Such is this act of Geo. It is the height of injustice when enforced in the *mildest* manner. But what will it be said when the present proceedings are ahead of that law? when acts are committed which no man in his senses will say they are in accordance with the law? The following is to the point:

The Rev. Mr. McLeod,[87] superintendent of the Methodist Missions in this nation, and not residing within the Georgia charter, lately returned from a visit to Tennessee. He merely passed this part of the nation a few weeks since, on his way to Creek path to fill an appointment previously made. On his way back to the Tennessee side of the Nation, where we believe he has generally made his stay, when but a few miles from Mount Wesley, he met the Guard conducting Messrs. Worcester and Trott[88] to their head quarters. He was arrested by them, ordered to dismount from his horse and take the line of march with the other prisoners.— Mr. Wells,[89] stationed at Chatooga, was with Mr. McLeod, and was about to be taken also, but on making proper representation, as to his location, he was permitted to go on his way if he thought proper. He followed on, however, leading Mr. McLeod's horse, supposing he would be released as soon as he got to Camp Gilmer,[90] as others have been who were arrested under similar circumstances.

Now under *what* law, under what provision of *any* law was Mr. McLeod arrested, and compelled to walk fifty or sixty miles? It becomes the good people of Georgia to see to these things. There are many in that state, we have not the least doubt, who advocated the extension of the laws over the Indians, who would deprecate such measures, if they were but properly informed of what is going on.

We wish to say a few words on another point. The State of Georgia is a Christian State—Its laws are founded on Christian principles, and the Governor, we suppose, is at least a nominal Christian. The Superiority of Christian laws over the rest of the world consists in their mildness.— The guilty are punished not in any way which may partake of cruelty, but *in mercy*. It is therefore, in the constitution of Georgia, most properly made the duty of the Governor to execute the laws *in mercy*. It has appeared to us, however, in some of the circumstances we have related in the execution of the Georgia laws over this nation, that there has been exhibited too much of a vindictive spirit. The case of Mr. Worcester was certainly one which demanded, at least, forbearance and that mercy which the Governor has in his oath promised to observe. He could not have removed without leaving his wife on a bed of sickness. His circumstances were known to the Guard, who we have reason to believe were disposed to be forbearing. His arrest, at this time, we are told, was founded on a direct order from the Governor for that purpose. The case, also, of the Cherokee we noticed last week as being under arrest, shows in what spirit Georgia laws are executed. It is said they found him digging gold, and when they were about to take him he took a gun to defend himself. After he was induced or made to lay that by, he took his knife. For this he was severely beaten on the head with a stick. On this part of the story we have nothing to say. But after he was in the power of the Guard—completely in their hands—when it was impossible that he could do them injury, he was chained to a waggon, and in that situation compelled to travel when they left Oougillogee. This is the information we have received.

Messrs. Worcester & Butler[91] are probably now in the jail of Gwinnett County, to await their trial at the next Superior Court. They will not think it worthwhile, we suppose, to give bail, as that would give them no security against another arrest. Look at the case of Mr. Trott. It is even reported here that Governor Gilmer has ordered his agent, that if Mr. Worcester gives bail and crosses the Chattahoochy river[92] on his return to his family, to have him again immediately arrested. That, however, makes no difference, as the case of Mr. Trott renders it certain that he would again be taken.

Since the foregoing was written, information has reached this place that Mr. McLeod, as we supposed, was discharged at the station.

It seems too that Mr. Wells, who is said above to have been in company with Mr. McLeod, received a severe blow with a stick from the hands of the Commanding officer. What the *crime* was we have not particularly understood.

Our neighbors, we perceive, are reviving their old argument, which we thought was nearly forgotten, viz: That the Cherokees ought to be removed beyond the Mississippi, *because* they are so wretched and can never be reclaimed where they are. The scarcity of provisions among us at this time they believe is a sufficient evidence that we are sinking fast, and their bowels of compassion are moved on our account. We lately published extracts from a communication of a Georgian, giving a wretched description of our wants. The public have been refreshed with other accounts of a like nature.— We will state fairly the argument of these wise and compassionate men. 'The Cherokees were a wretched people in the year 1830; they are far more so in 1831—some of them of both sexes are nearly naked and as nearly starved, several families having been known, which was not so a year ago, to subsist for three weeks on sap and roots; *therefore* the Cherokees are deteriorating.' As the argument goes they will be worse off a year hence than they are at present. Now we are very willing to meet them on this ground.— We are willing the whole question should turn upon this point. Let the coming year decide the matter. We will admit what has been said of our condition—we will admit that we are suffering for provisions, and that many are nearly starved and some compelled to sustain life by subsisting upon sap and roots, and that if our condition is not improved a year hence it will be sufficient evidence that we are deteriorating, and that we ought to be removed. On the other hand, if our affairs should be considerably improved, and if we should about that period be well supplied with provisions, it will demonstrably prove that we are not sinking, but sensibly rising from our degraded state, and therefore, as the argument is, we ought not to remove to the west of the Mississippi.— According to this mode of reasoning we have the most cheering prospects of a complete triumph: Notwithstanding the trouble, anxiety and disturbances occasioned by the whites, the people throughout the nation generally have used more than common industry in cultivating their farms, and there is now at this time a prospect of fine crops. If kind providence shall continue to grant us as good season as we have enjoyed, there will be more corn raised this year in the Cherokee Nation than at any other time since its existence.[93]

We beg our compassionate friends, therefore, not to put their benevolent purposes into effect right away, but to permit us a little longer to subsist on sap and roots. We are endeavoring to procure something more substantial. But if, with the aid of providence, we shall fail, we will then go to a land flowing with milk and honey, where, we presume, our kind friends intend we shall have every thing to our hearts' content without any exertion on our part.

CHEROKEE WOMEN, BEWARE

It is said the Georgia Guard have received orders, from the Governor we suppose, to inflict corporeal punishment on such females as shall hereafter be guilty of insulting them. We presume they are to be the judges of what constitutes *insult*. We will simply give our opinion upon this subject. According to our understanding of insult, we think, first, it is very undignified for a female to exercise it under any circumstances; and second, it is equally undignified for any gentleman to inflict a corporeal punishment on a female who may be guilty of such a crime.

August 27, 1831

TO THE READERS OF THE CHEROKEE PHOENIX

In the last two numbers of this paper I narrated very briefly some transactions which I conceived to be an invasion of the liberty of the press.[94] The circumstances attending my first interview with the Commander of the Georgia Guard were of such a nature, I thought, as to justify me in relating them to the public, and to give me sufficient reason in saying that I did not consider the movement in any other light but as an attempt to frown me down. My second interview with him, brought about as it was by force, by means of *armed men*, only confirmed the impressions I had first received. This movement is to me so extraordinary, so directly and openly in conflict with one great liberty guaranteed by the constitutions of the United States and the several states, that I feel impelled by a sense of duty to the public to recur to the subject again.

When I was first commanded before Col. Nelson, threats similar to the one he delivered had previously reached me through rumor. I had understood that one of the officers had said, if it were not for pity's sake, "he would whip me within an inch of my life." Another had declared, he would castigate & flagellate me. When, therefore, messengers came to my house with a request that I should walk up and have an interview with

Nelson before he left the place, I partly anticipated what the object was. I, however, readily consented to go, supposing, if his intention was really to deliver a formal threat of personal chastisement, I might be able to learn from him what particular part of the Phoenix they considered objectionable, as abusive and slanderous, demanding such satisfaction. Consequently in the course of our conversation, I requested him to point to a particular part of the paper which was so offensive to him. He did not specify but spoke of the Phoenix in its general course and character. I had intended, if any specification had been made, and if I had been permitted to speak and to explain fairly and freely upon the subject, to say to him that I stood ready to do him justice if I had injured him. I had intended to tell him that there was a wide difference between a deliberate falsehood and a mere misstatement. I was not conscious of being guilty of the former, but that it was more likely I had made some misstatements in attempting to relate particulars founded upon information; that if I was convinced of any such error I was prepared at all times to repair the wrong. But I obtained no opportunity to say these things—I found there was a determination to consider me a libeller without making a single specification, and that the rod was to bring me to my senses without allowing me the privilege of making reparation, if indeed I had been (as a nominal editor) guilty of slandering and abusing the Guard. It is true Col. Nelson spoke of falsehoods told by missionaries directly, and through me, but I could not learn where they were to be found in the Cherokee Phoenix.

Such in substance had been the nature of our interview when messengers again came to me with a request similar to the first. I refused to go according to my own ideas of propriety. I did not think I was bound to obey every summon that may be sent to me, particularly when I had reason to believe that the object was by no means a friendly one. I could not, according to my sense of honor, leave my own appropriate duties to attend to the call of any person, who pretended to act only in his private capacity, merely for the purpose of hearing a lecture & a threat of personal chastisement. I fully anticipated, when I refused to go, that I would be taken as a prisoner. When, therefore, I saw seven armed men approach my house I had no other idea but that I would be taken for refusing to comply with the call of Nelson. I was, consequently, not a little surprised to hear the question put to me, "Who fired that gun?" It is not for me to say whether they really thought I had shot at them, or had instigated another to do it. My impression at the time was, that this circumstance was seized as a pretext to take me and to bring me before Nelson; for there certainly was no investigation of the subject, and I was not kept under arrest five minutes after I arrived where he was. Be that as it may, I knew nothing of the firing of the gun, except merely hearing the report; and if it was really discharged at the Guard it was not done, I presume, within one hundred yards of my house. If it were not that I have Nelson's word that he arrested me for the firing of the gun, I should be firmly of the opinion, notwithstanding the circumstances under which that arrest was brought about, that my refusal to obey his call subjected me to the treatment I have received. Nelson's question to me, "Why did you not come when I sent for you," would confirm that opinion.

In my last I attempted to give the substance of his talk, delivered after I was relieved of arrest. I was not, certainly, in the least offended when he informed me that I was considered by them as an ignorant man. I knew they were welcome to their own opinions, and in regard to that one particular, I was sensible they were correct. I was conscious of ignorance myself, besides I had never placed myself before the public as a man of information. The intimation as to the part which the Missionaries have taken in conducting the Cherokee Phoenix, that is, in writing the editorial articles, is too foolish to demand any attention. I have said as much on that subject as I intend to say, unless any person, who believes or makes the assertion, will come out and attempt to prove that I have only been a tool in the hands of the Missionaries. I do not wish, however, to disguise the truth, that I entertain the highest regard for these persecuted men. I consider them to be men of the strictest integrity and veracity. Among them I have the honor to number some of my best and nearest friends, but they have as little desire to interfere with my duties as editor as to interfere with any other person.

The reader has already been informed that Col. Nelson became enraged* because I said, I did not care any thing about his threat. I have, also, already explained what I meant by that expression. I did not mean to dare his threat, or to intimate that the punishment, if inflicted, would be nothing to me. I believe I should feel as keenly as any other man the indignity offered to my person, if my back were indeed subjected to the lash; but yet that would be but a trifling consideration in my mind when compared with the dictates of my conscience, and what I consider to be the line of honesty. I could not abandon these on account of threats. That was my meaning. And why should I care about a threat if I really thought I was doing my duty, and felt not the workings of a guilty conscience? I should be unworthy of the confidence of my countrymen and friends, if, for fear of a personal chastisement, I should be guilty of a dereliction of duty.

In closing this article I would respectfully inquire, would a white man have been treated as I have been? If it is possible that a white editor can be treated in this manner, what would be the feelings of the people? In this free country, where the liberty of the press is solemnly guarantied, is this the way to obtain satisfaction for an alleged injury committed in a newspaper? I claim nothing but what I have a right to claim as a man—I complain of nothing of which a privileged white editor would not complain.— THE EDITOR

September 17, 1831

I, most readily, publish the communication of Col. Nelson, because, first, I consider the course he has now taken the most correct and honorable way to obtain satisfaction for an alleged wrong committed in a newspaper; and, second, because that communication *substantially* confirms my statements relating to our interview. It will be recollected that I did not profess to relate every thing that was said by Col. Nelson—my object was

*His expression, "I will mount you," has been misunderstood by some readers. They suppose he meant he would place me on a horse and take me off as a prisoner. It is a Southern phrase, meaning *he would fall upon and beat me*.

to give the substance, that is, to inform my readers that I was threatened with personal violence, & to state, what I understood to be the reason assigned. It did not enter into my mind that it was necessary, in order to do Col. Nelson or myself justice, to particularize every item of his conversation. A great deal of it I thought was not to the purpose, and still more I considered too foolish to demand any attention. The public, however, can now judge, having Nelson's own narrative and my statements to compare, whether I could possibly have had any motive to publish "mutilated accounts."

I cannot say that Col. Nelson has given a correct account of his conversation, that account being, or professing to be, a *particular* one. I do not now recollect to have heard many of his expressions he has introduced into his communication, and I think others which he has forgotten to relate; but that is to very little purpose, as his conversation throughout was nearly of the same tenor, and as my want of recollection may be attributed to my mental *indolence* in attending to his lecture, or to my *ignorance*—His expressions may have *escaped* me, or I may have *misunderstood* them.

On the letter of Col. Nelson, considering it as a communication, a few remarks may be necessary.

1. Whoever has been the "real editor" of the Cherokee Phoenix, he does unnecessary injustice to him when he says, that he had 'never failed to attribute their (Georgia Guard) acts to the worst passions of the human heart.' On this score I might very safely appeal to the reader, who must be supposed to recollect what has been said in this print in regard to the Guard. Sure I am if any such liberty has been taken with their acts and motives, by the editor, in any editorial article, I am ignorant of it.

2. He says they were "well informed" that Worcester was the real editor, and yet after Mr. Worcester has thought proper to publish a disclaimer, not a particle of evidence has been adduced to prove that he has been indeed the editor. Such a course is ungenerous, for if indeed they are "well informed" of that alleged fact, the public would be glad to be put in possession of the proofs. In this enlightened age and country a man is not, as we have been taught to believe, to be proclaimed guilty without some testimony.

3. By what kind of improved logic do they come to the conclusion that I am responsible for articles I never wrote, as they say, and yet complain bitterly 'of certain' communications to which are appended the names of persons who did not write them on the very ground, it would seem, that those who *penned* them are to be considered responsible? If Mr. Worcester has written the editorial articles, of which, they say, they are "well informed," how is my name, standing at the top of the paper, to *shield* him? If they can prove that he is the "real editor," why cannot the law reach him, and why should I be punished for the acts of another person? But if my name has really "shielded" my persecuted friend "from that punishment which his crimes have so justly merited," what shields his own name? He has 'appended' his name to certain statements—if those statements are not true, how is it that the law cannot reach him there, unshielded as he is by my name? My *indolence* and *ignorance* prevent me from understanding these matters.

4. There is one way in which Col. Nelson can obtain a complete and speedy satisfaction for all the injuries done to him in the Cherokee Phoenix. He says he informed me that "their (Missionaries) character for falsehoods was so well established, and their motive so well understood, that *censure* from them was *praise* to the Guard." Now it seems to me that if he can make it appear to the satisfaction of the public that these missionaries have conducted this paper, that one of them is the "real editor," he will at once gain his object, for whatever is said in the Phoenix, will be but *praise to the Guard*. This would settle the question at once, and instead of denouncing the paper they would have occasion to rejoice in its existence, if, under any circumstance, charity may be said to rejoice in iniquity.

5. Col. Nelson says he told me that there were not five lines of truth in the editorial articles relating to the Guard. Speaking of the same in my statement, I said, Col. Nelson "did not specify, but spoke of the Phoenix in its general course & character." Certainly I did not exaggerate here. To say that there have not been five lines of truth is saying too much. It is said that when a man attempts to prove *too much* he invalidates his testimony. Another expression is as equally unfortunate. "Impositions attempted to be passed upon the public, by inserting the most

slanderous communications with individuals' names appended to them, *who do not know the first letter of the alphabet*" &c. It will be seen he is not speaking here of those "more ignorant" men who presided as officers at certain meetings, where "indecorous preambles! & inflammatory resolutions"!! were passed, but of those we presume, who published accounts of their arrests by the Guard. He alludes to one in particular, & the only one who may be said to be too ignorant to write, but he does know the first letter of the Alphabet. I am told by those who know him best that he can read. And how did he abuse the Guard? The following sentence is copied from his communication: "In justice to the officers, and privates generally, I am bound to say that I was *friendly* and *politely* treated *by all*, except the above named Mr. Pope." As to the alleged imposition there was none. The readers of the Cherokee Phoenix were not informed that Benjamin Murray penned his communication himself—it was sufficient that he brought it to the office with his name "appended" to it.[95] As I told Col. Nelson, in our first conversation, Murray had a right to procure another person to write for him. Even General Jackson had "appended" his name to pieces he never wrote.

6. Something was really said of "real wrongs" done to the Cherokees by the missionaries in appropriating to themselves charities sent into the nation for the poor Indians—Col. Nelson thought if I was a patriot I ought to expose the evil. I can only say I have no right to speak of things which have no existence. Col. Nelson, I presume, was misinformed as to the object of the charities sent into the nation—but he was *credibly* informed by those who told him that they have never been distributed among the "poor and more indigent Cherokees."

7. What were the counsels which the Missionaries gave, and which, "if followed, would have been *treason* to the state and *destruction to the Cherokees*?" It is to be regretted that in all such grave charges so little attention should be paid to the proofs necessary to substantiate them. The testimony of respectable Cherokees will be credited, if not by the Georgia Courts, certainly by the public, and Col. N. will do immense good by revealing it. Georgia would soon get rid of the Missionaries without sending them to the Penitentiary.

8. Col. Nelson says I did not correctly state his hasty words closing our second interview I am pretty confident I stated them *substantially* as I heard them.— There were persons present who heard them I am willing an appeal should be made to them.

ELIAS BOUDINOT
Ed. of the Cher. Phoe.

September 17, 1831

We publish this week some letters of Governor Gilmer relating to the missionaries. He charges them, and other white men who are now suffering with them, with crimes, such as *sedition, opposing* the HUMANE policy of the Government, *exciting* the Indians &c., with these he has nothing to do in executing the law of the State. That law does not allege such charges, but it is very natural for the executive of the state now to hold these worthy men in the worst light possible, in order to 'misdirect' the public mind from the true state of the case, and to save the Government, of which he is the head, from that universal reprobation which it is destined to receive. We are not, therefore, surprised to hear him talk about what has been 'said,' 'believed,' or 'reported' of these missionaries. But the public will bear in mind that they have not been arrested, tried and sentenced to four years hard labor in the Penitentiary *for any of the charges the Governor alleges against them.* To the people of this nation, who know them best, & to most of our readers, it is not necessary that we should even say those charges are utterly unfounded.

The Governor is pleased to say that the rights of liberty, personal security and private property of the Indians are better protected under the laws of the state than heretofore. The Cherokees will laugh at this. They believe, and know by sad experience, the reverse to be the fact. There has been no personal security thus far, and liberty does not exist even in name, and as to property, it is sufficient that many, who may be said to have been under good circumstances heretofore, have been completely ruined since the administration of the Georgia laws commenced.

Governor Gilmer expresses the fullest conviction that the happiness and prosperity of the Cherokees depends upon their removal. It may be so after having made their existence here almost intolerable; but whatever the conviction of the Governor may be on this point, we presume the Cherokees will judge for themselves—They yet have no disposition to remove.

In his letter to Col. Sanford the Governor says—"Everything therefore, which is done in relation to them, (Cherokees) should have for its purpose, the accomplishment of that object" (their removal.) This is a precious confession. We knew this to be the case long ago. Every thing that has been done of late by Georgia and by the General Government—all the despotic acts that have been passed & the innumerable oppressions that have been countenanced by them, have been directed to that particular object, and we dare say the instructions of His Excellency on that point will be obeyed to the very iota.

November 12, 1831

It has been customary to charge the failure of attempts heretofore made to civilize and christianize the aborigines to the Indians themselves. Whence originated the common saying, "An Indian will still be an Indian."— Do what you will, he cannot be civilized—you cannot reclaim him from his wild habits—you may as well expect to change the spots of the Leopard as to effect any substantial renovation in his character—[96] he is as the wild Turkey, which at "night-fall seeks the tallest forest tree for his roosting place." Such assertions, although inconsistent with the general course of providence and the history of nations, have nevertheless been believed and acted upon by many well meaning persons.[97] Such persons do not sufficiently consider that causes, altogether different from those they have been in the habit of assigning, may have operated to frustrate the benevolent efforts made to reclaim the Indian. They do not, perhaps, think that as God has, of one blood, created all the nations of the earth, their circumstances, in a state of nature, must be somewhat the same, and therefore, in the history of mankind, we have no example upon which we can build the assertion, that it is impossible to civilize and christianize the Indian. On the contrary we have instances of nations, originally as ignorant and barbarous as the American natives, having risen from their degraded state to a high pitch of refinement—from the worst kind of paganism to the knowledge of the true God.

We have on more than one occasion remarked upon the difficulties which lie in the way of civilizing the Indians. Those difficulties have been fully developed in the history of the Cherokees within the last two years. They are such as no one can now mistake—their nature is fully revealed, and the source from whence they rise can no longer be a matter of doubt. They are not to be found in the "nature" of the Indians, which a man in high authority once said was as difficult to change as the Leopard his spots. It is not because they are, of all others, the most degraded and ignorant that they have not been brought to enjoy the blessings of a civilized life.— But it is because they have to contend with obstacles as numerous as they are peculiar.

With acommendable zeal the first Chief magistrate of the United States undertook to bring the Cherokees into the pale of civilization, by establishing friendly relations with them by treaties, and introducing the mechanic arts among them. He was indeed a "father" to them—They regarded him as such—They placed confidence in what he said, and well they might, for he was true to his promises. Of course the foundation for the improvement which the Cherokees have since made was laid under the patronage of that illustrious man. His successors followed his example and treated their "red children" as human beings, capable of improvement, and possessing rights derived from the source of all good, and guarantied by compacts as solemn as a great Republic could make. The attempts of those good men were attended with success, because they believed those attempts were feasible and acted accordingly.

Upon the same principle have acted those benevolent associations who have taken such a deep interest in the welfare of the Indians, and who may have expended so much time and money in extending the benign influence of religion. Those associations went hand in hand with the Government—it was a work of co-operation. God blessed their efforts. The Cherokees have been reclaimed from their wild habits—Instead of hunters they have become the cultivators of the soil—Instead of wild and ferocious savages, thirsting for blood, they have become the mild "citizens," the friends and brothers of the white man—Instead of the superstitious heathens, many of them have become the worshippers of the true God. Well would it have been if the cheering fruits of those labors had been fostered and encouraged by an enlightened community! But alas! no sooner was it made manifest that the Cherokees were becoming strongly attached to the ways and usages of civilized life, than was aroused the opposition of those from whom better things ought to have been expected. No sooner was it known that they had learned the proper use of the earth, and that they were now less likely to dispose of their lands for a mess of pottage, than they came in conflict with the cupidity and self-interest of those who ought to have been their benefactors—Then commenced a series of obstacles hard to overcome, and difficulties intended as a stumbling block, and unthought of before. The "Great Father" of the "red man" has lent his influence to encourage those difficulties. The *guardian* has deprived his *wards* of their rights—The sacred obligations of treaties and laws have been disregarded—The promises of Washington and Jefferson have not been fulfilled. The policy of the United States on Indian affairs has taken a different direction, for no other reason than that the Cherokees have so far become civilized as to appreciate a regular form of Government. They are now deprived of rights they once enjoyed—A neighboring power is now permitted to extend its withering hand over them—Their own laws, intended to regulate their society, to encourage virtue and to suppress vice, must now be abolished, and civilized acts, passed for the purpose of expelling them, must be substituted.—Their intelligent citizens who have been instructed through the means employed by former administrations, and through the efforts of benevolent societies, must be abused and insulted, represented as avaricious, feeding upon the poverty of the common Indians—the hostility of all those who want the Indian lands must be directed against them. That the Cherokees may be kept in ignorance, teachers who had settled among them by the approbation of the Government, for the best of all purposes, have been compelled to leave them by reason of laws unbecoming any civilized nation—Ministers of the Gospel, who might have, at this day of trial, administered to them the consolations of Religion, have been arrested, chained, dragged away before their eyes, tried as felons, and finally immured in prison with thieves and robbers.

Is not here an array of *difficulties*?— The truth is, while a portion of the community have been, in the most laudable manner, engaged in using efforts to civilize and christianize the Indian, another portion of the same community have been busy in counteracting those efforts. Cupidity and self-interest are at the bottom of all these difficulties—A desire *to possess* the Indian land is paramount to a desire to see him *established* on the soil as a *civilized* man.

December 21, 1831

> The following is an extract of a letter, from the Editor of this paper, who is now travelling through parts of the United States, on business connected with the nation—dated Augusta, Ga.[98]

On the second day after we left New Echota, we passed a place, about half way between Taloney and Daniel's, where we were told one of the officers of the Georgia Guard intends to settle. He has already made a commencement towards erecting some buildings. By what authority he intends to settle in the nation, and what business he professes to follow for a livelihood are not known. There is no good land near. He cannot of course follow farming—Nor can he follow merchandising, for there are no settlements or Cherokees in the neighborhood. It is his intention, likely, to open a public house, the place I am speaking of being on the main road leading from Georgia to Tennessee. It is probable, also, he intends to take possession of certain medicinal springs which I am told are to be found about a quarter of a mile from where he is building. As to the *authority*, it is as practiced of late, encouraged by the State of Georgia, and countenanced by the General Government.

At Gainsville[99] we saw Milledgeville papers containing the message of Governor Lumpkin[100] relating to the citation of Mr.

Justice Baldwin on the case of Messrs. Worcester and Butler.[101] We have heard very little said on the subject, and in fact on the general subject of Indian affairs. The people appear to be more indifferent than I expected to find them; and it is not at all improbable that, if it were not for the leading men, another demogogue who cannot obtain the votes of the people but by promising the *Indian land*,[102] the Cherokees would be permitted to remain peaceably on the soil of their fathers, and the authority of the Supreme Court of the United States would not be contempted. I am glad that it has so turned out that Mr. Baldwin, who is supposed to be favorable to the Georgia policy, has signed the citation. You will recollect the Chief Justice was very harshly dealt with last year, on Tassell's case, by the legislature and by most editors in the State.— His conduct was viewed in the light of *interference*. Whether the legislature will think proper to notice Mr. Baldwin's citation as they did the Chief Justice, I do not know. I think it probable, however, they will. Some of the editors are out upon Mr. Baldwin already. They view his conduct as an "outrage upon the dignity of the State." It is surprising how some of them, at least, will attempt to mislead the people. They must know that for a Judge of the Supreme Court to sign a citation is not an outrage upon the dignity of a state—it is a matter of course. Whether the court will take jurisdiction is another question.

Since we came to this place I have seen the *Federal Union*[103] which states that the House of Representatives of Georgia Legislature passed, a few days since, a bill authorizing the immediate survey and occupancy of the Cherokee country. The Senate had not yet acted upon it.[104] Be their course as it may it cannot effect the determination of the Cherokees. They have taken their stand and are contending for vital principles—They have counted the cost, and if the long protracted controversy between them and Georgia must end in the loss of their beloved country it must be so.[105] They must trust themselves to superintending providence, and to the guarantees and promises of good faith which the people of the United States have made. To take our lands by force is a serious matter—it is fraught with considerations full of interest to the people of Georgia themselves and to the whole Union.— A respectable portion of Georgia view it in that light. It would be robbery to all intent and purposes. And would the General Government look on with indifference and see its solemn pledges trampled in the dust? "There is a Lion in the way" whether the Government of the United States interferes or not—The integrity of the Union is at stake. As respects the Cherokees, their duty is plain—they cannot err. They reside on the land which God gave them—they are surrounded with guarantees which this Republic has voluntarily made for their protection and which once formed a sufficient security against oppression. If those guaranties must now be violated with impunity for purposes altogether selfish, the sin will not be at our door, but at the door of our *oppressor* and our faithless *Guardian*.

NOTES

[1]*Laws*, 85.

[2]Because only 18 percent of the households in the Nation contained members who could read English, Cherokee types were necesary if the paper reached most citizens. The Prudential Committee of the American Board reported in October 1827 that "punches have been cut, and types cast, after the model of Guess's alphabet at the foundry of Messrs. Baker and Greele, Boston." *Report of the American Board of Commissioners for Foreign Missions* (Boston, 1827), 111. Since the press and types did not arrive until 1828, the prospectus had to be printed in English only. For the Cherokee alphabet, see pp. 48-58.

[3]According to Boudinot, Cherokee translations of articles proved to be "by far the most arduous part of our labor." *Cherokee Phoenix*, May 6, 1828. Consequently, most material reprinted from English language journals appeared only in the original language. Laws of the Cherokee Nation, selections from the Bible, editorials, and letters to the editor usually were published in both languages. Scripture sometimes appeared only in Cherokee. In general, however, the *Phoenix* published far more English material than Cherokee. The Council was keenly aware of the discrepancy and the difficulties involved in translating all copy into Cherokee. In 1829 Edward Graves was hired to translate proceedings of the Council for publication in the *Phoenix*, and Stephen Foreman was appointed assistant editor to translate public documents and English news into Cherokee. *Laws*, 135, 144.

[4]Boudinot obtained most news items and "miscellancous articles" that were not local in subject from the approximately 100 newspapers with which he exchanged copies.

[5]Boudinot had hoped to begin publication in January, but no paper arrived with the press, and the printer had to go to Knoxville for a supply. An excellent account, written by John F. Wheeler, relates these early days at the

printing office in New Echota and describes the technical aspects of producing a bilingual newspaper. See James C. Pilling, *Bibliography of the Iroquoian Languages* (Washington, D. C., 1888), 41–42. Harris left after the first year, and Wheeler became the chief printer. In 1831 the name of John Candy, who was Cherokee, began to appear as printer of the *Phoenix*.

[6]Many people attributed the purchase of the press to the U.S. government or to missionary societies. Boudinot viewed the press as a source of national pride, and he constantly reiterated the fact that the Cherokee Council appropriated funds obtained by contribution and from annuities for the press.

[7]The law which specified the responsibilities of the editor of the *Phoenix* provided that "he is also expressly empowered to use his discretion in every respect, in order that the Nation may be benefitted by the institution." *Laws*, 86. Nevertheless, the Council did issue directives to the editor occasionally (see below), and the Cherokee Constitution of 1827 did not guarantee freedom of the press.

[8]Boudinot managed to become embroiled in a dispute with the Methodist missionary, N. D. Scales, who advocated in a letter to the *Phoenix* "itinerating schools" instead of permanent mission stations. Boudinot's published comments questioned both the Methodists' educational method and Scales's contention that the denomination had 700 members. Boudinot did not publish Scales's acrimonious reply, but he did make a qualified apology. Next, in a letter to a Tennessee newspaper, Scales accused Samuel Austin Worcester, a white American Board missionary, of being the real editor of the *Phoenix*. Boudinot countered with an "unequivocal denial." One consequence of this exchange was a Council injunction on the publication of "scurrilous communication and sectarian religious material." *Phoenix*, May 28,1828, June 18, 1828, Nov. 12, 1828; *Laws*, 114. The correspondence published in the *Phoenix* has been reprinted with annotation in Kilpatrick and Kilpatrick, *New Echota Letters*, 34–40.

[9]Boudinot was a Presbyterian.

[10]Proverbs 15:1.

[11]In the Feb. 28 issue, Boudinot reprinted excerpts from a Georgia legislative report that asserted "the absolute jurisdictional right of the said state" to Cherokee land within its borders.

[12]Many people including Andrew Jackson believed that a majority of the Cherokees favored migration and that wealthy and powerful chiefs prevented the masses from negotiating a removal treaty. U.S. Senate, *Indian Removal*, 5 vols. (S. Doc. 512, 23d Cong., 1st sess.), 2:186–87, 113. Actually, the vast majority of Cherokees opposed removal, and those who ultimately signed a removal treaty were fairly well-to-do and certainly not representative of the majority.

[13]The 1828 presidential campaigns of John Quincy Adams, the incumbent, and Andrew Jackson, who won, were among the most vituperative in the history of the United States. The Cherokees desperately hoped that Adams would be reelected because he had discarded a fraudulent treaty made with the Creeks. Glendon G. Van Deusen, *The Jacksonian Era, 1828–1848* (New York, 1959), 26–27; Debo, 88–95.

[14]The *Phoenix* cost $2.50 if paid in advance, $3.00 if paid within six months, and $3.50 if paid at the end of the year. People who read only Cherokee paid

$2.00 in advance and $2.50 at the end of the year. A subscription was considered to be continued unless the subscriber notified Boudinot otherwise, and Boudinot found that he did have "occasion to complain" of delinquency in payment.

[15]The Committee on Indian Affairs of the U.S. House of Representatives passed a resolution appropriating $50,000 "to enable the President of the United States to extinguish the title of the Cherokee Indians." *Phoenix*, Feb. 28, 1828.

[16]Richard Henry Wilde of Augusta, Ga.

[17]Although the American Board of Commissioners was technically interdenominational, most missionaries among the Cherokees were Presbyterians.

[18]In this same issue, "Oakfuskie" charged that "our Marshals are asleep on the watch tower" and that they "adhere to the policy of picking money from the National pocket without rendering the required services." He maintained that the Light Horse Companies, which district courts and marshals replaced, were far more successful at enforcing the law because they apprehended, tried, convicted, and punished criminals on the spot.

[19]About 6,000 Chickasaws, who had resided primarily in Mississippi north of the Choctaw Nation, finally moved to Indian territory under the provisions of the Treaty of Pontotoc signed Oct. 20, 1832. According to the terms of the treaty, the Chickasaws paid for their own removal out of funds arising from the sale of tribal lands. Kappler, 2:356–62; Grant Foreman, *Indian Removal: The Emigration of the Five Civilized Tribes of Indians* (Norman, Okla., 1932), 193–226.

[20]The actual population was about 15,000.

[21]Boudinot became a member of the executive committee of the Cherokee Temperance Society founded in 1829. The temperance movement was not confined to the Cherokee Nation. Many prominent reformers, such as Dr. Benjamin Rush, and well-known ministers, including Lyman Beecher, William Ellery Channing, and Theodore Parker, were advocates of temperance. In 1826 Dr. Justin Edwards of Andover Theological Seminary and other like-minded individuals established the American Society for the Promotion of Temperance, which was modeled on the American Board of Commissioners for Foreign Missions. See Alice Felt Tyler, *Freedom's Ferment: Phases of American Social History from the Colonial Period to the Outbreak of the Civil War* (Minneapolis, 1944), 308–50, and Ian R. Tyrrell, *Sobering Up: From Temperance to Prohibition in Antebellum America, 1800–1860* (Westport, Conn., 1979).

[22]The Council prohibited "ardent spirits" within three miles of a court or Council meeting site in 1822 and at "ball plays, all night dances and other public gatherings" in 1825. Those who violated this ordinance were subject to "having all their liquors wasted." *Laws*, 26, 36.

[23]This correspondent had attended an Indian dance for the first time in order to "obtain a knowledge of the manners and customs of those unfortunate children of nature."

[24]Despite "an era of reformation," Cherokees continued to perform traditional dances into the 20th century. See Frank G. Speck and Leonard Broom, *Cherokee Dance and Drama* (Berkeley, Cal., 1951); Gilbert, 321–29.

[25]The Cherokee ball play, or stick ball, was more than a mere game. Sometimes called "the little brother to war," the ballgame involved ritual and danger. The ballgame was a device for settling disputes not serious enough for war and a means of keeping men fit in case war did occur. Southeastern Indians still engage in ball games. See James Mooney, "The Cherokee Ball Play," *American Anthropologist* 13 (1890):105–32; Raymond D. Fogelson, "The Cherokee Ball Game: A Study in Southeastern Ethnology" (Ph.D. diss., Univ. of Pennsylvania, 1962); Mark Reed, "Reflections on Cherokee Stickball," *Journal of Cherokee Studies* 2 (1977):195–200.

[26]Hominy.

[27]Europeans did not consider hunting, fishing, and war to be "work," and so they believed that Cherokee men were lazy and Cherokee women were virtual slaves. Women did, in fact, perform most of the manual labor: they farmed, gathered wood, carried water, and made most household goods. But women also had considerable freedom and power in aboriginal Cherokee society. See Theda Perdue, "The Traditional Status of Cherokee Women," *Furman Studies*, 26 (1980):19–25.

[28]Kappler, 2:29–33.

[29]The agent who was most actively involved in the implementation of the "civilization" program inaugurated by Washington was Return J. Meigs. For Meigs's career among the Cherokees (1801–1823), see Henry Thompson Malone, "Return Jonathan Meigs—Indian Agent Extraordinary," *East Tennessee Historical Society's Publications* 28 (1956):3–22.

[30]According to the calculations of Samuel Austin Worcester in 1830, 1,084 Cherokees were members of Protestant churches. *Phoenix*, May 8, 1830.

[31]Boudinot and Worcester collaborated on *Cherokee Hymns Compiled from Several Authors and Revised*, one of their first joint ventures.

[32]Once again Boudinot stressed the importance of a separate political existence to Indian survival.

[33]Georgia's discriminatory legislation was scheduled to take effect for Cherokees residing within the state on June 1, 1830.

[34]War and disease had reduced the once numerous Catawbas of upper South Carolina to approximately 110 individuals. Charles M. Hudson, "The Catawba Indians of South Carolina: A Question of Ethnic Survival" in *Southeastern Indians Since the Removal Era*, ed. Walter Williams (Athens, Ga., 1979), 114.

[35]The Council had hoped that Boudinot's journey of 1826 would raise enough money for a seminary (or high school) as well as a press. The mission schools generally offered only an elementary education, and Cherokees who sought higher education had to go outside the Nation. When the Foreign Mission School, which Boudinot had attended, closed in 1827, the need for a secondary school in the Cherokee Nation became more acute. The Council, however, never appropriated funds, and well-to-do Cherokees often sent their children to white academies.

[36]The treaty of 1819 provided that a tract of land within the ceded territory be sold and the proceeds invested in stock. Interest or dividends would be used "to diffuse the benefits of education among the Cherokee nation." Kappler, 2:177–81.

[37]A clan is composed of people who believe they have a common ancestor

even though that ancestor can no longer be identified. Cherokee clans were matrilineal; that is, a person belonged to the clan of his mother and his only kinsmen were those who could be traced through women. The best study of Cherokee clans and the practice of blood vengeance is Reid, *A Law of Blood.*

[38]On Apr. 10, 1810, representatives of the seven clans met and abolished blood vengeance. *Laws*, p. 4. Shadowy evidence exists that the practice continued. In 1829, for example, the Council passed an act that warned that anyone who killed Noochorwee, who had been convicted of murder and given a reprieve, would "experience the consequences of the law, as if it had been done to him in a state of innocence." Obviously, there was fear that someone would seek vengeance. Ibid., 12. Gabriel suggests that Boudinot's own death was an act of vengeance, while accounts of the Council that condemned him indicate that his kinsmen made the decision and thus relieved the executioners of any fear of retaliation under the old law of blood. Gabriel, 177; and Wilkins, 320–21.

[39]Boudinot published an address by President Jackson to the Creeks and a letter from Secretary of War John H. Eaton to the Cherokee delegation to Washington. Jackson informed the Creeks that they must become subject to the oppressive laws of Alabama if they remained in the state, and Eaton told the Cherokees that they resided on their land only by "permission" of the states, which retained "original sovereignty." Eaton also reprimanded the Cherokees for writing a constitution that established a formal, republican government since Georgia interpreted this as a direct challenge to the state's sovereignty. For the administration's position, see Satz, 9–38.

[40]While Jefferson, Madison, and Monroe encouraged "civilization," they did not discount removal to the land acquired in the Louisiana purchase. See Prucha, 211–49.

[41]See pp. 107-8.

[42]He is referring to the Constitution of 1827. See *Laws*, 118–30.

[43]White communities on the Cherokee Nation's border with Georgia.

[44]The delegation headed by John Ross, the principal chief, sent a memorial to Congress that protested the imminent extension of Georgia law over the Cherokees. U.S. House, "Memorial of John Ross, and Others, Representatives of the Cherokee Nation of Indians" (H. Doc. 145, 20th Cong., 2nd sess., 1827).

[45]A newspaper published in Milledgeville, then the capital of Georgia.

[46]The Cherokees also owned slaves, and their legislature passed laws to protect and regulate the institution of slavery. See Halliburton; and Perdue, *Slavery*.

[47]"Intruders" were whites who moved illegally onto Indian land. Most were squatters; a few "bought" their land from Indians in violation of U.S. and Cherokee laws prohibiting individual purchases and sales of Indian land. For an analysis of the problem of intruders on Indian land and attempts by the United States to prevent such incursions, see Prucha, 139–87.

[48]Col. Hugh Montgomery was the U.S. agent among the Cherokees.

[49]These were houses abandoned by Cherokees who chose to emigrate under the terms of the 1828 treaty with the Arkansas Cherokees. The emigrants could not sell the houses under Cherokee law; Cherokee land was

owned in common and reverted to the Nation when the occupant removed. *Laws*, 113, 139–41.

[50]John Ross was principal chief and Major Ridge, uncle of Boudinot, was his counselor.

[51]In 1829 gold was discovered on Cherokee land, and the next year Georgia Gov. George R. Gilmer prohibited whites and Indians from mining gold. See Fletcher Green, "Georgia's Forgotten Industry: Gold Mining," *Georgia Historical Quarterly* 19 (1935):93–111.

[52]Whites in Cherokee territory were already under the jurisdiction of Georgia. Therefore, arrest warrants had to be obtained in Georgia.

[53]The federal government appraised the improvements of those Cherokees who had emigrated under the terms of the 1828 treaty so that their claims could be paid.

[54]U.S. House, "Report on Removal of Indians from Georgia" (H. Doc. 227, 21st Cong., 1st sess., 1830).

[55]Cherokee hunting grounds were primarily in what is today West Virginia, Tennessee, and Kentucky. This territory was ceded in a series of transactions in the 18th and early 19th centuries. See Charles C. Royce, *The Cherokee Nation of Indians* (5th Annual Report, Bureau of American Ethnology; rpt., Chicago, 1975).

[56]For a study of the Cherokee economic situation, see McLoughlin and Conser, 678–703.

[57]See pp. 100-2.

[58]Meigs conducted a census in 1810, and the Cherokee Council authorized a census in 1824.

[59]Hugh L. White of Tennessee, chairman of the House Committee on Indian Affairs, supported the Indian Removal Act, which authorized the president to negotiate removal treaties. The Senate version of the bill passed on May 28, 1830. *U.S. Stat.*, 4:411–12.

[60]Theodore Frelinghuysen of New Jersey tried to amend the act so that current treaties could not be violated.

[61]Boudinot is alluding to the U.S. Supreme Court.

[62]Peleg Sprague of New Jersey and Thomas Clayton of Delaware.

[63]The Indian Removal Act appropriated funds for negotiations. Boudinot feared that the money would be used to bribe unauthorized chiefs to make a treaty. The Council shared this apprehension and had passed an act in Oct. 1829 that committed to writing the law imposing the death penalty on anyone who ceded land without authorization. *Laws*, 136–37.

[64]A Georgia county adjoining the Cherokee Nation.

[65]The capital of Georgia.

[66]Augustin Smith Clayton of the Superior Court of Gwinnett County, Ga.

[67]John Marshall.

[68]George R. Gilmer, governor of Georgia, 1829–31, 1837–39.

[69]Led by John C. Calhoun, nullifiers contended that the states created the union and that when the union exceeded powers expressly granted it, a state could nullify that action. South Carolina sought to nullify protective tariffs passed by Congress. The classic statement of the theory of nullification is Calhoun's *A Disquisition on Government*, ed. Richard K. Cralle (New York, 1943).

[70]*Acts of Georgia* (1829):145–46.

[71]Many whites believed that the missionaries actually operated the Cherokee government and that they encouraged the Cherokees to resist removal. Since a number of the missionaries were from New England, southerners were even more suspicious of their motives. Missionaries were the first arrested under the new Georgia law. See below.

[72]In 1830, the Georgia legislature suspended operation of the Cherokee Council and courts and established a militia, the Georgia Guard, to patrol the Nation. *Acts of Georgia* (1830), 114–18, 154–55.

[73]Samuel Austin Worcester, a missionary of the American Board of Commissioners for Foreign Missions, collaborated with Boudinot on translations of hymns, tracts, and the New Testament. See Bass; and Kilpatrick and Kilpatrick, *New Echota Letters*.

[74]A Georgia county.

[75]Col. Charles H. Nelson.

[76]Col. John W. A. Sanford.

[77]John F. Wheeler was the white printer of the *Phoenix*.

[78]Clayton based his decision on the assistance that the federal government provided for mission schools. The receipt and expenditure of government funds, he reasoned, made the missionaries government agents. Worcester was also postmaster at New Echota, the Cherokee capital.

[79]The Intercourse Act of 1802 recognized Indian land titles as established by treaty. Only another treaty between an Indian nation and the U.S. government (and not a state legislative act or an individual purchase) could alter that title. *U.S. Stat.*, 2:139–46.

[80]In 1830 the Georgia legislature authorized the survey of Cherokee land and the distribution of plots in a lottery. The law specified that Indians were not to be forcibly evicted from tracts they actually occupied. *Acts of Georgia* (1830), 127–43.

[81]See pp. 112-13.

[82]Georgia appointed an agent to rent abandoned Cherokee improvements to whites, with the proceeds going to the state.

[83]The Cherokees had asked the U. S. Supreme court for an injunction against the enforcement of Georgia laws within the Nation. The Nation brought the case before the Supreme Court on the supposition that Indian tribes were the same as foreign countries. The Court refused to rule in the case on the grounds that the Cherokee Nation was not a foreign government but a "domestic dependent nation." 5 Peters 1. Boudinot was correct about the implications of the case.

[84]William T. Barry was the postmaster general of the United States.

[85]See Prucha, 102–38.

[86]This anonymous Latin maxim was cited by Cicero and used by Racine, Voltaire, and others.

[87]Dickson C. McLeod was the Methodist missionary at New Echota.

[88]James J. Trott was a Methodist missionary whose wife was Cherokee.

[89]Martin Wells.

[90]Headquarters of the Georgia Guard.

[91]Dr. Elizur Butler and Rev. Samuel A. Worcester of the American Board were the only people to serve sentences in the Georgia penitentiary for violating the law against whites in Cherokee territory.

[92]The boundary between the Cherokee Nation and Georgia.

[93]Even in 1835 when the situation was more serious, many Cherokees produced not only enough corn for their own use but also some for sale. Census of 1835 (Henderson Roll), Record Group 75, National Archives, Washington, D. C. McLoughlin and Conger calculated that in Tennessee, Cherokees harvested an average of 313.54 bushels of corn per farm; in Alabama, 342.76; in North Carolina, 109.79; and in Georgia, 154.26.

[94]The *Phoenix*, which had wide circulation outside the Cherokee Nation, was a thorn in Georgia's side. The continuation of the paper after the arrest of the missionaries and its consistent defense of Cherokee rights challenged Georgia's version of the Cherokee "problem." Surprisingly, the state did not legislate the paper out of existence (as it did the Cherokee Council and court system) and did not seize the press until 1835, after it had ceased operation.

[95]Benjamin Murray was a twenty-year-old white man arrested by the Georgia Guard. The commanding officer, according to Murray's letter, "pronounced me as belonging to a certain Mr. Pope of Wilks County who is one of said guard. He, savage like, shouldered his musket and used as much authority over me as if he had captured me in Africa & brought me to Georgia for his use." Murray's mother managed to have him freed by testifying that he had not reached adulthood. *Phoenix*, May 7, 1831.

[96]"Can the Ethiopian change his skin, or the leopard his spots?" Jeremiah 13:23.

[97]For the dominant attitudes of whites toward Indians, see Roy Harvey Pearce, *The Savages of America: A Study of the Indian and the Idea of Civilization* (Baltimore, 1953); Robert F. Berkhofer, Jr., *The White Man's Indian: The History of an Idea from Columbus to the Present* (New York, 1978).

[98]Boudinot was raising money for the continuation of the paper.

[99]The county seat of Hall County, Ga.

[100]Wilson Lumpkin, governor of Georgia, 1831–35. For Lumpkin's views, see his *The Removal of the Cherokee Indians from Georgia*, 2 vols. (New York, 1907).

[101]On Sept. 16, 1831, 11 white men were convicted of illegal residence in Cherokee territory; that is, they had refused to take the oath of allegiance to Georgia. Nine decided to take the oath and accept executive clemency. Worcester and Butler chose to go to prison under a sentence of four years. Associate Supreme Court Justice Henry Baldwin ordered the state to present arguments before the Court as to why the missionaries' conviction should not be overturned. Lumpkin, who became governor on Nov. 9, declined to appear. For an excellent account of the state's position, see Carl Jackson Vipperman, "Wilson Lumpkin and Cherokee Removal," 57–65.

[102]Georgians began popularly electing their governors in 1825, and until 1832 when the tariff also became a major issue, they tended to vote for the man who took the strongest stand against the Indians. As a result, political rhetoric was virulently anti-Cherokee. See Coleman, 130–34.

[103]A Milledgeville newspaper.

[104]The bill passed, and Lumpkin sent in armed surveyors in April 1832, *Acts of Georgia* (1831), 74–75, 164–67. See Vipperman, "Lumpkin and Removal," 70–75; and Douglas C. Wilms, "Georgia's Land Lottery of 1832," *Chronicles of Oklahoma* 52 (1974):52–60.

[105]While he was on this journey, Boudinot began to have reservations about continued resistance to removal. When he returned home, he suggested that the Cherokees should consider negotiation. This stand brought him into conflict with the Nation's leaders, who forbade him to publish his views in the *Phoenix*. Boudinot resigned.

Letters and Other Papers Relating to Cherokee Affairs: Being a Reply to Sundry Publications Authorized by John Ross

by

Elias Boudinot,
Formerly Editor of the
Cherokee Phoenix

« « « Boudinot arrived in Washington shortly after the *Worcester* v. *Georgia* decision, and he became convinced that the federal government would not act to free the missionaries. The Cherokees, he believed, were powerless, and their only alternative was removal. Restrained by the Cherokee authorities from publicizing his views, Boudinot resigned as editor of the *Cherokee Phoenix*, and the possibility of debating the removal issue in the Cherokee Nation disappeared. Even the Council ceased to be an open forum; in 1834 Major Ridge, John Ridge, and David Vann were impeached for favoring removal. Harrassment and threats of violence, however, did not deter the small group that advocated negotiation, and in December 1835 they signed a removal treaty. Some of the signers of the Treaty of New Echota were no doubt motivated by the prospect of financial gain; others, including John Ridge, had political ambitions they believed could be served by the treaty. Boudinot, on the other hand, promoted removal in part out of loyalty to his family but primarily because of his concern for "the moral condition of this people."

The people for whom he expressed such deep concern did not rally to his cause. In fact, they came to vilify Boudinot and impugn his motives, and they looked to Principal Chief John Ross to preserve them in their homeland. Ross was indefatigable in his attempts to have the treaty abrogated or, when that seemed impossible, to have it amended in order to provide better terms for the Cherokees. In order to gain support in the United States for the Cherokees, Ross encouraged sympathetic whites to publicize the plight of his people, and he himself authored two pamphlets. These publications harshly criticized members of the Treaty Party for their unauthorized negotiations and branded them as traitors.

Boudinot replied in "Letters and Other Papers Relating to Cherokee Affairs: Being a Reply to Sundry Publications Authorized by John Ross." In this pamphlet Boudinot maintained that removal or extermination were the Cherokees' only alternatives. He insisted that Ross's initial refusal to negotiate, his subsequent attempts to have the treaty discarded or amended, and his ultimate haggling over terms only prolonged the suffering of the Cherokee people. First published in Athens, Georgia, in 1837, the pamphlet became public record as Senate Document 121, 25th Congress, 2nd session.

Boudinot was unjustified in most of his accusations. First of all, Ross remained in office beyond his term because, given the extraordinary circumstances of the Georgian invasion, no elections could be held, and the Council ratified this arrangement. Furthermore, little evidence exists to support Boudinot's contention that Ross purposefully misled both the Cherokees and the United States by telling the former that he would not cede their land and the latter that he would agree to a treaty. Ross did employ a variety of delay tactics. He hoped that the United States would tire of the Cherokee controversy, some other issue such as the tariff would divert interest, or a new administration would prove more sympathetic to the Cherokees. Ross also believed that when the Georgians discovered that the Cherokee country was red clay hills instead of the Garden of Eden, they would content themselves with the gold mines and relinquish their claim to the entire region in exchange for a cash settlement. These may have been unreasonable expectations, but they were probably genuine and they were certainly shared by the vast majority of Cherokees. In the final analysis, the wealthy, acculturated principal chief and not the editor filled with missionary zeal represented the sentiments of the Cherokee people. Perhaps this realization, even more than the controversy over removal, accounts for the obvious bitterness in Boudinot's last published work.

A number of modern scholars have examined the removal issue. In *Stand Watie and the Agony of the Cherokee Nation* (Memphis, 1979), Kenny A. Franks advocated the treaty party's position on Cherokee removal. A sympathetic but more evenhanded discussion can be found in Thurman Wilkins, *Cherokee Tragedy: The Story of the Ridge Family and the Decimation of a People* (New York, 1970). John Ross's position has been objectively presented by his biographers. See Gary E. Moulton, *John Ross, Cherokee Chief* (Athens, Ga., 1978), and Rachel Caroline Eaton, *John Ross and the Cherokee Indians* (Menasha, Wis., 1914). The Ridge family's own defense can be found in Edward E. Dale and Gaston Litton, eds., *Cherokee Cavaliers: Forty Years of Cherokee History as Told in the Correspondence of the Ridge-Watie-Boudinot Family* (Norman, Okla., 1939), which will be countered by the publication of Moulton's edition of the John Ross papers. The writings of two white supporters of Cherokee rights are also important for an understanding of the issue. See Clemens de Baillou, ed., *John Howard Payne to His Countrymen* (Athens, Ga., 1961), and Francis Paul Prucha, ed., *Cherokee Removal: The "William Penn" Essays and Other Writings by Jeremiah Evarts* (Knoxville, 1981). Two anthologies that include the most cogent arguments by contemporaries and the conflicting interpretations of modern scholars are Louis Filler and Allen Gutman, eds., *The Removal of the Cherokee Nation: Manifest Destiny or National Dishonor* (Lexington, Mass., 1962), and Allen Gutman, ed., *States' Rights and Indian Removal: The Cherokee Nation v. The State of Georgia* (Boston, 1965).

For the development of the U. S. government's removal policy, see Reginald Horsman, *The Origin of Indian Removal, 1815–1824* (East Lansing, Mich., 1970). Jackson's implementation of that policy is dealt with in Ronald N. Satz, *American Indian Policy in the Jacksonian Era* (Lincoln, Neb., 1975). A psychoanalytical approach to Jackson's interaction with Indians can be found in Michael Paul Rogin, *Fathers and Children: Andrew Jackson and the Subjugation of the American Indian* (New York, 1975). The classic defense of Jackson is Francis Paul Prucha, "Andrew Jackson's Indian Policy: A Reassessment," *Journal of American History* 56 (1969): 527–39. Far less sympathetic to Jackson is Dale Van Every, *Disinherited: The Lost Birthright of the American Indian* (New York, 1966).

TO THE PUBLIC

What is termed the "Cherokee question" may be considered in two points of view: the controversy with the States and the General Government, and the controversy among the Cherokees themselves.[1] The first has been agitated in so many ways, and before so many tribunals, that it is needless, for any good purpose, to remark upon it at this place. The latter is founded upon the question of a remedy, to extricate the Cherokees from their difficulties, in consequence of their conflict with the States. Upon this point, less has been said or known before the public, but it has not been the less interesting to the Cherokees. It is here where different views and different feelings has been excited.

"What is to be done?" was a national inquiry, after we found that all our efforts to obtain redress from the General Government, *on the land of our fathers*, had been of no avail. The first rupture among ourselves was the moment we presumed to answer that question. To a portion of the Cherokee people it early became evident that the interest of their countrymen, and the happiness of their posterity, depended upon an entire change of policy. Instead of contending uselessly against superior power, the only course left, was, to yield to circumstances over which they had no control.

In all difficulties of this kind, between the United States and the Cherokees, the only mode of settling them has been by treaties; consequently, when a portion of our people became convinced that no other measures would avail, they became the *advocates of a treaty*, as the only means to extricate the Cherokees from their perplexities—hence they were called *the Treaty Party*. Those who maintained the old policy, were known as the *Anti Treaty Party*. At the head of the latter has been Mr. John Ross.

It would be of no purpose now to describe these Indian political parties, or to enter into a particular history of the rise, progress, and the present state of the dissensions which have distracted the Cherokees. It is enough to say that our parties have been similar to other political parties found among the whites. They have been characterized by high feeling, and not unfrequently, by undue asperity. It is easy to conceive of the disadvantages under which the first mentioned party must have labored. To advocate a treaty was to declare war against the established habits of thinking peculiar to the aborigines. It was to come in contact with settled prejudices—with the deep rooted attachment for the soil of our forefathers.[2] Aside from these natural obstacles, the influence of the chiefs,[3] who were ready to take advantage of the well known feelings of the Cherokees, in reference to their lands, was put in active requisition against us.

It is worthy of notice that, in this contest, we have had to bear no small share of obloquy, arising from our very principles, from our opposition to the views and measures of what is termed the *constituted authorities* of the nation, and from the illusive appearance of having a vast majority opposed to us.[4] That obloquy was increased by the manner in which we were represented to our people. *Traitors—land sellers—interested persons*, &c., were terms calculated to stir up prejudice and opposition. To represent us in these various lights to our own people, we supposed to be a matter of course, judging from the nature of all political contests. But we have lately been arraigned before the American public—a tribunal to which we, as Cherokees, are not properly amenable in this affair—in our own family disputes. Mr. Ross has made sundry publications of late, by the aid of writers whom he has employed for the purpose, which have arraigned us to that tribunal.[5] He has called upon the public to award its judgment against us. He has represented us as a disaffected faction, opposed to him, the constituted chief of this nation—He represents us as a small minority opposed to the will of the people—that we have ceded their lands without their authority, and against their expressed injunctions.[6]— These are matters which concern the Cherokees themselves, the result of which must be left to their posterity to judge.

Without replying to these charges in this place, we will state what *we* suppose to be the great cause of our present difficulties—our present dissensions. A *want of proper information among the people*. We charge Mr. Ross with having deluded them with expectations incompatible with, and injurious to, their interest. He has prevented the discussion of this interesting matter, by systematic measures, at a time when discussion was of the most vital importance.[7] By that means the people have been kept ignorant of their true condition. They have been taught to feel and expect what *could not* be realized—and what Mr. Ross himself must have known *would not* be realized. This great delusion has lasted to this day. Now, in view of such a state of things, we cannot conceive of the acts of a *minority* to be so reprehensible or unjust as are represented Mr. Ross. If one hundred persons are ignorant of their true situation, and are so completely blinded as not to see the destruction that awaits them, we can see strong reasons to justify the action of a minority of fifty persons—to do what the majority *would do* if they understood their condition—to save a *nation* from political thraldom and moral degradation.[8] It is not intended to discuss the question here, but simply to show that a great deal may be said on both sides—besides, the reader will recollect that it is in reference to an Indian community, and to very extraordinary circumstances.

The original error was in the refusal of the leaders and advisers of this nation to discuss the question which is now agitated only in the last extremity, and in closing every avenue by which the people might be reached with correct information. That was an error which cannot now be retrieved, and which has thrown us into inextricable difficulties. The *Treaty Party* is not to blame for this—We sounded the alarm in time—we called upon the *authorities of the nation* to see to what these matters were tending —to save the nation by timely action—we asked, we entreated, we implored.—But we were met at the very threshhold as *enemies of our country*. The same system of opposition has been waged against us to this day.

For an illustration of these remarks, the following papers are presented to the public, as a proper introduction to the two letters which will occupy the principal portion of these pages.

[*The following article appeared in the Cherokee Phoenix of August 11, 1832.*]

TO THE READERS OF THE CHEROKEE PHOENIX.

The subscriber takes this opportunity to inform the readers of the Cherokee Phoenix that he has resigned his station as Editor. Some of the reasons which have induced him to take this step are contained in the following letter addressed to the principal chief.

RED HILL, CHEROKEE NATION, Aug. 1st, 1832.

TO JOHN ROSS, Esq. Principal Chief of the Cherokee Nation.

SIR—According to the intimation I gave you some time since, I hereby tender to you my resignation as editor of the Cherokee Phoenix. In taking this step it may not be necessary to give my reasons *in full*; it is, however, due to you, to myself, and my countrymen, to avoid misrepresentations, to state the following:

1. I believe the continuation of the Phoenix, and my services as its Editor, have answered *all the purposes* that it can be expected to answer hereafter. Two of the great objects which the nation had in view in supporting the paper were, the defence of our *rights*, and the proper representation of our *grievances* to the people of the United States.[9] In regard to the *former*, we can add nothing to the full and thorough investigation that has taken place, especially after the decision of the Supreme Court, which has forever closed the question of our conventional rights. In regard to the *latter*, we can say nothing which will have more effect upon the community, than what we have already said. The public is as fully apprised as we can ever expect it to be, of our *grievances*. It knows our troubles, and yet never was it more silent than at present. It is engrossed in other local and sectional interests.[10]

2. The two great and important objects of the paper not now existing as heretofore, and the nation being in great want of funds, it is unnecessary to continue the *expenses* in supporting it.[11]

3. Were I to continue as Editor, I should feel myself in a most peculiar and delicate situation. I do not know whether I could, at the same time, satisfy my own views, and the views of the authorities of the nation. My situation would then be as embarrassing as it would be peculiar and delicate. I do conscientiously believe it to be the duty of every citizen to reflect upon the dangers with which we are surrounded—to view the darkness which seems to lie before our people—our prospects, and the evils with which we are threatened—to talk over all these matters, and, if possible, come to some definite and satisfactory conclusion, while there is time, as to what ought to be done in the last alternative. I could not consent to be the conductor of the

paper without having the right and privilege of discussing these important matters—and from what I have seen and heard, were I to assume that privilege, my usefulness would be paralyzed by being considered, as I have already been, an enemy to the interests of my country and people. I love my country and I love my people, as my own heart bears me witness, and for that very reason I should deem it my duty to tell them the whole truth, or what I believe to be the truth. I cannot tell them that we will be reinstated in our rights, when I have no such hope, and after our leading, active, and true friends in Congress, and elsewhere, have signified to us that they can do us no good.

4. I have now been more than four years in service of the nation,[12] and my *inclination* is to retire from the arduous duties in which I have been engaged, and which have been far from being *beneficial* to my health and happiness, except the happiness of doing good, and being useful to my country. When, therefore, the chance of usefulness, in my present employment, is in a great measure *lessened*, the inclination to retire is *increased*.

I hope the foregoing reasons, stated in a few words, will be sufficient to guard me against misapprehension and misrepresentations which may be likely to arise from the step I have taken. Let me again assure you that I love my country and my people, and I pray God that the evils which we so much fear may be averted from us by His merciful interposition.

I have the honor to be, sir,
Yours, very respectfully,
ELIAS BOUDINOT.

In communicating the foregoing to the General Council, the Principal Chief also submitted the following message:

To the Committee and Council in
General Council convened:

Agreeably to the request of Mr. Elias Boudinot, I lay before you his letter of resignation as Editor of the Cherokee Phoenix, which, in part, will show his reasons for the step he has taken. I cannot agree in opinion with Mr. Boudinot, that the continuation of the Phoenix has "*answered all the purposes that it can be expected to answer hereafter*;" although the representation of our *grievances* in defence of our *rights* have been fully made, and *thoroughly investigated*, and the Supreme Court has forever closed the question of our *conventional rights*, and the American public at this time may be more silent on the subject of our *grievances* than heretofore, yet I deem it to be essentially important that the paper should be kept up. It is an incontrovertible fact, that the circulation of the paper has been greatly instrumental in the diffusion of science and general knowledge among our own citizens. The pecuniary embarrassments of the nation by no means ought to influence you to discontinue the paper, if a suitable person can be found to conduct it.[13] At your last session, you authorized the Editor to take a journey throughout the United States, with the view of collecting money for the support of the Phoenix, and the express purpose of meeting the expenses incidental to the printing and Editorial departments of that paper. After such collections having been made, would it be politic, would it be wise, or would it be right to discontinue the paper, and apply the money for other purposes,* when the interest of the nation would seem to demand its continuance?—The *views* of the *public authorities* should continue and ever be in accordance with the *will of the people*; and the *views of the Editor of the National paper* be the same. The toleration of *diversified views* to the columns of such a paper would not fail to create fermentation and confusion among our citizens, and in the end prove injurious to the welfare of the nation. The love of our country and people demands *unity of sentiment and action* for the good of all.[14] The truth, and the whole truth, has always been, and must still continue to be, told. Our *rights* have been sustained, and whether they will eventually be protected unto us, or wantonly wrested from us forever, are subjects of speculation in the minds of many; but when we

*It is a little singular, after having made such an avowal in regard to the proper appropriation of a few thousand collected by the Editor, that Mr. Ross should, within three or four months after, draw this same money from the Cherokee Treasury, to be expended by him and his fellow delegates at Washington, *and not leave one cent* "for the expenses incidental to the printing and Editorial departments of the paper."

reflect upon the honor, magnanimity, and *binding obligations* of the General Government, and the peculiar character of its constitutonal system, we cannot but hope and believe that *justice* will yet be extended to our nation. By doing so, there can be no cause for just complaint from any quarter against the United States; much less for violence and disunion among the States. Under these views of the subject, I deem it necessary that the vacancy occasioned by the resignation of the Editor be filled by some suitable person.

JOHN ROSS.

RED CLAY, *August* 4, 1832.

A few futher explanations may here be necessary.

When I say that the continuation of the Phoenix has answered all the purposes that it could be expected to answer hereafter, I mean the purposes intended to be effected *out* of the nation. The political rights of the Cherokees cannot be restored or secured by a continued *investigation*, or a repetition of the numerous and aggravated *grievances* which they have already laid before the American People.

* * *

I cannot agree with the Principal Chief in regard to the admission of "*diversified views*" in the columns of the paper.[15] I am for making the situation of the Cherokees a *question* of momentous interest, subject to a free and friendly discussion among ourselves, as the only way to ascertain the will of the people as to what ought to be done in the last alternative. What are our *hopes* and *prospects*? What are our *dangers* and *difficulties*? What are the *reasons* of our hopes and prospects? What would be the consequences of such a step, and of such a one? are questions of no ordinary interest, and ought, in my view, to be fully considered.—That the time to consider these matters has arrived I verily believe, from event that have taken place, and are now taking place. Nor am I alone in this belief—our worthy delegation, three of our most intelligent citizens,[16] in whose patriotism I have the utmost confidence, would, no doubt, sustain me, from a proper view of things while they were at the seat of Government. And what say our friends in Congress? Have they not fully apprised us that they cannot effect any substantial good for us? Have not a number of them, whose motives are above suspicion, communicated their views in writing for our information?[17] And has not an Hon. Judge of the Supreme Court made a similar communication, stating that the operation of the late decision of the Supreme Court cannot extend to our relief, unless the Executive felt itself bound to enforce the treaties? And does President Jackson feel himself bound to obey the Supreme Court, and to execute the treaties? On this point the reader is referred to another article under the editorial head.*[18]

*The following is the article referred to: "There is a doctrine laid down in the veto Message of the President, returning the Bill to recharter the Bank of the United States, which bears directly upon the interest of the Cherokees; it is, that the *Executive is not bound by the decisions of the Supreme Court.*[19] That such was the opinion of the President it was frequently intimated after the decision of the court in the case of the Missionaries, but it has not been before publicly and officially avowed. If General Jackson acts upon this assumption of Executive prerogative, the Cherokees will have nothing to hope from his interference. Indeed, we need not go to his official declaration to find out whether he will support the Court or not. We see he does not—the system of oppression carried on by acts declared to be unconstitutional by the highest tribunal of the country, is permitted to proceed steadily to its final consummation, and the Chief Magistrate the land, to whom is intrusted the execution of the laws, views with apparent complacence the mischief as it progresses.

However unpleasant the fact may be to us, yet it is a fact which our eyes see fully demonstrated every day, that the President of the United States *does not* take the first step to defend the rights of the Cherokees under the decision of the Supreme Court. But this is not all—he now officially tells us that he is *not bound* by that decision, and, by inference, intends to *disregard* it—according to the doctrine in the veto Message, he will disregard it even when he is called upon by a regular process from the Supreme Court. But supposing he obeys and executes the mandate of the court, that will bring no relief to the Cherokees; for the nation, we take it, of the tribunal which issues the mandate terminates in the persons of the individuals incarcerated in the Penitentiary.[20]

What sort of hope have we then from a President who feels himself under no obligation *to execute*, but has an inclination *to disregard* the laws and treaties, as interpreted by a proper branch of the Government? We have nothing to expect from such an executive; and if the President is disposed to do as he pleases in this affair, the remedy is not with us, but with the people of the United States.—We shall see whether that remedy will be promptly applied."

Such being the facts on one side, how is the case on the other? Has not our oppressor, presuming upon her power, and overlooking the sacred obligations of right, not only infringed upon our political rights, but has actually, to all intents and purposes, taken possession of one-half of our country, and is now on the point of consummating her acts by conveying it to her citizens? Already have the commissioners, who are to superintend the *drawings of the land lottery*, been summoned to appear at Milledgeville.[21] Now, to trust merely upon contingencies, and to ease our minds with undefined hopes, when the danger is immediate and appalling, does not seem to me to be altogether satisfactory. And think, for a moment, my countrymen, the danger to be apprehended from an overwhelming white population—a population not unfrequently overcharged with high notions of color, dignity, and greatness—at once overbearing and impudent to those whom, in their sovereign pleasure, they consider as their inferiors.[22] They should have, our sons and daughters, be slaves indeed. Such a population, and the evils and vices it would bring with it, the chief of which would be the deluging the country with ardent spirits, would create an enemy more pernicious and destructive to the Cherokees than "the pestilence that walketh in darkness, and the destruction that wasteth at noon-day."[23]

It is the presenting the serious and momentous things to the people, what I mean by *telling them the truth*. And I am inclined to believe that it is the best, if not the only way to find out what the *will of the people* is.

Were it not that my motives have been misapprehended by some, and wilfully misrepresented by others, I should not have published my letter of resignation, nor troubled the reader with the foregoing explanations. But it is due to myself and to my countrymen, for whom the above remarks are intended, that I should at least say what I have said.

In taking leave of my readers and patrons, I must express my gratitude for the great forbearance and allowances with which I have been treated by them. They have had frequent occasion to exercise that forbearance. In return, I can only say, I have done what I could, and as my limited abilities and means would allow.—I have served my countrymen, I hope with fidelity, through evil as well as good report, and I know I have the witness in my own heart, that I have had, and do still have, their interest uppermost in my mind. In retiring, I have made it a matter of conscience. In a different sphere of employment, I trust to be more useful than I can be as Editor of the Cherokee Phoenix.

ELIAS BOUDINOT.

The opinion by Mr. Ross, that "diversified views" ought not to be inserted in the Phoenix, was sufficient for practical purposes. My successor denounced the foregoing in no measured terms—he made a personal attack, in his very first number, I think, upon some of the Treaty Party—impugned their motives, and allowed himself a free scope in speaking of our views, designs, &c.[24] I thought justice required at my hands a suitable answer, explaining more fully the views I had advanced in the preceding article, which I supposed must have been misapprehended by the Editor.—But the order had gone out—no "diversified views" were to be admitted, so the poor privilege of *explaining my views* was not allowed. The paper that I had prepared for that purpose was returned to me, with a declaration that it was not the *will of the authorities of the nation* that it should be published. I present that paper, as I have preserved it.

[The following paper was prepared for publication in the Cherokee Phoenix, in answer to an editorial article of that paper, censuring the political views and conduct of the writer. Although it was in reply to remarks of a personal nature, yet it was refused admittance, *because it discussed matters which the authorities of the nation had decided should not be discussed.* In a note to the writer, the Editor says: "It must be borne in mind, that the authorities of the nation are opposed to the introduction of controversial matter in the Phoenix, and especially of making it a *point* of changing our situation a matter of discussion. Your communication, while it points out the passages of my address, as having dealt hard with you, would on the other hand, if published and answered, which I could not possibly avoid, involve that momentous *point*, and an endless controversy might be the consequence. To avoid this course would be compatible with the policy of the nation, and my bounden duty. Therefore, I have thought it expedient to withhold its publication."

ELIJAH HICKS.]

To the Editor of the Cherokee Phoenix:

Sir,—I have read in your last paper the remarks which you have been pleased to bestow upon my letter of resignation. I regret that the common courtesy, that of noticing the retirement of a brother editor, which some of the conductors of the papers with which I exchanged seem to have exercised towards me, should have made it necessary for you to direct your attention to that letter. It is hardly entitled to the importance you have given it. I certainly did not think but that it would be "like the fleeting wind, to be heard of no more." As you have, however, bestowed some remarks upon its merits, it may not be improper for me to recur to such parts of it, by way of explanation, as seem to have been misapprehended by you, and to correct the impression which may be created in the mind of the reader by the *import* of your language.

I have no objection to your subjecting any remarks which I may have published while I was honored with the management of the Cherokee Phoenix to your editorial scrutiny, provided such remarks or sentiments are presented to the public *just what they are*. I have nothing to recall from what I have said—I am willing that my words should speak for themselves, and that reprehension should be cast upon them where they *deserve* reprehension.

When we write in a language which we understand but imperfectly, and which is not our mother tongue, we are liable, as I know by experience, to use words or phrases which do not express our meaning. Such, I take it, is the case in the very first sentence of your remarks, where you represent my letter as "setting forth my *indisposition* to sustain the cause of the Cherokees." You did not mean, I presume, what these words would seem to imply; because, in my letter and explanations upon it, as your readers will recollect, I say nothing as to what my "disposition" is to sustain the cause of the Cherokees. In my *letter*, my object was merely to give a few reasons why I thought it necessary to leave my station as editor.—In my *explanations*, I alluded to some of the great, and, in my views, *insurmountable difficulties*, that are in the way of our rights being secured to us. If I had said any thing about my *disposition*, or *inclination*, if you please, I would have said that it was *strong—as strong as ever*.

One who has not read my letter would suppose that there has been an important change of sentiment in my views in regard to the all-engrossing subject among us, from such expressions as the following, which I find in your remarks: "The right of the late Editor to *change* his *opinions*, on questions involving the dearest rights of the Cherokees"—"The *change* of *sentiment* of the Editor, which this letter would seem to indicate, as despairing of the redress of our wrongs," &c. Such change of opinions or sentiments, that is, in regard to the rights of the Cherokees, and the redress of our wrongs, is not, however, implied in my letter. As to the first, you could not have meant that I had undergone such a complete "revolution" as to *deny* the 'dearest rights" of the Cherokees, or that I ever *questioned* them. As to the latter, I do not know whether, in my public capacity, I have ever expressed the opinion that our rights *would certainly be redressed*—I have the impression that I have never, however desirous I have been that such should be the case. I have been careful not to commit myself on this point, and thus create hopes, which, by possibility, to say the least, would exist only to be disappointed and frustrated. To say, then, which I have thought it my duty, in frankness, to say to my countrymen, that I do not believe that our rights will be secured to us, is not in opposition to any previous opinion expressed.

You seem, however, to intimate that I have *favored a treaty* with the Government. Your readers will recollect that I said nothing about a treaty, but urged the importance of considering our situation, and coming to some definite and satisfactory conclusion as to what ought to be done in the *last alternative*. My views as to what ought to be done *may* be somewhat different from those I formerly entertained—but if they are, they are such, in my humble opinion, as are *patriotic*, and I know they are founded upon mature and most serious reflection.[25]

I should consider myself very hardly dealt with if I thought that you really intended to convey the idea that I was now *no more* a patriot. You could not have meant what these words would seem to imply—"As a *breach* in the *patriotic rank* of the Cherokee."—"However valuable the services of this once devoted *patriot*—we must bear the *loss*. The *loss* is but a drop from the bucket." There is nothing in my letter of resignation, or in my explanations, which shows a want of patriotic views and motives—my motives certainly were of the most patriotic kind. But it is needless to enlarge. My past acts will speak for themselves, and I am willing to be tried and tested for the future. I will give you a definition of the patriotism by which I profess myself to be actuated.

In one word, I may say that my patriotism consists in the *love of the country*,[26] and *the love of the People*. These are intimately connected, yet they are not altogether inseparable. They are inseparable if the people are made the first victim, for in that case the country must go also, and there must be an end of the objects of our patriotism. But if the country is lost, or is likely to be lost to all human appearance, and the people still exist, may I not, with a patriotism true and commendable, make a *question* for the safety of the remaining object of my affection?

In applying the above definition of patriotism to my conduct, I can but say that I have come to the unpleasant and most disagreeable conclusion (whether that conclusion be correct is another question) that our lands, or a large portion of them, are about to be seized and taken from us. Now, as a friend of my people, I cannot say *peace, peace,* when there is no peace. I cannot ease their minds with any expectation of a calm, when the vessel is already tossed to and fro, and threatened to be shattered to pieces by an approaching tempest. If I really believe there is danger, I must act consistently, and give the alarm—tell my countrymen our true, or what I believe to be our true, situation. In the case under consideration, I am induced to believe there is danger, "immediate and appalling," and that it becomes the people of this country to weigh the matter rightly, act wisely, not rashly, and choose a course that will come nearest benefitting the nation. When we come to the last crisis, (and my opinion is, that we are that point,) one of three things *must* be chosen. 1. Nature's right of all nations to resist and fight in the defence of our lands. 2. Submit and peaceably come under the dominion of the oppressor, and suffer, which we most assuredly must if we make that choice, a *moral death*! 3. Avoid the two first by a removal. Now the article which has given rise to your remarks merely suggests the importance of making choice of one of the three evils, (for evils they are,) in time. In saying this, I do not disguise that I, as one of the nation, have an opinion on this delicate point, and am willing to express it when occasion requires. But this is not the place and time to express it, for we are merely considering the "merits" of my letter of resignation.

It may be said, to consider the matter now is premature. It may be so. If it is, the error which I commit is an error of *judgment*, not of the *heart*, and cannot, of course, be attributed to any want of patriotism. If it is premature to consider this matter, it must be because there is still hope that our rights will be "redressed." That hope, I have already said, is "undefined," and rests upon "contingencies." The contingencies of which I speak do not at all terminate in the election of a President, although that may not indeed be now, as our good friend of the N.Y. Spectator seems to suppose, one of the contingencies. He is better able to judge than I am. But suppose the present incumbent is not re-elected, and that another individual succeeds him, whose sentiments on the Indian question are correct, and is disposed to do us justice?[27] I still make it a question whether our rights can be restored to us, for the new President cannot take his seat until the 4th of March, 1833,[28] and there is, to say the least a *great danger* of the enemy having a complete possession of one-half of our country before that time.—Can the Chief Magistrate then, however disposed he may be to do right, remove all intruders, to whom the protection of a State is pledged, and place us *in peace*, upon our former privileges, *under the present circumstances of the country*? But there is still another contingency in regard to the contemplated change in the administration. Suppose the new President succeeds in restoring, to us our rights? What security have we that the restoration of our rights will be permanent, and that a President similar to the present one will not succeed the one who does us justice, and thus the game will not be played over anew? I can hardly consent to trust the peace and happiness of our people to political changes and party triumphs. Unfortunately for us, the Indian question has been made a party and sectional question.

Your expression, "the loss is but a drop in the bucket," may be interpreted in two ways. It may mean that my opinions or exertions as a individual are nothing compared to the nation, and, of course, the *loss* to them is but of little moment—or it may mean that I am *detached* from the nation, and that no one approves of the views I have given in my letter of resignation. If you mean the first, you are certainly correct, for my opinions or exertions are of little consequence—they are but a "drop from the bucket." If you mean the second, I will only say that I am not *detached from*, but *attached to*, the nation, and that there are those connected with the Judicial, Executive, and Legislative departments of our little Government, men of intelligence and patriotism, who cordially approve of the remarks and suggestions contained in the article upon which you have commented.

In alluding to a letter signed by a number of our friends in Congress, addressed to Mr. Ross, and another from one of the Judges of the Supreme Court, I had no other object than to show my readers the views entertained by those gentlemen on the subject, and to strengthen, by such high authority, the opinions I had expressed. I thought those views, coming as they did from such a quarter, were worthy of all attention and respect, and I had every reason to believe that the motives of those who communicated them were of the purest kind.

Respectfully,

E. BOUDINOT.

OCTOBER 2, 1832.

Thus was the press muzzled and the avenue by which we could reach the people closed against us! Although we could not get a hearing in that way, we still persisted, and continued to give the alarm, as opportunities presented. Attempts were made to discuss the matter in the Councils of the Nation. There were members of those Councils who had independence enough to speak their minds. But what was the result? These members, namely, Messrs. Major Ridge, John Ridge, and

David Vann, were *impeached* for holding *opinions* that were contrary to those entertained by the authorities! Not having access to the records of the Council, I am not able to give a copy of what was preferred as an impeachment—but it was a curious paper. The charge was not for *acts*, but for *opinions*. At a proper time the persons charged demanded a hearing, and called upon the National Committee to try them for the offence alleged against them. What is a little singular, *they would not try them*, nor withdraw the impeachment, for no other reason, I apprehend, than that discussion might be elicited, to avoid which seemed to be their object, while they kept the individuals arraigned before them *under censure*, and finally to effect their expulsion. This they soon accomplished. The persons impeached left the Council in disgust. *This was the second triumph over discussion*. It was enough to alarm those who foresaw the point to which these things were tending. It was a most extraordinary spectacle to see a few leading men acting in this extraordinary way, under cover of the *will of the people*, when those people were purposely kept from discussion and truth, by which alone they could be enabled to exercise *their will* to good and beneficial purposes.

Soon after this, the friends of free discussion met, and adopted the following resolutions, as containing principles by which they professed to be actuated.

RESOLUTIONS.

Whereas, a crisis of the utmost importance, in the affairs of the Cherokee people has arrived, requiring from every individual the most serious reflection and the expression of views as to the present condition and future prospects of the Nation; and whereas a portion of the Cherokees have entertained opinions which have been represented as hostile to the true interest and happiness of the people, merely because they have not agreed with the Chiefs and leading men; and as these opinions have not heretofore been properly made known, therefore.

Resolved, That it is our decided opinion, founded upon the melancholy experience of the Cherokees within the last two years, and upon facts which history has furnished us in regard to other Indian nations, that our people cannot exist amidst a white population, subject to laws which they have no hand in making, and which they do not understand; that the suppression of the Cherokee Government, which connected this people in a distinct community, will not only check their progress in improvement and advancement in knowledge, but, by means of numerous influences and temptations which this new state of things has created, will completely destroy every thing like civilization among them, and ultimately reduce them to poverty, misery, and wretchedness.

Resolved, That, considering the progress of the States authorities in this country, the distribution and settlement of the lands, the organization of counties, the erection of county seats and Courthouses, and other indications of a determined course on the part of the surrounding States, and considering, on the other hand, the repeated refusal of the President and Congress of the United States to interfere in our behalf, we have come to the conclusion that this nation cannot be reinstated in its present location, and that the question left to us and to every Cherokee, is, whether it is more desirable to remain here, with all the embarrassments with which we must be surrounded, or to seek a country where we *may* enjoy our own laws, and live under our own vine and fig-tree.

Resolved, That in expressing the opinion that this nation cannot be reinstated, we do it from a thorough conviction of its truth—that we never will encourage our confiding people with hopes that can never be realized, and with expectations that will assuredly be disappointed—that however unwelcome and painful the truth may be to them, and however unkindly it may be received from us, we cannot, as *patriots* and well-wishers of the Indian race, shrink from doing our duty in expressing our decided convictions. That we scorn the charge of selfishness and a want of patriotic feelings alleged against us by some of our countrymen, while we can appeal to our consciences and the searcher of all hearts for the rectitude of our motives and intentions.

Resolved, That, although *we love the land* of our fathers, and should leave the place of our nativity with as much regret as any of our citizens, we consider the lot of the *Exile* immeasurably more to be preferred than a submission to the laws of the States, and thus becoming witnesses of the ruin and degradation of the Cherokee people.

Resolved, That we are firmly of the opinion, that a large majority of the Cherokee people would prefer to remove, if the true state of their condition was properly made known to them.—[29] We believe that if they were told that they had nothing to expect from further efforts to regain their rights as a *distinct community*, and that the only alternatives left to them is either to remain amidst a white population, subject to the white man's laws, or to remove to another country, where they *may* enjoy peace and happiness, they would unhesitatingly prefer the latter.

Resolved, That we were desirous to leave our Chiefs and leading men to seek a country for their people, but as they have thought proper not to do any thing towards the ultimate removal of the nation, we know of none to which the Cherokees can go as asylum but that possessed by our brethren west of the Mississippi; that we are willing to unite with them under a proper guaranty from the United States that the lands shall be secured to us, and that we shall be governed by our own laws and regulations.

Resolved, That we consider the policy pursued by the Red Clay Council, in continuing a useless struggle from year to year, as destructive to the present peace and future happiness of the Cherokees, because it is evident to every observer that while this struggle is going on, their difficulties will be accumulating, until they are ruined in their property and character, and the only remedy that will then be proposed in their case will be, *submission to the laws of the States* by taking reservations.[30]

Resolved, That we consider the fate of our poor brethren, the Creeks, to be a sufficient warning to all those who may finally subject the Cherokees to the laws of the States by giving them reservations.[31]

Resolved, That we will never consent to have our own rights and the rights of our posterity, sold "*prospectively*" to the laws of the States by our Chiefs, in any compact or "compromise" into which they may choose to enter with the Government—that we cannot be satisfied with any thing less than a release from State Legislation—but, while we do not intend to have our own political interests compromised, we shall not oppose those who prefer to remain subject to State laws.

Resolved, That we were disposed to contend for what we considered to be our own rights, as long as there was any hope of relief *to the nation*, but that we never can consent to the waste of our public moneys in instituting and prosecuting suits which will result only to individual advantage.[32]

Resolved, That it is with great surprise and mortification we have noticed the idea attempted to be conveyed to the minds of our people that the *nation* can be relieved by the courts of Georgia—that we regard the appealing to those Courts, *by the nation*, for redress, as an entire departure from the true policy maintained by the Cherokees in their struggle for national existence.[33]

NOVEMBER, 1834.

A candid statement of views, such as the foregoing, by the leading men of this nation, was all that was necessary to terminate our difficulties in peace. But Mr. Ross has pursued a mysterious course with a "plain and unsophisticated people", to borrow his own expression. "The final adjustment of the existing difficulties," may mean in as many ways as there are words in the sentence, and it is no exaggeration to say that nine out of ten of our whole population do not comprehend it. That has been the favorite expression of Mr. Ross when, I suppose, his intention has been to *allude* to a treaty—It is his favorite expression yet. These cautious expressions, which may mean this or that, have had mischievous tendency upon the minds of the Cherokees. What they need is plain dealing. Tell them the truth in a plain and simple language, and they will understand it. It is this that we have not been able yet to induce Mr. Ross and his friends to do. Even as late as October, 1835, at the memorable council, of which more will be said in one of the two following letters, we found it difficult to bring them to the decided point—to acknowledge to the people that a treaty was necessary, and that it *ought* to be made. And when we thought that we had succeeded in the compromise, it was in such a way that the people did not at last understand it.

At the council alluded to, a conference was held between the representatives of the two parties, for the purpose of coming to some friendly understanding. Our object was to bring the other side to acknowledge the vital principle, which they had never done, that nothing but a treaty could save the Cherokees. We knew that if we got them to that point, and the principle was declared to the people, the whole delusion under which the Cherokees were laboring would vanish away, and that a treaty would be speedily made, and this vexatious question for ever put to an end. While the principle was acknowledged in our conferences and discussions, we could not induce them to bring it *before the people*. As samples of our modes of thinking, and the manner of approaching the delicate subject, the two following propositions are submitted; the first, offered by the Treaty party, and the other by the Ross party:

PROPOSITIONS OFFERED BY THE TREATY PARTY.

Whereas, the following persons, viz: John Martin, George M. Waters, Richard Taylor, John F. Balridge, and John Benge, on the one part, and George Chambers, Charles Vann, John Ridge, Elias Boudinot, and John Gunter,[34] on the other part, have met, to consider and deliberate upon the difficulties of the Cherokee people, and to unite upon some plan of relief; they have accordingly agreed to the following resolutions, as expressing their views, and would recommend the same to the serious consideration of the Cherokee people:

Resolved, That the Cherokees cannot be relieved from their peculiar difficulties and afflicted condition, by a continued application to the General Government for redress under the treaties and laws of the United States.

Resolved, That an arrangement with the Government, by a general treaty, is the only remedy that can be applied to relieve the Cherokees.

Resolved, That a treaty ought to be made upon the basis of preserving the Cherokee people, as a distinct and separate community, and that in a convention to make the arrangement, all parties and all interests ought to be fairly and fully represented.

Resolved, That the increasing difficulties of our people demand a speedy remedy.

Resolved, That an arrangement with the Government ought to be made within the limits of the Cherokee country.

RED CLAY, *October* 21, 1835.

PROPOSITIONS OFFERED BY THE ROSS PARTY.

The undersigned persons, being selected by the Principal Chief of the Cherokee nation to confer with certain other persons of the Treaty or Ridge party for the purpose of an endeavor to unite the two parties in a course that may eventuate in the general good of their common country, propose, 1st. The present provisional arrangement will have to be disposed of by a general vote of the people. 2d. Should the Commissioners have full powers to make a treaty,[35] there is no doubt the authorities of the nation will receive them with respect and attention. 3d. Should no proposition be received from the commissioners for a treaty upon just and liberal terms, it is presumed the recommendation of the Principal Chief to the national Council will be acted upon; that is to say, the appointment of another delegation to Washington, for the purpose of effecting a final adjustment of our difficulties. It is also presumed that the delegation will have power to act upon any matter in relation to a treaty, &c., that may be submitted to them before their departure for Washington.

In conclusion, the undersigned will in good feeling say to the conferees of the opposite party, that they will recommend one of their party to the Principal Chief, &c., as a delegate, which they have no doubt will be received with attention.

GEORGE M. WATERS,
JOHN MARTIN,
R. TAYLOR,
JOHN BENGE,
JOHN BALDRIDGE.

RED CLAY, *October* 21, 1835.

We could not agree to an instrument so *indefinite* as the preceding, and the others would not agree to ours, because it was too *definite*. Shortly after, however, an agreement was entered into and signed, which formed the compromise between the parties, and with the violation of which we have been charged by Mr. Ross. That matter is discussed in the following letter, addressed to a friend:

WASHINGTON, *May* 16, 1836.

SIR—Among the documents accompanying Mr. Ross's protest against the Treaty, I notice one which purports to be a compromise entered into at Red Clay,[36] in the month of October last, by the two parties into which the Cherokee Nation was then divided.—That paper is in the words following, to wit:

"The Committees of Conference on the subject of uniting the parties of the Nation into one, and harmonizing and associating together as one people, in any treaty which may take place between the United States and the Cherokee Nation, in order to relieve the last from its distressed and afflicted condition, have agreed, that is to say, Major George M. Waters, Judge John Martin, Richard Taylor, John Balridge, and John Benge, acting under the instructions of John Ross, principal Chief, on the one part, and George Chambers, John Gunter, John Ridge, Charles Vann, and Elias Boudinot, on the other, acting under the instructions of Major Ridge and others, of the treaty party, have agreed to bury in oblivion all unfriendly feelings and act unitedly in [any][37] treaty [arrangement] with the United States for the relief of their nation—that the number of Delegates to be chosen by the [General Council] and people [here present] shall consist of nineteen members, to act for the nation, with full powers. That of this number there shall be three chosen of the treaty party, and nominated and appointed in the same way as the others, their authority to be joint and equal, to be confirmed by the people [here present.] This agreement then and in the case only to be binding at once upon the parties. The Cherokee press is the property of the Nation; and, as we have become friends, no more publications shall be made either against the one or the other of the parties, because they are now united, [and should be surrendered to the proper authorities of the Nation.] In concluding, speeches of peace and reconciliation shall be made, of a prudent and judicious character, to the people, in order to do away any unpleasant feelings which may exist. Given under our hands and seals, this the 24th October, 1835, at Red Clay, in the Cherokee Nation."

Signed,
GEORGE M. WATERS,
JOHN RIDGE,
JOHN MARTIN,
CHARLES VANN,
his
JOHN x BALRIDGE,
mark
his
GEORGE x CHAMBERS,
mark
his
JOHN x BENGE,
mark
JOHN GUNTER,
R. TAYLOR,
ELIAS BOUDINOT.

We are charged by Mr. Ross, in his communication to the Executive and the Senate, with having violated the above arrangement, from the fact that we attended the Council at New Echota, and entered into a treaty with the Commissioner of the United States. This charge of bad faith is a matter of some importance, intended to affect our characters for consistency and integrity.—In order to defend ourselves, it is necessary for us to show, either that the charge is false, or, in other words, that we have faithfully fulfilled the compromise in its letter and spirit; or to show that it is not obligatory upon us. I propose to do the latter in this communication. Every one loves a good name, and wishes to bequeath that good name to his posterity. It is this universal and commendable feeling which has impelled me to address this letter to you, to remove the unfavorable impressions which *may* have been created by reading the papers above referred to. We are then not guilty of bad faith, because—

1. The foregoing document is not the compromise we signed at Red Clay. If this declaration astounds you, it is nevertheless true. I suppose our opponents would compel us to observe the compromise, the whole compromise, and *nothing but* the compromise, just as it was signed by the ten conferees. One party has no right to take away any part of it, or to make any additions, without the consent of the other. If either is done, it is no more a compromise, and the obligation to observe it is therefore destroyed.—Now, to apply this principle to the matter in hand—while the ink with which the ten conferees had thought proper to inscribe their agreement was hardly dry, Mr. John Ross, who now professes such obedience to the will of the people, and to have no will of his own, added such parts of sentences as I have included in brackets in the foregoing agreement. It is no reason to say that it was done with the consent of one of the conferees. One entire party cannot bind in this manner the other; much less can one individual bind both the contracting parties. It is true, Mr. John Ridge, from motives truly conciliatory and patriotic, in order to prevent the consequences of such despicable quibbling as Mr. Ross was then making, after the whole affair had been concluded and signed by men of his own appointment, agreed that the additions should be made. But his other four associates knew nothing about it—it was done with the presumption that they would, for the sake of good understanding, waive the matter, which they undoubtedly would have done if an infraction of a far more important nature had not subsequently been committed upon the foregoing agreement by the other party, and circumstances had not taken

place to defeat the purposes of the compromise. This then leads me to consider—

2. That we are not guilty of bad faith, because one of the two principles upon which the ten conferees agreed to unite and become friends, was disregarded and violated by Mr. Ross, in the appointment of a delegation to negotiate with the United States.—All compromises are effected by concessions. So it was in this case. The concession to the treaty party was, *that a treaty should be made*; to the Ross party, *that the majority of the persons by whom the negotiations were to be carried on should belong to that party.* This was a matter of bargain,[38] made very explicit. *Three* individuals were to be appointed as delegates from one party, and *sixteen* from the other. The execution of it, that is, in the appointment of the Delegation, was entrusted to Mr. Ross; and did he comply with its essential provision, *that sixteen only should be chosen out of his party?* Not satisfied with the great preponderance and advantage we had already given him in that compromise, certainly too much so for our interest and honor, he disregarded it by having *seventeen* appointed, viz: John Ross, Lewis Ross, Richard Taylor, James Brown, John F. Balridge, John Benge, John Martin, Elijah Hicks, Richard Fields, Joseph Vann, John Huss, Sleeping Rabbit, Soft Shell Turtle, Thomas Foreman, Jesse Bushyhead, Peter and James Daniel. Now, sir, what right had he to add one to the number which had been agreed upon?[39] What right had he to say that *seventeen* should be appointed, when the conferees, the proper Representatives of the two parties, had settled upon the number *sixteen*? And if he could add one, without asking our consent, and without our knowledge, he could add ten. And yet this is the man who would bind us to the letter and spirit of our agreement, and expose us to the world as faithless and wicked persons, after having, by his arbitrary acts, and ambiguous proceedings, as I shall show in the course of this letter, deprived us of the means of fulfilling the engagements which that compromise had imposed upon us.

Where, then, may the charge of bad faith properly rest? Certainly the two instances I have here given will be considered by every impartial judge as most palpable violations of the letter of the agreement, and sufficient to exonerate the other party from its obligations. Upon those violations it became null and void. But so desirous were we that a treaty should be made, and made speedily, as upon that depended the destiny of the suffering Cherokees, we were willing to overlook these acts of Mr. Ross, and to waive such objections as we very properly might have raised in reference to those acts. If a treaty, for which we had so long contended against such overwhelming odds, could only be made upon just and equitable principles, for the relief of our countrymen sunk in misery and degradation, it was all we cared—and it was not until we had lost every ray of hope that our compromise would lead to that happy result, from a series of evasions and ambiguous proceedings of the other side, in violation of the *spirit* of our agreement, that we resorted to the course we have done, which now forms the ground of complaint by Mr. Ross.

I shall now proceed to note down some of the proceedings of the other party, which I have termed *ambiguous* and as *violations* of the *spirit* of our agreement, and which has rendered the execution of the compromise impossible.

1. You will see, in the foregoing agreement, that the result of the conference was to be explained, and speeches of conciliation delivered by prominent members of both parties. In the execution of this part of our agreement, an additional indignity was cast upon us. How was the matter explained? Were the congregated Cherokees informed of the unhappy situation of their country and affairs, which had been the cause of their divisions into parties? Were they informed that all were brethren, fellow-sufferers, and of course ought not to charge each other with the difficulties under which they were laboring? That those difficulties can never now be settled except by a treaty and a cession of the land, and that the ten men who had the matter under consideration had so decided? Was such the explanation? Mr. Ross, who took upon himself that part of the business, represented us as a faction returning to our allegiance, and agreeing to support the measures of "the constituted authorities of the nation to close the difficulties with the United States, by a final adjustment, to be made there or elsewhere." What was ambiguous and doubtful in these words was made more so by their interpretation into the Cherokee language. What do you suppose would

be the understanding of an ignorant, prejudiced Cherokee, from such an explanation as that—one who had been constantly flattered and deluded with the expectation of an entire re-establishment in his country, and one who had been taught to believe that nothing prevented that reinstatement but the existence of a party favorable to a treaty and removal? I say, what would be his understanding? The most natural in the world.—"The constituted authorities love the land, and are striving to save it. They have been prevented from succeeding, thus far, by the treaty party, who wish to sell the land. That party has now united with the proper chiefs—*Therefore*, the country is now saved." Such was precisely the reasoning of these deluded people, the victims of misguided confidence. They were rejoicing by audible assents, while such *lucid* explanations were flowing from the lips of the *Indian* Chief, to be *interpreted* into his *native* language,[40] and while the speaker of the Council was expressing in a speech his willingness to receive, with extended arms, his children who had strayed from the right path, but had now returned to their duty.—Now, was all this in accordance with our agreement? Did we sign that compromise to be thus degraded and exposed to a gazing multitude as servile sycophants, deserting the great cause of *Cherokee emancipation*, upon which we had staked our all? No! It was a base violation of the *spirit* of that compromise.

2. The second item in these novel proceedings, is in the production, nature, and adoption of the powers with which the twenty delegates were to be instructed in the "final adjustment of the difficulties with the United States." It is a fact worthy of your notice, that, notwithstanding Mr. Ross professes such obedience to the will of his people, and to do nothing but what they desire him to do, yet he is the father, if not the writer, of every decree, order, or power, that comes from the Committee and Council at Red Clay. The powers in question had a similar origin; and what do you suppose they were? Were they such as were demanded by the state of things, plain, direct and decided? No. far from it—they were evasive, unmeaning, and undecided; such as might be understood by one person, in one way, according to his inclination; and in another way, by another person, according to *his* inclination, as was precisely the case in

this instance, as I shall show in the progress of this letter. I regret that I cannot have access to those written powers, in order to show the correctness of these remarks by quotations; but you may rest assured that I shall allege nothing but what is contained in them.

At the call of the public crier, the Cherokees, to the number of about one thousand, were collected around a stand, to hear some important communication from their Chief. Mr. Ross soon appeared, with a bundle of papers in his hand, which turned out to be the nomination of the twenty delegates, and their powers. They were all written out, ready to receive the assent and signatures of the multitude, who stood around the chief with indescribable anxiety, to hear some important development, or a suggestion of some plan that would result in their relief. Mr. Ross commenced to read an instrument of writing, drawn in the form of resolutions, to be adopted or approved by the people, granting powers to the twenty delegates, of which number he was one. Those powers, to an English reader, or to a person understanding the English language, may be understood as being ample and sufficient. They authorized the delegation to terminate the difficulties with the United States, by a treaty arrangement, either there or elsewhere. They gave them full power to negotiate, upon what principles they pleased, in any manner they pleased, and for any amount they pleased. In fine, they were unlimited, discretionary powers. So far, it was well enough, only that they were too extensive to be intrusted to twenty irresponsible persons. In addition to the fullest extent of authority which the people had conferred upon their delegation, they were made to declare that *they would be bound by all the acts of that delegation*. What will be your surprise when I tell you that those resolutions, containing such a declaration, were accompanied with a protest, in which the people are made to say, that *they will never consent to a treaty made upon the basis of the five millions of dollars*![41]

After the resolutions and the protest had been interpreted into the Cherokee language, (for all the communications of Mr. Ross to the Cherokees are made through an interpreter,) a question was put to the people whether they were willing to confirm them. The repeated cries of yes, yes, fully indicated the direction the current was moving. After this they were desired to sign those papers; about one thousand persons registered their names. It is worthy of notice that in obtaining their assent, the usual method was not observed; that is, that those who were in favor of confirming should say yes—and those of the contrary opinion should say no. Now I ask, were all these unmeaning words and unusual proceedings in accordance with the *spirit* of our compromise? Were they calculated to teach the poor Cherokees their true condition, and to result in, what was designed at least by one of the contracting parties, a speedy relief by a treaty arrangement? You will learn the answer to these queries by the *impressions* which were created in the minds of the multitude.

3. We must judge of things by their effects—and what were the effects of the proceedings I have just narrated? Let the conflicting opinions entertained by the people after the termination of those proceedings supply you with the correct answer. Mr. Ross, whether designedly or not, could not have taken a better course than he did take to confuse the minds of the people in reference to the nature and extent of the powers that had been conferred upon the delegation. I have already stated how one class, the largest class, of the Cherokees, whose prejudices and inclinations ran in a particular channel, understood the explanation made upon our compromise. That understanding was but strengthened by the subsequent proceedings. Although they had signed an instrument of writing conveying from them full powers to the select committee of twenty to dispose of their country, yet for want of proper explanation and interpretation of those powers, and because the terms to *sell* or *to cede* were not contained in them—especially because they were accompanied by a protest, to which I have already called your attention, *they never dreamt that the land would be sold.* On the contrary, they thought, by conferring those very powers, with the circumstances attending them, *they had saved the land.* They were under the impression that the danger of losing their country proceeded from the anxiety and exertions of the Government to purchase it, and as they had now declared never to submit to a treaty made upon the basis of the five millions of Dollars, the Government would cease those exertions, and consequently their lands would be secured—and furthermore, they thought

that the delegation were empowered to carry into effect the determination only, and for no other purpose whatever. Although this account will give you but an unfavorable opinion of the understanding of the Cherokees, and perhaps less so of the political honesty of those who were the instruments of this most wretched delusion, yet it is incumbent upon me to relate the whole truth, especially as this humiliating truth is necessary to the defence of my own character. Mistaken people! While they were congratulating themselves in the happy termination of their council, and the entire *overthrow*, as they thought, of the opposition—while they were expressing their joy, and spreading the glad news in every direction, as they dispersed from Red Clay, that the land was now saved, the delegation, with powers in their hands which to them may mean any thing or nothing, continued on the council ground, to add further stock to this mass of equivocating.

Such were the impressions entertained by one class of the Cherokees—but there was another to be satisfied—the intelligence of the country—those who understood the situation of the Cherokees, and foresaw the consequences of persisting to reject the propositions for a treaty, those who believed that a treaty was inevitable, and ought to be made speedily. Entertaining such views, it was natural to receive every favorable indication of a willingness in the people to cede their lands. What more could be desired by them, therefore, than the full discretionary powers that had now been conferred upon the delegation? The people had now waived all opposition, and had surrendered their country. So carried away were they with this much desired state of things, that they entirely overlooked the insidious *protest*, with which the powers for a treaty were encumbered. They thought that the difficulties which had so long oppressed the Cherokees were now in a fair way of being terminated. This consideration gave them much satisfaction, and *they* left the council ground with rejoicings founded upon *impressions just the reverse* of those I have described in the preceding paragraph.

But here is not all. How ambiguous must be those powers that are not understood by those upon whom they are conferred. The delegation partook of the confusion of opinions that possessed the people. A portion of them considered themselves clothed with full and unqualified powers; some, that they could make a partial cession, but could not treat upon money basis, as the people had resolved "never to submit to a treaty made upon the basis of the five millions of dollars." Some, for the *same* reason, thought they were authorized to cede the entire country for money, but for a sum *exceeding* five millions of dollars—and others disclaimed the right of selling one foot of land, alleging that the *people had not granted the authority*. These last were certainly correct according to the understanding of a majority of the people.

In all this confusion, what was the understanding of the author of the resolutions containing the powers in question? At the very first meeting of the delegation, I called his attention to the doubtful terms in which those resolutions were couched, and wished to know the practical effects the declaration of the people, that they would never consent to a treaty made upon the basis of the five millions of dollars, was likely to have upon our future deliberations. Was this declaration considered as a limitation in our instructions? Was it a sufficient obstacle to prevent us from treating upon that basis? If so intended, it was a matter of great moment. For what were the facts in reference to this particular matter? A previous delegation, of which Mr. Ross was the leader, had made propositions to make a partial cession, which the Government rejected. They then proposed to sell the entire country for the genteel sum of *twenty millions* of dollars, which also, the Government rejected. They then proposed to refer the matter to the Senate for its award, giving a written obligation to be bound by the award, whatever it might be, and to induce their people to accept of the same. That award was made, authorizing the President to give the Cherokees "for their lands and possessions not exceeding five millions of dollars." Now, here is a resolution containing a declaration of upwards of one thousand Cherokees, *that they will never consent to a treaty made upon the basis of that award*. Supposing we proceed to Washington city, and shall not be able to treat upon any other basis but the basis established by the Senate, will that declaration prevent us from treating? Are we so limited and instructed by the people? Mr. Ross said he thought we were! This avowal, under the circumstances it was made, appeared to me equivalent to an avowal *that no treaty would be concluded.*

The various opinions which I have briefly described were quickly disseminated through the nation. Conflicting views were advanced as to the object of the delegation—the great body of the people being under the impression that it was *to secure the land*, the others supposing it was *to sell the land.* When a portion of the delegation corroborated the latter opinion, it created considerable uneasiness, especially in a particular section of the country where nothing of that kind was dreamed of. "We have just returned," they said, "from Red Clay, where the treaty was voted down and where we declared we would never consent to a treaty; and how comes this delegation to claim the right of ceding the country?"—To satisfy themselves, they sent an embassy to Mr. Ross, wishing to have a direct information upon that point—to know what what was actually their intention. It is easy to apprehend what *ought* to have been the reply of a candid person, under Ross's circumstances, possessing, as he did, the entire confidence of an ignorant and confiding people—It ought to have been plain, direct, and unequivocal, such as this: "I have done what I could to have our nation reinstated—I have failed. There is now no other alternative, for the salvation of the Cherokees, but to make a treaty, and *to treat is to sell the land.*" But what was his reply? He told them that they may rest assured that he was their friend, and that the delegation *would not leave them in a worse situation than they were in.*[42] Poor consolation to a perishing people! Whether those to whom this reply of the *Delphic Oracle* was sent were *satisfied* and *appeased*, I have not had the means of ascertaining. I leave it to you now, to say whether all these proceedings were in accordance with the *spirit* of our compromise.

4. The last upon which I propose to speak, is the *predetermination* of Mr. Ross and the majority of the delegation not to negotiate in the Cherokee country, but at all events to proceed to the city of Washington. It is true, in the compromise, we speak of a treaty *to be* made, or which *may be* made, but we never presumed one moment but that, under the circumstances then existing, a treaty *would be made on the ground.* A commis-

sioner of the United States was there,[43] prepared to negotiate with the Cherokees upon the very basis recommended by the Senate of the United States, and acceded to in advance by a previous delegation, headed by Mr. Ross himself. We could not imagine, therefore, how Mr. Ross could consistently refuse to act in accordance with that obligation. When the matter was brought before the people, that is, when the compromise and the resolutions were presented for their confirmation, the expression "here or *elsewhere*," was used by Mr. Ross, in speaking of *where* the delegation may carry on the negotiations.—Mr. Ross distinctly used that expressed, and it as so interpreted into the Cherokee language, although, it seems, it was not so written, for in perusing the resolutions a day or so after, I noticed the word *Washington* was used in the place of *elsewhere*.

There was another expression used in the papers to which I have so often recurred, which no one but those in the secret imagined could have any bearing upon the future course of the delegation. When they were clothed with power to negotiate "here or *elsewhere*," with a commissioner of the United States, the expression *having full powers* was used. That is, with a commissioner *having full powers*. Now, to us, all these were harmless expressions, and we never one moment supposed that any advantage would be or could be taken. But have patience while I expose the intrigue and insincerity of these very men who now charge us with a violation of faith, and are so vociferous in their denunciations against us, *because they would not permit us to fulfil our obligations to them*. You will say, how can that be? I will tell you how *it has been*.

All the preliminary arrangements for negotiations being made on the part of the Cherokees—the Delegation appointed, and powers conferred upon them—the Commissioner of the United States was accordingly informed of it, and requested to state what time he would wish to confer with the Delegation. He appointed a certain hour of the day, at which time the first conference took place.—The Commissioner presented his letter of appointment from the Secretary of War. He said he was authorized by the President of the United States to enter into a treaty with the Cherokees East, for all their lands, under the basis awarded by the Senate at its last session. He then went into a particular history of the circumstances which brought about that award. So far as the amount was concerned, it was a settled question—it was settled by the Senate, at the request of Mr. Ross—of course the President could not transcend that amount. He was, therefore, instructed to go just so far as the Senate had permitted the President to go, and now he stood ready to negotiate with the Cherokees to the extent of his powers, *and a little beyond.*

The consultation which took place after the above conference, fully brought to light the designs and the system of evasion that had been carried on during the memorable council. *Doubts* were now suggested whether they could treat with the Commissioner, from the fact that he was acting under a letter of the Secretary of War, and not under a *commission* from the President! "We are authorized," said Mr. Ross and his friends, "to treat with a commissioner *having full powers*—But certainly this man has not full powers, because he has no commission from the President.[44] However, this objection *may* be waived. Yet we cannot treat with him, because he proposed to negotiate only upon the basis and principles which the people have *already rejected*, in the declaration that they *never will consent to a treaty made upon the basis of the five millions of dollars*." Upon these two positions they planted themselves, and proved impregnable to the assaults of the Commissioner. But did they gain their object by simply refusing to treat? Would that satisfy them, or satisfy the people, many of whom were anxiously watching the result of the expected negotiations, and trembling in anticipation of the fearful consequences, in case no treaty was made? One step further, they gained the point at which they were aiming during the whole council. "Although," they said, "we cannot negotiate with the present Commissioner, *according to our instructions*, yet from the *power* we are intrusted with, to negotiate here or at *Washington*, (*Washington* was now openly avowed,) we can go to the Seat of Government, and make a treaty under the eye of the President himself." No sooner said, than a pretended determination was made, to take a step already *predetermined.*—Without offering any propositions themselves, it was decided to put an end to the negotiations, and to proceed as speedily as possible to Washington City. Upon this decision the grand delegation, into whose hands the destiny of a nation was committed, dispersed to their homes, after having appointed a certain time to leave for Washington, and after being notified by the Commissioner to attend another Council at New Echota, on the 21st December following.

Such was the end of all the movements at Red Clay. The leaders and principal actors in all these transactions, had come together with a settled determination to evade the Commissioner and his propositions. All their movements tended to that point—all their papers were drawn for that purpose—all their talks, speeches, and explanations, were evasive, dark, and unmeaning. They accomplished their object by a system of delusion. To one portion of the Cherokees they were the saviours of the land—to the other, agents by whom a cession of the land was to be made. With these two characters, directly opposite, they were about to proceed to Washington, when official communications were addressed to them by order of the President, informing them that they would not be received by him as a delegation—that he would negotiate no treaty with them in Washington—that if a treaty was made it must be made in the Cherokee country, with the commissioner then there, and according to the basis settled by the Senate.[45] In this state of things, what was the duty of these men, who had abstracted the entire power of the nation into their own hands? It was not necessary to consider whether the determination of the President was right or wrong, but what, under the circumstances, was practicable to be done—and this must depend upon the question, whether the President had declared *the truth*, and whether he would *adhere* to his declaration. If he was likely to adhere to what he had said, then it became a matter of serious consideration, whether the Delegation ought to push forward to Washington, reckless of all consequences. In this critical moment, did they act as wise men—as practical, *common sense men*—as patriotic men, unswayed by personal predilections and prejudices? Did they choose the least *of two evils*; to meet the Commissioner at New Echota, to re-open negotiations, and, if necessary, to leave the whole matter to the people? No—they plunged into a fearful *uncertainty*, by rushing in the very face of the official declaration *that they would not be received by the*

President. They accordingly left the Cherokee country about the 1st of December, on their way to the seat of Government.

Now sir, under the circumstances which I have briefly enumerated, what was the course which patriotism suggested to me and my associates, who had agreed to a compromise for the purpose of effecting one great object, the relief of the Cherokees, *by a treaty*? For that object *alone* the compromise was made, and to effect *that only* it was binding. Now was it likely to be accomplished? This was the sole question for us to decide, and we decided in the negative, because, 1. A treaty *could not* be made by the Delegation at Washington, according to the official notification. 2. Because they *would not* make a treaty upon the only basis that it could be made.—But what was to be done? Were we to sit under the impression that we had tied our hands by the compromise, and see the "Constituted Authorities," as they are pleased to style themselves, lead a suffering community to destruction, by a system of delusion? We did not so judge our duty. There was still an opening, by which the very purpose of the compromise, the execution of which by the other party had now been rendered hopeless, might yet be carried into effect—and that was to attend the Council at New Echota on the 21st of December, appointed by the Commissioners of the United States, for the purpose of entering into negotiations with the *Cherokee People*. We did attend, with a respectable portion of our countrymen;[46] and the result of our deliberations at the council was, the treaty now before the Senate, and which has furnished to Mr. Ross the charge to which I have been replying.

There is another fact connected with this subject, which will show the unreasonableness of the charge alleged against us. During the negotiations at New Echota, it was suggested that possibly we might be mistaken in supposing that Mr. Ross's Delegation *would not* or *could not* make a treaty—that the President might receive them and negotiate with them, and that they might propose to treat upon the basis offered by the Government. Measures were taken to meet such possible contingencies. The Delegation who were appointed to accompany the treaty to Washington, were, therefore, expressly instructed to lay no obstacle in the way of the first Delegation, if they found that they had been received, and were in a course of negotiations with the Government, or were likely to consummate a better treaty. This trust was faithfully fulfilled, as you will see from the following letter addressed by the second Delegation to the first.

WASHINGTON CITY, *February* 5, 1836.

Messrs. John Ross and others, Cherokee Delegation, now in Washington City.

GENTLEMEN:—The undersigned, a delegation appointed at a General Council held in New Echota, in December last, and convened agreeably to a public notice signed by William Carroll and J. F. Schermerhorn, Commissioners of the United States to negotiate with the Cherokees east, herewith submit to your consideration the accompanying articles of a treaty. We do this in compliance with the instructions of the Council, which will be found in the copy of the journal also herewith submitted.

It is needless, gentlemen, to speak at large upon the imperious considerations and urgent necessity which has compelled your constituents at home to negotiate this treaty. Those considerations and that necessity are found in the suffering condition of our people, the *urgency* of some relief, and the *uncertainty* of it, as was apprehended, from the fact that you were officially informed, before you left the Cherokee country, that the President of the United States would not receive your delegation; and that if a treaty was made, it must be made with the people at home, according to the instructions given to the Commissioners, one of whom was then in the country. That uncertainty was also greatly increased from similar declarations that were made to the council at New Echota, and the circumstances that had brought about the award of the Senate last winter, and a certain protest, signed at Red Clay and appended to the instrument of writing, that gave you authority as a Delegation, declaring that the award of the Senate, made upon the reference of our Delegation, *would never be accepted.*

It appeared to the Council, therefore, that there was no other alternative left but either to linger out another miserable year, subject to all the privations incident upon the oppressive legislations of the States, or immediately to settle the perplexed difficulties by a treaty arrangement.

In doing what the people have done at New Echota, it was with no view to lay any obstacles in your way. They were desirous that the matter should have been settled by you, if practicable, and they have instructed us, as their Delegation, to proceed in such a manner as not to retard any good work that you may have done, or can do, for the benefit of the Cherokees. In compliance, therefore, with that instruction, we assure you of the heartfelt satisfaction that it would give us, and certainly our constituents, if you have settled, or can settle, our difficulties with the Government by a treaty. The treaty we now present to you, was signed, as the best that can be obtained from the Government—So it was considered by those who signed it. If, upon a perusal of it, you will, in your wisdom, consider that a better can be made, and will be enabled to effect one, it will rejoice us much, and we will congratulate our country in the happy consummation.

You will perceive, from the copy of the journal we herewith transmit, that we are instructed, in case that you have not already made, or are able to make, a better, to urge the ratification of this treaty, and we shall proceed to the performance of that duty as soon as we shall be satisfied upon that point. As the case is very urgent, the misery of our people accumulating every day, we trust we may be enable soon to know your prospects and views upon this most important matter. If you think the treaty we send you is the best that can be obtained from the Government, of which *we* are decidedly convinced, but will propose any modification or alternation which will be to the advantage of our people, we shall be happy in lending you any assistance in our power.

Major RIDGE,
JAMES FOSTER,
LONG SHERE,
and others.

To this letter Mr. Ross has not deigned to give a reply, and I infer his prospects of making, not to say a *better* treaty, from a letter of the Commissioner of Indian Affairs, addressed to him and his associates, of which the following is an extract:

"The delegation of the Cherokee nation, of which some of you were members, and which visited this city last winter, was emphatically assured during the last session of Congress, and that assurance was officially repeated in the course of the following autumn, that no delegation would be received here to make a treaty; and in defiance of that notification, you have come on and presented yourselves for that purpose. How could you, under such circumstances, imagine that you would be received by the Department as the duly constituted representatives of the Cherokee people? It is not easy to account for that strange error of opinion, unless it arose from the courtesy with which you were treated, when you called upon the President and Secretary of War." [The letter from which the foregoing is extracted, is dated February 13, 1836.]

In this state of things, utterly unable himself to consummate a treaty, which he may think preferable, Mr. Ross is using his influence to defeat the only measure that can give relief to his suffering people. Why is it? Does he expect a better treaty? And has he plans in operation to induce such an expectation? It is not pretended. He says he is doing the *will* of the people, and he holds their authority—*they* are opposed, and it is enough. The will of the people! The opposition of the people!! This has been the cry for the last five years, until that people have become but a mere wreck of what they once were—all their institutions and improvements utterly destroyed—their energy enervated—their moral character debased, corrupted and ruined. The whole of that catastrophe, I mean aside from the mere loss of the soil, a trifle in consideration with other matters, which has overwhelmed and crushed the Cherokees, might have been averted, if Mr. Ross, instead of identifying himself with the contemptible prejudice founded upon the *love of the land*, had met the crisis manfully as it became him to do, and unfolded to his confiding people the sure termination of all these things, they might now have been a happy and prosperous community, a monument of his forecase and wise administration as an Indian chief. But, no Sir—he has dragged an ignorant train, wrought upon by near sighted prejudice and stupid obstinacy, to the last brink of destruction; and now, when he would take the same measures, that he has so long discarded, to save his followers from the dreadful dilemma in which he has placed them, he cannot even have that poor consolation. He stands surrounded by a hungry, naked and destitute people—surprised at his unwise course, and confounded at his near sighted policy.

Very respectfully,
ELIAS BOUDINOT.

NEW ECHOTA, Nov. 25, 1836.

To MR. JOHN ROSS:

SIR—In the foregoing letter addressed to a friend, at first not intended for publication, I have taken the liberty to comment upon your course in reference to our political concerns, especially in reference to that part of it least injustice, although what reference I have made to certain papers and documents was altogether from memory. My object was to give facts—not so much to state how the powers conferred upon the delegation were drawn, but *how they were understood*, and what *action* took place upon them. On this point I am not mistaken—I cannot be mistaken in reference to transactions which occurred before my eyes and in my hearing. The facts stated by me can be proved by legal testimony. I could produce affidavits, if your friends would allow me the use of their testimony, that even your Vice-Chief[47] did not think that you were authorized to dispose of the land—I can produce affidavits to show that at least one of the "regular" delegation expressed himself vehemently against the cession of land, upon the ground that you were not authorized to make a cession, and this, too, at the time when you were presenting yourself to the Government as specially authorized for that purpose—I can produce affidavits from the people, whose will, you say, must regulate your conduct in all cases, to show that you were never understood, by the majority of those people, to have received the authority in question.[48]

What then? perhaps you will say. I answer, according to those facts, you must either have been deceiving your people or deceiving the Government. If you were acting in accordance with the will of the people, as you allege you were, then you were deceiving the Government, when you presented yourself as specially authorized to make a cession of the land—and if you were in earnest with the Government, you were deceiving your people, for you were acting against their will, and against their authority, *as they understood that authority*. I care not how plainly the powers under which you attempted to act were written, or how it is possible they can otherwise be understood than they are generally understood by English readers—that has nothing to do with the understanding of the people, to whom all their political information has been communicated by written papers, couched, not unfrequently, in very ambiguous terms, and through the medium of interpreters not always capable of conveying the true sense or meaning of the English.

But upon this point I need not proceed further. I have already stated that the letter to which I have here briefly alluded, was not written with a view to its publication. Even your memorial to the Senate, protesting against the New Echota Treaty, in which you make very free with my name, was not sufficient to provoke me to publish it.[49] I have, however, met with two printed pamphlets, one purporting to be a memorial of a minority of your Delegation to the House of Representatives; and the other a letter to a friend, signed with your name, and dated July 2d, 1836.[50] In these there is an evident attempt to present my character to the public in an obnoxious light. You have *indirectly* charged me with hypocrisy, servility, duplicity, and the like, which, if true, must forever degrade me in the eye of a virtuous community. You present those charges under such circumstances, and in such a way, as to be taken for truth by persons unacquainted with our affairs, especially if I were to sit still and permit your aspersions to go abroad without a reply. I am therefore called upon by the duty I owe to myself, and to the community, whose good opinion, of course, every one must desire to possess, to make the foregoing letter public, and to add another addressed to yourself.

In this controversy, I am well aware of the disadvantages

under which I labor. I am but an humble individual, and I do not claim anything incidental to any station or calling to recommend me to the sympathies of the public. You, on the other hand, have presented yourself as the "*Principal Chief*," a title, under other times, and under other circumstances, conferred upon you by an Indian community, but to which, I perceive, when those circumstances have long since ceased to exist, you cling with the most unyielding pertinacity.[51] You present yourself, also, as a *persecuted* chief; and you know well the advantage which that title must give, by exciting the sympathies of the public towards you, and its execrations upon your alleged persecutors. You claim, likewise, to be the *favorite* chief, whom the Cherokees are accustomed to honor, and you even go so far as to strike a comparison between yourself and the illustrious Washington. All these claims and pretensions, and your charges against me, are held forth to the public by a *hired* but a practised pen.[52] Against this whole array of titles, claims, pretensions, charges, &c. I can bring nothing but what clear conscience and integrity will furnish me, dressed up by the aid of my own limited abilities and feeble pen.

Among the many charges that have been made against me and my associates during this unhappy controversy, is that of being *interested persons*. This has been often repeated, and some have gone so far as to say that we have been *bought* or *bribed*, and hence our *subserviency* to the Government in this matter. I perceive, in your communications, you employ the term *interested*, which you evidently intend to apply to us. We do not deny that we are deeply interested in the result of this question—as Cherokees, and in common with other Cherokees, we cannot but be deeply interested. To represent us in any other light, is an unprovoked assault upon our reputation.

But the charge, that we have been actuated, in all our efforts to effect a treaty for the removal of the Cherokees, by *interested motives*, has so often been made, you have finally undertaken to endorse it, and it is in that light you attempt to represent me. I do not now particularly refer to what you have said in your communication, but to what you have repeatedly alleged to these confiding people. What is the nature of those interested motives? Are they political or pecuniary? The former is too insignificant to deserve notice.[53] That you mean the latter, in other words, that, by the consummation of a treaty, I am to be benefitted in a pecuniary point of view, or to receive some special advantage, it is easy to surmise.[54] I may here content myself by denying the allegation, and throwing the burden of proof upon you, according to the maxim of all civilized nations, that the accuser must prove his charges before the accused can be accounted guilty.

And where is your proof in support of this grave charge? You are acquainted with Indian treaties, and you understand the mode of forming them, and securing special advantages. You have made such treaties, and you have seen such *special advantages* secured in them. Are they not found upon the very face of the instruments themselves? And are not the names of the persons to be thus benefitted broadly inscribed upon them? *You know it is so*, universally so, where special reservations are given. Where then can you find, in the treaty which you so much oppose, and which you allege has been the result of self-interest, my name identified with any thing that will give me any pecuniary advantage over my fellowcountrymen? Perhaps you will answer, that my name is found among the committee of thirteen to transact all the business of the Indians, and hence I have secured to myself a lucrative office.[55] It so happens, however, which will be sufficient for my defence in this respect, that not one cent is provided, under the treaty, even for the *expenses* of the committee.

It may be said, perhaps, that notwithstanding I have taken precaution to prevent any showing of self-interest upon the face of the treaty, I am, nevertheless, to reap some great pecuniary advantage under its execution or operation. The execution of the treaty has now sufficiently progressed either to confirm or refute that assertion. And how is it? Instead of I being benefitted over my fellows, it is *you*. Any person need but look to the lists of valuations, to be convinced upon this point.[56] And how is it possible that I can receive any extra pecuniary advantage under the present treaty?—To be sure, I might have had the same opportunities with some of my countrymen to speculate upon the ignorance and credulity of our citizens—I could as easily have taken advantage of their weakness, and ingratiated myself into their good favor, by pretending to be a land lover, and deluding them with hopes and expectations which I myself did not believe would be realized; and under that deep delusion into which our people have been thrown, I could have purchased their possessions and claims for a trifle, and thus have enriched myself upon the spoils of my countrymen but I have detested that vile speculation. I have seen others engaged in it, and those too, who were understood to be your friends, and consequently opposed to a treaty. What speculation have I made, then, which you might allege the treaty was made to confirm to me?

Again—It is well known that while you were adding one farm after another, and stretching your fences over hills and dales, from river to river, and through swamps and forests, no doubt, for I can conceive no other substantial reason for such unusual conduct, with a view to these very times—I say, while you were making these great preparations, which have now turned out to be a pecuniary advantage to you, I was here, toiling, at the most trying time of our difficulties, for the defence of our rights, in an arduous employment, and with a nominal salary of three hundred dollars only, entirely neglecting my own pecuniary interest. You know it is so—it is too notorious to call for denial; and yet you would present me as being actuated, in this affair, by interested motives!

Another of your charges is, that I acted a hypocritical part in going with the "got up" Delegation, after having declined to go with the "regular" Delegation. To prove my hypocyrisy, you have published my letter of resignation. A bare inspection of that letter must show the unreasonableness of that charge. Will you not admit that I had a right to resign my station as a delegate for ample reasons, or such as I considered ample reasons, as set forth in the foregoing letter; and, having so resigned, that I had the right to go with another Delegation, whose principles of action were more congenial to my views? Even, then, upon the very ground you seem to condemn me, I am not so culpable as you would make out. I did accept an appointment as one of the "Regular Delegation," at Red Clay, and did intend to act in good faith towards you, and did so act as long I believed, not that *you* had acted in good faith towards me and my associates, but that there was a prospect of a treaty being made, for which object *alone* I had accepted the appointment. How long I could consistently flatter myself with such a belief will appear from the history of the transactions at Red Clay, as narrated in the proceding letter. I say then, upon that view of the ease, I had the right to resign as a member of your Delegation, and to go with another; and I see no reason why you should brand me with hypocrisy, if I chose not to be invested with a seeming authority which proved, to my satisfaction, to be fraud upon the good sense of every Cherokee capable of the least discernment.

But, Sir, even under such circumstances, I was not disposed to take a step which would expose me to any charges from you, however groundless or unjust they might be. It is well known to my friends, that after the compromise was made, even after *you had violated it*, I was desirous that the Commissioner should waive his instructions to convene a council at New Echota, and go with you to Washington. It is well known to many that Mr. Ridge and myself urged that course upon the Commissioner, for the purpose of conciliation and closing our difficulties in peace, and on account of the very urgency that we used, the good understanding that had subsisted between the Commissioner and us was interrupted. These are facts that can be corroborated by ample testimony, are well known as many of your friends, and may be known to you, and yet I see you have labored hard to prove that we acted hypocritically.—Notwithstanding all your equivocations and violations of the compromise, and the utter uncertainty which your proceedings had rendered the question of a treaty, I had still concluded, with the most extreme reluctance, as you may well suppose from that uncertainty, to go with you to Washington. And let me say, *I should have gone*, against my judgment, were it not for reasons of a domestic nature. Upon the existence of these reasons I sat down and wrote you the letter you have published.

That charge is also founded upon the fact that I signed, while a member of your Delegation, certain papers containing views directly opposite to those I have since expressed, and upon which I have acted.[57] I should have presumed that you would have been the last person to have brought forward such a charge founded upon such a reason. You knew very well, and you now know very well, that all the members of the Delegation were *required* to sign those papers, not as the sense of each delegate, but as the sense of the majority of them. That was your decision, for I expressly made the question at the time you brought forward those papers. I gave you sufficient intimation that I should sign them against my judgement, which I did, and for which act I have been superlatively ashamed ever since.

In connection with this part of my letter, I will say a word or two in reference to a charge you have made against Mr. Ridge.[58] "This being his fourth entire revolution in politics within as many months: varying as often as the moon, without the excuse of lunacy for his change." Let us see how this is. In the first place, what are we to understand by the term *politics*? And what have been the politics of Mr. Ridge and those who have acted with him? You know they have been identified with a treaty, as the only measure to relieve these people, while yours have been opposed to a treaty. These have been the only politics known in this country, as existing among the Cherokees themselves. Your charge against Mr. Ridge is then this—in going with you to Washington, as one of the "regular" Delegation, he changed his views in reference to a treaty, and in leaving your Delegation to advocate the New Echota Treaty, he retraced his steps, and became the *advocate* of a measure which he *opposed* while with you. This is your misrepresentation, and it is precisely with what I have charged you in the foregoing letter as a violation of the spirit of our compromise, when you "represented us as a faction returning to our allegiance." We went for a treaty—Hence our opposition to you, because you were opposed to it; now could we act with you in concert until you had agreed that a treaty should be made. That was the principle upon which the compromise was founded—they were the politics of Mr. Ridge and his associates. If Mr. Ridge was convinced that you were not disposed to fulfil your obligations which that compromise imposed upon you, hence no treaty was likely to be made by you and your "regular" delegation, he acted but consistently, and in accordance with his politics, to leave you and advocate the New Echota treaty. What you term as the "revolution in politics" is only an adherence to his political principles. He stuck to you as long as there was a bare probability of your doing what the compromise called for, and he left you as soon as he was satisfied that even that bare probability did not exist.

Besides the circumstances which I have enumerated in the preceding letter as obstacles in the accomplishment of a treaty contemplated in the compromise, I will state one other, which was enough to raise doubts, at least in the mind of Mr. Ridge, as to the sincerity of your professions. And it will give an apt illustration of your oft repeated declaration, *that you do the will of the people*!

There appeared in the public prints a statement signed by John Howard Payne, giving an account of his captivity by the Georgia Guard, accompanied by an address from the Cherokees to the people of the United States, written by the same person at your request and approved by you—and if we are to believe the writer, that address was intended to be circulated and signed by the Cherokee people.[59] Now, what is important to be known is this—that address was written, approved and printed *after* the compromise was made, and after the delegation (of which you were but one) had been appointed. And what is material to the proper understanding of this matter is another consideration—the compromise professed to *bury in oblivion* all the ill feeling that had subsisted between the parties, and had conferred *equal power* upon *each* of the delegation, for the purposes for which they were appointed. Now let us see in what way you *presumed* to speak for the Cherokee people, without their knowledge, and without the knowledge of any other but the *one* whom you employed to write for you—a stranger, and of course not the most capable to understand our complicated difficulties. I have not that address by me, but I copy what was noted, as the subjects discussed in it, by another person, immediately after reading it.[60]

"It is a dramatical appeal from the President to the people. It argues that they are compelled to treat—that the Government price is too small—that the Cherokees do not wish to go to the west—to a country remote, unhealthy, and undesirable—that if they are compelled to treat they would prefer to be allowed citizenship in counties and towns. It speaks of some of their own countrymen as having been *seduced* from their policy by the

United States—their press taken, and their own people induced to publish *falsehoods* against their Chiefs."[61]

This is a correct statement of what was discussed in that address, and I need not do more than present in juxtaposition to that statement, the compromise which *buried in oblivion all party differences*, and your declaration *that you do the will of the people*. At any rate, it is a most beautiful illustration of what you say in your letter—"It is I who serve under them, not they under me!" Just look at it. An individual member of a delegation composed of twenty persons, upon the eve of commencing important duties intrusted to all *collectively*, without consulting his associates, employs a stranger to write an address of the Cherokee people—an address digested, prepared, and *approved* without the knowledge of the people for whom it was intended, and *to be sent to them for their signatures*—an address containing dishonorable allusions to some of the delegation, and avowing political doctrines abhorrent to the people, at least never agitated by them—an address intended to commit, in advance, the nation to the views of *one* out of a delegation of *twenty* persons! This may be the way to do the will of the people, and to obey their *commands*, or *to serve under them*—If it is, I must confess my entire ignorance of such matters.

This address Mr. Ridge did not see until he reached Athens, Tennessee, on his way to Washington. What impressions it produced upon his mind will be seen from the letter he addressed you at that place.

ATHENS, TENNESSEE, *4th December*, 1836.

MR. JOHN ROSS.

SIR—I have the honor to decline going on with you to Washington City, after having read John Howard Payne's statement and the Cherokee address to the people of the United States, prepared, no doubt, at your request and suggestions. That address unfolds to me your views of policy diametrically opposite to mine and my friends, who will never consent to be citizens of the States, or receive money to buy land in a foreign country.[62] I trust that whatever you do, if you can effect a treaty, that the rights of the poor Indians, who are now nearly naked and homeless, will not be disregarded. Neither do I believe waging a political war, by appealing from the treaty making power of the United States, will be of any service to our people, but will result in their ruin.

Respectfully, your friend,
JOHN RIDGE.

The reason he did not return and leave you at that time was your urgent entreaty that he would go on, which he did—still hoping that you might be disposed and enabled to effect a treaty for the removal of the Cherokees. It was not until that hope was eradicated by your continued evasive and non-committal policy, and the refusal of the Government to negotiate with you at Washington, that he broke his connexion with you, to do the best the times and circumstances presented. This you have called "resolution in politics."—*It is an adherence to political principles*.

One of your defences is in reference to the charge that has been made against you as a reservee.[63] It is said that, in a former treaty, negotiated too, by yourself, you secured a tract of land in fee simple, upon the condition that you were in future to remain a citizen of the U. States. According to that condition, it has been alleged, you cannot claim any rights as an Indian.[64] I am not disposed to go so far, or even to say that you really did obligate yourself to become a citizen of the United States. Be that as it may, my objection to you as a reservee has been identified with my objection to the entire system. I am opposed to it upon the very ground on which you say you took the reservation, viz: Because it despenses *special grants* to few individuals. It gives ground for that very charge of selfinterested motives, which has been so profusely heaped upon me and my associates, but whether with an *equal appearance* of truth, I leave you to say, and the public to judge.[65]

But what further I have to say upon this subject is in reference to the *manner* in which you have explained this matter. I am sorry to be compelled to say any thing which will have the appearance of charging you with a want of justice or integrity. "But those who dwell in a glass house ought to beware how they throw stones out of it." This controversy is not of my seeking. If you think I am too personal, I wish you to bear in mind what you have said in reference to me. Your account of the matter is as follows: "There was a tract of land given to my ancestors by the Cherokee Nation. In the year 1819, the United States thought proper to secure six hundred and forty acres of that tract to me, as a *special* reservation." Now, sir, I am not disposed to say, from this statement, that you have stated what is not true, but I allege that you have not stated the *whole* truth. It is true that the Cherokees did give your ancestors a certain tract of land; whether for services rendered, or as a gift, it is not material for us to know; but *it is not true* that the land was given to them *exclusively*, but it was given to them and the ancestors of Watts *jointly*. It is true, as you state, that at the treaty of 1819, you being one of the principal negotiators on the part of the Cherokees, the grant to the certain tract of land was confirmed to you *exclusively*, as a "*special*" reservation. Why Watts, who had an equal interest in that land, and which interest it was your bounden duty, as a man of honor, to see protected and defended, instead of taking advantage of his weakness, and the circumstances which grew out of your position, was excluded from an equal participation in that land, is not, perhaps, for me to say; but it behooves you, as you have triumphantly referred to that transaction, to satisfy the public upon this matter. Will you deny it? Can you deny it? Or will you say that it was done with the consent or concurrence of Watts? You cannot even *pretend* to say so, because the contrary is too notorious in this country. Watts did complain, bitterly complain of the gross injustice done towards him; but what could a poor ignorant man accomplish with a Diplomatist? His complaints and demands for justice were unheard, and his murmurings soon hushed into silence.

It has been suggested, from the words, "of that tract," only a portion of that land was confirmed to you, and consequently no injustice was done to Watts. True, if a portion of that land was given to you *exclusively*. But it was not so. There was a *joint* ownership between yourself and Watts, and you had no more right to dispose of one foot of that land, without his knowledge and consent, than you had to dispose of the whole. But is it true that only a part of the original gift was confirmed to you, which impression, it has been supposed, you intended to convey by the words "of that tract?" I have made inquiries as to this matter, and I am told that your special reservation of 610 acres included *the whole* of the original gift, and took in some which had never been granted, in order *to make up the deficiency*.

What should have urged you to such an act of injustice has been a matter of surmise. Some have supposed that you thought it was right, from the circumstance that Watts, in the year 1817, or thereabouts, had enrolled to remove the Arkansas. That cannot alter the case, because his enrolment could not affect his *individual property*.[66] And it seems *you* did not consider his rights as a *Cherokee citizen* affected, because he has been, and for aught I know, is still considered a member of your Red Clay Council.

Another of your defences is in reference to the charge that your policy has been to get the money of the nation into your hands. The extent that I have intended to charge you is, that your policy has been to get the money into the hands of what you call the *Constituted Authorities*. I need not spend time to prove that, for you avow it yourself in your letter, and you contend for its propriety. While you justify that policy, you make a "monstrous misrepresentation" when you say that the treaty throws our money into the hands of frontier agents. You will find *no such provision* in the treaty. It seems that you have been hard run to find real objections, so that you have been compelled to make imaginary objections. The only agent known in the treaty, and the only one responsible to the Cherokees for the disbursement of the money, according to the provisions of the treaty, is the United States. This is in accordance with the universal practice established in all our past treaties with the Government.[67]

Now what is your wish—what is your policy? You would place the five millions in the hands of the *authorities of the nation*—their receipt of course, would discharge the United States. Let the least reflecting mind think for a moment, of the operation of such a policy. *Responsibility* is an essential ingredient in all money operations. And where is the responsibility of the Red Clay Council equal to the proper disbursement of $5,000,000? A bare statement will show your policy to be consummately ridiculous. Will you say that the *authorities* of the nation is a sufficient security? What do you mean by that oft repeated word, when you know there is *no* authority of the nation? You cannot, I may say you do not even pretend to execute a ten dollar judgement. And what if there was authority? A single fact in the proceedings of the consituted council will answer for an illustration.

Some years since, I think in the year 1824, an arrearage to a considerable amount was paid to the Nation by the United States. Not being in immediate want of the money, the *Constituted Authorities* (there was some show of authority then) passed an act to loan it to the citizens of the Nation in sums not exceeding five hundred dollars. I cannot say how much was loaned out, but thus much I can safely affirm—a large portion of what was loaned, perhaps to the amount of four or five thousand dollars, *has never been collected to this day.* Here is a sample to show how well your council would discharge the trust were the five millions placed in their hands.[68]

"If ever I hold an office in the Nation of my compatriots, it must be from *their election*, not the nomination of an executive of another country." "I am only one of their agents and their *elected* Chief." And, again—"*The people* saw and understood it, and determined to preserve both without changing the spirit of our laws, though they were forced to modify the mode of their fulfilment." With what *scrupulous fidelity* you make the assertions in these extracts will be seen from the following short and simple statement of facts, which you cannot gainsay:

According to a provision of the Cherokee Constitution, the office of the Principal Chief, and the members of the Council are to be filled, the latter by election of the people, for two years, and the former by the General Council, for four years. The last election held was in the month of August, of 1830, and the next was to have been held in 1832. In the same year, in the month of October, came the election, by the Council, for the Principal Chief. On the accont of a law of the State of Georgia, there was no election held in August, 1832; and, consequently, the members of the Council, who were, according to the Constitution, to elect the Principal Chief in the month of October following, were not elected. In this state of things, the members of the Council, whose term of service was about to expire, took the following measures, at a called council held, I think, in the month of August. I will be short. They passed a resolution appointing twenty-four men, selected (by the Council) from the Cherokee people then on the ground, the aggregate number of which did not *exceed* two hundred. These twenty-four men were required to meet, as the resolution expressed it, in *convention*. I claim to know something of this matter, because I was a member of the *convention*. Two propositions were introduced—1. That the Cherokee Government should be continued *as it was* for two years. This was my proposition. 2. That the Cherokee Government should be continued as it was *while our difficulties lasted*. The latter prevailed, and it was sent to the Council as the *advice* of the *Convention*, which the Council very gravely *accepted*, and referred to the people *on the ground* for their confirmation. The members of the Council, the Chiefs, and all, accordingly retained their seats after the expiration of their term of office prescribed in the constitution, and have retained them ever since.[69]

Such is the simple history of this matter. For aught I know, this may be only a *modification* of the mode of fulfilling the Cherokee laws, although it has seemed to me to be an entire change of the principles of the Government. And by some new kind of construction it may be considered by *you* as the act *of the people*, although I can safely venture in the assertion, that three out of five do not even know, *to this day*, that such transactions even transpired. And for aught I know you may hold your office by the *election of the people*, and may be their "elected Chief," although there has been *no election* since the constitution, under which you cannot pretend to hold your present office.

I find your letter a passage or two which confirm a point discussed in the preceding letter. I have stated there that, according to the ambiguous terms in which your powers were drawn, from the fact that the Cherokees were made to declare, in a protest, that they would never consent to a treaty made upon the basis of the five million Dollars, it was altogether uncertain whether a treaty would be made by you at Washington, even if the President received you, and was willing to negotiate with you. The passages to which I allude are these: "Three times have the Cherokee people formally and openly rejected conditions substantially the same as these. We were commissioned by the people, under express injunctions, not to bind the nation to such conditions." And again, "who (the nation) unanimously protested, in open assembly, against any Treaty on the basis of the five millions, under any circumstances; and therefore, had I been ever so much disposed to regard the *opinion* as an *award*, the VETO OF THE NATION settled the matter finally." The *injunctions* and the *veto of the nation* are that which I have characterized "the insidious protest," which the people were made to declare, while they were supposed to be giving full and discretionary powers. With your construction of that protest, the question of a Treaty depended entirely upon the contingency whether the President would negotiate with you upon bases different from those he proposed to negotiate. You declared, and you say the people declared, that you would not negotiate a Treaty *upon those bases*—on the other hand, the President declared he would not negotiate *upon any other bases*. Who was to succeed in this strife? If I had the *weakness* to believe that General Jackson would succeed, and if I acted upon that belief, I hope you will not charge me as wanting to the best interests of my country.

It is a little singular that while you declare the New Echota Treaty to be "deceptive to the world and a fraud upon the Cherokee People," although it was made in the face of day and in the eye of the nation, to prove your assertion, you resort to matters which are deceptive and fraudulent. It is deceptive to say that the great body of the Cherokees are opposed *understandingly* to the New Echota Treaty, and that they have *understandingly* authorized you to make another with which they would be better pleased. The fact is, these Cherokees, perhaps, have never spent one moment's thought beyond that of *loving* and *securing* the land upon which they live—their whole instructions has tended to that point. According to that instruction, and the impressions produced in their minds by your want of candor and plain dealing, a portion of the Cherokees may be opposed to the New Echota Treaty, but not more than they would be to any other, *as long as they understood you as trying to reinstate them in their country.* This is the whole secret of this much talked of opposition. Is it right to humor this delusion? Be candid with them—tell them that their country cannot be saved, and that you want their authority to sell, yes, *to sell* it—an authority which you have alleged to the Government you have received, and you will see to where this opposition against a removal will go.

Again,—it is a "fraud upon the world" to say that "upwards of fifteen thousand Cherokees have protested against the Treaty, solemnly declaring they will never acquiesce," and to produce before the world a paper containing that number of signatures. Let us see how this matter is. I will quote another sentence. "The Cherokee people, in two protests, the one signed by twelve thousand seven hundred and fourteen persons, and the other by three thousand two hundred and fifty persons, spoke for themselves against the Treaty." In order to illustrate these, I take another from your memorial. "The Cherokee population has recently been reported by the War Department to be 18,000."[70] Of these 18,000, there are upwards of 1,000 Blacks, who, you will not allege, have been among the signers. Of the remaining sixteen or seventeen thousand (for I have not the census before me) upwards of one thousand, at the lowest estimate, had been registered for removal, none of whom, it is likely, would have signed any protest. Here are then about 15,000, probably less, to do what? To "*protest*," "SOLEMNLY DECLARE," to "sign," to SPEAK FOR THEMSELVES against the Treaty! I must confess my impotency to unravel such a mystery as this. A *population* of 15,000 furnish 15,000 who are able and competent *to declare* and *to speak for themselves*! I suppose, however, we are required to believe it implicitly. This must indeed be a wise and precocious nation. Well may you say, "that owing to the intelligence of the Cherokee people, they have a correct knowledge of their own rights."

In your memorial to the House of Representatives, in order to make the acts of the "unauthorized minority" the more obnoxious, you attempt a most flagrant deception upon the public. In order that I may not seem to misrepresent you, I will quote your language. "The Cherokees were happy and prosperous under a scrupulous observance of Treaty stipulations by the Government of the United States, and from the fostering hand extended over them, they made rapid advances in civilization, morals, and in the arts and sciences. Little did they anticipate, that when taught to feel and think as the American citizen, and to have with him a common interest, they were to be *despoiled by their guardian*, to become strangers and wanderers in the land of their fathers, forced to return to the savage life, and to seek a new home in the wilds of the far west, and that without their consent. An instrument purporting to be a Treaty with the Cherokee people, has recently been made public by the President of the U. States, that will have such an operation, if carried into effect."

Now you evidently intend to convey the impression, and such would be the view of a person unacquainted with the true facts of the case would take from your language, that the evils you have enumerated *are the results of the "instrument purporting to be a treaty"*—that the Cherokees are "despoiled by their guardian" by *means* of that instrument; that previous to the making and publishing of the instrument the Cherokees were in that happy and prosperous condition you have mentioned. Is all this so? Have we indeed been the instruments of despoiling our nation? Have we destroyed their happiness, checked their civilization, and corrupted their morals? The question again recurs, is all this true? At a distance, and with persons who have heard all that they know about Cherokee affairs through vague mediums, and by means of such statements as you have been accustomed of late to send to the world, what you seem to have alleged in the above extract may be taken for truth. But those who have watched attentively the progress of the Cherokee controversy from its commencement to the present time those who know what was actually the condition of the Cherokees before the making and publishing the "instrument" in question; that they had already "become strangers and wanderers in the land of their fathers"—those who have seen their happiness destroyed, their civilization checked, and their morals corrupted, by circumstances long before existing—those who know the entire prostration of the Cherokee Government, and that you are clinging only to an empty title—all these must know that you have attempted to produce an impression not in accordance with facts; that instead of the despoliation being in consequence of the "instrument," the "instrument" has been the result of the despoliation. We cannot consent to this unfair mode of presenting us to the public—We have suffered too much, in common with our citizens in this general despoliation, to submit silently to such aspersions cast upon us in an indirect way.

Without the hazard of being presumed vain, I can with propriety ask you, who have done more to stem the progress of despoliation which has overtaken this people than those whom you have now represented as the despoilers of their country? Who have been willing to do more—to suffer more, while doing and suffering was likely to be of any avail? To be sure, with their views of what they owed to their countrymen, and what they believed, in the sight of God, to be their duty, they did not resist the only measure, by which an entire despoliation could be prevented, to the extent that you have done.

Aside from your objections to the New Echota Treaty, upon the ground that it was made by a minority, and by persons unauthorized to make it, (which, by the bye, if true, is no new thing in Cherokee negotiations, as some of the signers of your memorials can testify,) you express your opposition to the details of it. I am not disposed to enter into a defence of the treaty. I am not foolish enough to tell you that it is unexceptionable. I have not been disposed to make *my will*, or my *opinion* as the *sine qua non* in this matter. It is true, I have agreed to that instrument, and signed it, but it does not follow that the details are such as I would wish, or that I can find no objection to the composition, which makes the treaty liable to bear different constructions. But I waive my objections—I take the treaty as the best that can be done for the Cherokees, under present circumstances—a treaty that will place them in a *better* condition than they *now* are. On this principle my actions have been founded in reference to the treaty, and I have no doubt of the correctness of that principle.

But let us see how you present your objections to some of the details of the Treaty—and first, your objection to the title which is proposed to be given to the Cherokees for the Western country.

The third article of the treaty provides, "The United States also agree that the lands above ceded by the treaty of Feb. 14, 1833,[71] including the outlet, and those ceded by this treaty, shall

all be included in one patent, executed to the Cherokee nation of Indians by the President of the United States, according to the provisions of the act of May 28, 1830."[72] The provision of that act of Congress is as follows: "That in the making of such exchange or exchanges, it shall and may be lawful for the President solemnly to assure the tribe or nation with which the exchange is made, that the United States will forever secure and guaranty to them, their heirs or successors, the Country so exchanged with them, and, if they prefer it, that the United States will cause a patent or grant to be made and executed to them for the same; *Provided, always*, that such lands shall revert to the United States if the Indians became extinct, or abandon the same."

The fifth article of the Treaty provides—"The United States hereby covenant and agree, that the lands ceded to the Cherokee nation in the foregoing article shall in no future time, without their consent, be included within the territorial limits or jurisdiction of any State or Territory. But they shall secure to the Cherokee nation the right, by their national Councils, to make and carry into effect all such laws as they may deem necessary," &c.

These are the promises from which you have formed a most curious inference, by a course of reasoning which cannot even be entitled sophistical. I present these matters only to show how unfair you are even when you *pretend* to reason. But to illustrate your logic—"The pretended Treaty *expressly avows*," you say, "That it is under the law containing the clause above quoted, and other similar laws, that the transfer is made; and the Indian tribe is to be subject, not only to those laws already existing, but to such laws as may be made hereafter." When the Treaty refers *only* to the act of May 28, how do you make out that it "*expressly avows*" that the transfer is made, under the law and "*other similar laws*," and the Indian title is to be subject to "*those laws*" and those "*which may be made hereafter*!" The treaty provides that the lands ceded to the Cherokees "*shall in no future time, without their consent*, be included within the territorial limits or jurisdiction of any State or Territory." Now let us see how gravely and wisely you reason upon that. "Suppose it should suit the policy of the United States, hereafter, to pass a law organizing a territorial government upon the Cherokee lands west?

Those laws necessarily destroy the character of the Cherokee nation as a distinct community; the nation becomes *legally extinct*; and the lands *revert to the United States*." The act of May says, if the *Indians* become *extinct*, then the lands shall revert, &c. You infer hence that the law organizing a territorial Government upon the Cherokee lands, which can be done only with their consent, according to the Treaty, will make the *nation extinct*, and the lands will hence revert to the United States. This is *splendid reasoning*, no doubt.— It is the first time I have heard *Indian extinction* to mean *legal extinction*.

But to state the matter in a short way. According to the provisions of the Treaty, a patent is to be given by the President of the United States for all the Cherokee lands West, agreeably to the provisions of the act of May 28, 1830—that act secures those lands to the Cherokees by a guarantee as strong as the United States can make it, with a single proviso, that if the *Indians* become *extinct* or remove, then those lands shall revert to the United States—according to the treaty, in no future time is a territorial government to be formed over those lands, *without the consent of the Cherokees*. From these plain provisions you build an argument to show that the Indian title is subject, not only to the act of May, 1830, and to *similar* acts, but to *other acts which may hereafter be made*—that if the Government *should see fit* to organize a territory over the Cherokee country, the *Nation* will become *legally extinct*, and the lands will revert to the United States; and hence the title pretended to be given in the treaty is good for nothing! This no doubt is conclusive reasoning *from the premises*![73]

Again—To show your unfairness in argument, and how you present your objections to the treaty by perverting its language, I will quote what you say in regard to the introduction of "useful farmers, mechanics," &c. "But this very article" (the article providing the intruders into the Cherokee country should be removed by order of the President of the United States) "is clogged with a worse than neutralizing condition—a condition that it is not to prevent the introduction of useful farmers, mechanics, and teachers: under which denomination some future Executive of the United States may find it convenient, hereafter, to overwhelm the original population," &c. I consider this a most palpable perversion, which the writer of your letter (may be from misinformation) has attempted to impose upon the public. He has left out a most important clause in the provision, which gives entirely a different construction, from what has been attempted to be impressed upon the reader—*according to treaty stipulations*. That is, the article referred to "is not intended to prevent the residence of useful farmers, mechanics, and teachers, for the instruction of Indians, *according to treaty stipulations*;" which must be understood as meaning the *consent* of the Cherokees given in *treaty stipulations*.

A similar perversion is made upon what the treaty stipulates respecting military posts and roads, which, you say, may be made at any time and at any place. You leave out what the treaty avows to be the object, and for which object alone, those military posts and military roads may be made—*for the interest and protection of the Cherokee Country*. And how is this objection consistent with your past *entreaties* to the Government for military aid and protection?[74] Have you not made one application after another for the establishment of the military in this country, for the interest of this nation? And have you not been willing that such a military should have the use of as much land, timber, &c, as may be necessary for the purpose and for the object, *the interest and protection of the Cherokee Country*? I cannot conceive why *you* should become so sensitive in regard to this matter. Is it because the treaty obligates the U. States to do the very thing you have been asking and entreating may be done? Understand me—I am not speaking of the advantages or disadvantages of a military—nor do I say that no *evils* will result from it. Such evils which *may* result if it should so "suit policy of the United States," are incidental to our very condition and the nature of our connexion with the Government of the U. States—to our weakness and dependence, and the power of the U. States. The military has been necessary to our safety and interest heretofore, and it *may be* necessary hereafter. That it *may* be put to pernicious and oppressive purposes is another question, and a contingency, as I say, *incidental to our very condition*. But what remedy do you propose? You cannot prevent those possible evils, of which you speak, "if it should suit the policy of the United States," by running in the very face of the Government, and by striving to retain, entirely, an independent existence, which is impracticable, and perhaps not desirable. If you want to avoid those evils resulting from the military, and the application of a supervisory power by the United States, which they *have always* exercised, and *will always* exercise over the Cherokee country, whether the treaty gives the power or not, (for it is claimed by the Constitution,) you will have to work differently. You must either go out of the limits of the United States, which has been alleged by some is your object, or you must pursue a contrary course—instead of *receding, approach* this great people by a modified connexion; a connexion that will somewhat identify your interest with theirs, and theirs with yours.

And let me stop here, while I am upon this subject, and inquire of a very curious avowal in your letter, after having said so much about the danger, from the treaty, of destroying "the character of the Cherokee Nation as a distinct community." I quote your language—"Now, the fact is, we never have objected to become citizens of the United States, and to conform to her laws." How does that accord with your sensibility, lest "the character of the Cherokee Nation, as a distinct community," should be destroyed? But is it true, as a matter of fact, that the Cherokees "never have objected to become citizens of the United States and to conform to her laws?" You mean, no doubt, that the Cherokees have *expressed* a willingness to become citizens, because, you say, they "have *required* the protection and the privileges of her laws to accompany that conformity on their part."[75] The question recurs, have they expressed such a willingness? Those who know that this matter has never been formally agitated by this people, and so far as it has been agitated, the universal voice has been the reverse of what you have stated, will see your following declarations fully illustrated: "I must here beg leave to observe that I have never yet been placed in a position which could render my individual decison conclusive upon any matters of this nature." And again—"It is I who serve under them, not they under me." This declaration, that you do the will of the people, has been so repeatedly made that it has become doubtful whether it is so or not; particularly when you undertake to give your *individual decision* or *opinion* of the Cherokee people, on a matter of vital importance.

In your letter and memorial you speak very decidedly for the nation, where you had no right or authority to do so, and where your declarations have not been supported by subsequent facts. Even where you undertake to give the views and decision of the "regular" delegation, it is far from being true that those views and that decision have accorded with their acts. One example will suffice. "Neither myself nor any other member of the regular delegation to Washington can, without violating our most sacred engagements, ever recognize that paper as a Treaty, by assenting to its terms, or the mode of its execution." You are understood to have made a similar declaration repeatedly since your return from Washington.—It is enough to mislead those who have no mind of their own, (and there are not a few here, notwithstanding "the intelligence of the Cherokee people," and "their correct knowledge of their own rights," common place expressions, which all *true patriots* must need make,)—I say it is enough to mislead such—they think that you really have never, and will never assent to the terms of the treaty in any manner whatever. Many have acted to their great injury, as they think, upon such high example. But what is the fact? Without presuming to be very confident as to what *you* have done—although it is not doubted that you have assented to the terms of the treaty, by consenting to the valuation of your place, and by sending your agent to show your property in order to be valued—I can refer you to the acts of the majority of the "regular" delegation.[76] Be your acts as they may, what I now wish you to understand me as saying is this—*Even where you undertake to give the views and decision of the "regular" delegation, it is far from being true that those views and that decision have accorded with their acts.* How is it but an assent to the terms of the treaty, and to the mode of its execution, to claim the advantages which that treaty secures to individuals? And how many of your "regular" delegation have done that? How many have, I will not say *consented*, but *entreated* to have their valuations made according to the mode prescribed in the Treaty? How many claim all the rights which the Treaty gives them? How many have even acceded to the grand principle of the treaty, a *removal*, and are now foremost in going to our new country? I need not mention who and how many, nor do I make these queries in order to place them in a disadvantageous position in reference to what you have undertaken *to assert* for them. I commend them for what they are doing—it is the right course—it is the right policy, and the only one to convince the mass of our people who have NOT intelligence enough, or "correct knowledge" of the extent of their difficulties to guide them in these matters. The point is this—What you have asserted as your decision, and the decision of your immediate associates of the "regular" delegation, has been contradicted by your acts, as they are understood here, and the acts of the majority of that delegation. It is not presumable then, and I may say it is not certain, that you have been as premature in speaking for *the people*; and will not the result of your confident assertions prove as unfortunate as in the case already stated?

I will trouble you with one more topic, and then I will close this letter.

It is with sincere regret that I notice you say little or nothing about the moral condition of this people, as affected by present circumstances. I have searched in vain, in all your late communications, for some indication of your sensibility upon this point. You seem to be absorbed altogether in the pecuniary aspects of this nation's affairs—hence your extravagant demands for the lands we are compelled to relinquish—your ideas of the value of the gold mines, (which, if they had been peaceably possessed by the Cherokees, would have ruined them as soon as the operation of the State laws have done) of the value of our marble quarries, our mountains and forests.[77] Indeed, you seem to have forgotten that your people are a community of moral beings, capable of an elevation to an equal standing with the most civilized and virtuous, or a deterioration to the level of the most degraded of our race. Upon what principle, then, could you have made the assertion that you are reported to have made, "that the Cherokees had not suffered one-half what their country was worth," but upon the principle of valuing your nation in dollars and cents? If you meant simply the physical sufferings of this people, your assertion may be listened to with some patience; but can it be possible that you, who have claimed to be their leader and guardian, have forgotten that there is another kind of suffering which they have endured, and will endure as long as they are kept in these perplexities, of *a far more important nature*? Can it be possible that you consider the mere pains and privations of the body, and the loss of a paltry sum of money, of a paramount importance to the depression of the mind, and the degradation and pollution of the soul? That the difficulties under which they are laboring, originating from the operation of the State laws, and their absorption by a white population, *will* affect them in that light, I need not here stop to argue with you: that they have *already* affected them is a fact too palpable, too notorious for us to deny it. That they will *increase* to affect them, in proportion to the delay of applying the remedy, we need only judge from past experience. How then can you reconcile your conscience and your sense of what is demanded by the best interest of your people, first with your incessant opposition to *a* treaty, and then your opposition to *the* treaty, because circumstances which had accumulated upon the nation by your delays, had compelled, if you please, a minority to make it; and forsooth it does not secure just such a title to the western lands as you may wish; and because a sufficient sum of *money* is not obtained for the "invaluable" gold mines, marble quarries, mountains, and forests of our country! How can you persist in deluding your people with phantoms, and in your opposition to that which alone is practicable, when you see them dying a moral death.

To be sure, from your account of the condition and circumstances of the Cherokees, the public may form an idea different from what my remarks may seem to convey. When applied to a portion of our people, confined mostly to whites intermarried among us, and the descendants of whites, your account is probably correct, divesting it of all the exaggeration with which you have encircled it. But look at the mass—look at the entire population as it now is, and say, can you see any indication of a progressing improvement—anything that can encourage a philanthropist? You know that it is almost a dreary waste. I care not if I am accounted a slanderer of my country's reputation—every observing man in this nation knows that I speak the words of truth and soberness. In the light that I consider my countrymen, not as mere animals, and to judge of their happiness by their condition as such, which to be sure is bad enough, but as moral beings, to be affected for better or for worse, by moral circumstances, I say their condition is wretched. Look, my dear sir, around you, and see the progress that vice and immorality have already made! See the spread of intemperance and the wretchedness and misery it has already occasioned! I need not reason with a man of your sense and discernment, and of your observation, to show the debasing character of that vice to our people—you will find an argument in every tippling shop in the country—you will find its cruel effects in the bloody tragedies that are frequently occurring—in the frequent convictions and executions for murders, and in the tears and groans of the widows and fatherless, rendered homeless, naked and hungry, by this vile curse of our race. And has it stopped its cruel ravages with the lower or poorer classes of our people? Are the higher orders, if I may so speak, left untainted? While there are honorable exceptions in all classes, a security for a future renovation under other circumstances, it is not to be denied that, as a people, we are making a rapid tendency to a general immorality and debasement. What more evidence do we need, to prove this general tendency, than the slow but sure insinuation of the lower vices into our female population? Oh! it is heart-rending to think of these things, much more to speak of them—but the world *will* know them—the world *does* know them, and we need not try to hide our shame.

Now, sir, can you say that in all this the Cherokees had not *suffered* one half what their country was worth? Can you presume to be spending your whole time in opposing *a* treaty, then in trying, as you say, to make a *better* treaty, that is to get more money, a full compensation for your gold mines, your marble quarries, your forests, your water courses—I say, can you be doing all this while the canker is eating the very vitals of this nation? Perish your gold mines and your money, if, in the pursuit of them, the moral credit of this people, their happiness and their existence are to be sacrificed!

If the dark picture which I have here drawn is a true one, and no candid person will say it is an exaggerated one, can we see a brighter prospect ahead? In another country, and under other circumstances, there is a *better* prospect. Removal, then, is the only remedy—the only *practicable* remedy. By it there *may be* finally a renovation—our people *may* rise from their very ashes to become prosperous and happy, and a credit to our race. Such has been and is now my opinion, and under such a settled opinion I have acted in all this affair. My language has been, "fly for your lives"—it is now the same. I would say to my countrymen, you among the rest, fly from the moral pestilence that will finally destroy our nation.

What is the prospect in reference to *your* plan of relief, if you are understood at all to have any plan? It is dark and gloomy beyond description. Subject the Cherokees to the laws of the States in their present condition? It matters not how favorable those laws may be, instead of remedying the evil you would only rivet the chains and fasten the manacles of their servitude and degradation. The final destiny of our race, under such circumstances, is too revolting to think of. Its course *must* be downward, until it finally becomes extinct or is merged in another race, more ignoble and more detested. Take my word for it, it is the sure consummation, if you succeed in preventing the removal of your people. The time will come when there will be only here and there those who can be called upon to sign a protest, or to vote against a treaty for their removal—when the few remnants of our once happy and improving nation will be viewed by posterity with curious and gazing interest, as relics of a brave and noble race. Are our people destined to such a catastrophe? Are we to run the race of all our brethren who have gone before us, and of whom hardly any thing is known but their name, and, perhaps, only here and there a solitary being, walking, "as a ghost over the ashes of his fathers," to remind a stranger that such a race *once* existed? May God preserve us from such a destiny.

I have the honor to be, Sir,
Your obedient and humble servant,

E. BOUDINOT.

NOTES

[1]In the spring of 1832 while traveling in the United States with his cousin John Ridge, Boudinot decided that the Cherokees should negotiate with the United States. A group known as the Ridge faction or Treaty Party began to coalesce around the leadership of Boudinot, John Ridge, and Major Ridge. Andrew Ross, brother of the principal chief, and David Vann, a member of the Council, were also prominent members of the group. The Treaty Party, however, represented only a small faction of the Cherokees. The majority followed Principal Chief John Ross, who originally refused to negotiate and finally, when a treaty proved unavoidable, held out for the best possible terms for the Cherokees.

[2]The Cherokees conceived of their homeland as the center of the world and the Indian territory as near the edge. Because they associated west with death, conservatives (people who held on to traditional beliefs) were understandably reluctant to accept removal west of the Mississippi.

[3]In addition to Ross, Assistant Principal Chief George Lowrey, President of the Committee Lewis Ross, and Chief Justice and Treasurer John Martin opposed removal. It is doubtful that these chiefs had as much influence as Boudinot suggests. In 1830 Samuel A. Worcester wrote a letter to a member of the Cherokee delegation in Washington, which Boudinot published in the *Phoenix* on May 8, 1830, and he observed: "Nothing is plainer, than that it is the earnest wish of the whole body of the people to remain where they are. They are not overawed by the chiefs. Individuals may be overawed by *popular opinion*, but *not by the chiefs*. On the other hand, if there were a chief in favor of removal, *he* would be overawed *by the people*. He would know that he could not open his mouth in favor of such a proposition, but on pain, not only of the failure of his reelection, but of popular odium and scorn."

[4]Even with the objectivity that time presumably brings to controversy, the "vast majority" still appear to have been opposed to removal.

[5]John Ross published two pamphlets in which he set forth his reasons for opposing removal. See pp. 200, 206-7. He received advice on these pamphlets from John Howard Payne, who had visited Ross in 1835 and had been arrested along with his host by the Georgia Guard. Payne, better known perhaps as the composer of "Home Sweet Home," became a champion of Cherokee rights.

[6]However rationally and responsibly the Treaty Party believed it acted, the fact remains that the party *was* a "small minority opposed to the will of the people."

[7]Boudinot had wanted to open the columns of the *Cherokee Phoenix* to a debate of the issue. Principal Chief John Ross and the majority of the Council believed that the newspaper as an official organ of the Cherokee Nation should present only the Nation's position. Furthermore, Ross feared that whites would perceive an open debate as a weakening of the Cherokees' resolve to resist removal. Consequently, Boudinot was enjoined from publishing any dissenting opinions. Unable to accept censorship, Boudinot resigned.

[8]This comment gives rise to speculation about the influence of Boudinot's

Calvinist education on his political ideas. It seems to be a latter-day version of the 17th-century Puritan doctrine of election.

[9]These were not the objectives mentioned in the prospectus. See pp. 89-90.

[10]He probably meant the tariff of 1832, which South Carolina nullified. Northerners supported the tariff while southerners opposed it. For the relationship between the nullification crisis and the removal of the Cherokees, see Edwin A. Miles, "After John Marshall's Decision: *Worcester v. Georgia* and the Nullification Crisis," *Journal of Southern History* 39 (1973):519–44.

[11]The Council subsidized the *Phoenix* out of the Nation's annuity, that is, money paid annually by the federal government under the terms of previous treaties. In 1830 in an attempt to bankrupt the Cherokee government, the Office of Indian Affairs instructed the agent to distribute the annuity on a per capita basis rather than paying it into the National treasury. The Cherokees demonstrated their dissatisfaction with this arrangement by refusing to accept individual payments, which amounted to less than 50 cents each. The empty National treasury meant that the Cherokees had to rely on contributions for their delegations to Washington and their lawyers. In 1835, after the Cherokees voted overwhelmingly to deposit the entire sum in the treasury, the federal government paid the annuity but suspended it in 1836 and restored it once again in 1837.

[12]Boudinot had been editor of the *Phoenix* for four years. He also served the Nation as clerk of the Council in 1825, 1826, and 1827.

[13]Elijah Hicks, Ross's brother-in-law, became editor of the *Phoenix*, which was published until 1834. In 1835 the Georgia Guard accompanied by Boudinot's brother, Stand Watie, confiscated the press and types in order to prevent Ross from using them to present his case.

[14]Ross expressed the traditional Cherokee approach to politics in which councils reached a consensus and chiefs had no power to enforce their will. In a letter published in the *Gentleman's Magazine* (Aug. 1733), Gen. James Edward Oglethorpe, the founder of Georgia, wrote: "Their Kings can do no more than *persuade*. . . . They reason together till they have brought each other into some unanimous Resolution."

[15]The Constitution of the Cherokee Nation (1827) did not protect freedom of the press, and the Council clearly viewed the *Phoenix* as an organ of the government.

[16]The delegation of 1831–32 was composed of John Martin, John Ridge, and William Shorey Coodey.

[17]Many people, including supporters of the Cherokees, feared that federal recognition of Cherokee rights would encourage Georgia (as well as Alabama and Mississippi, which had passed similar laws) to join South Carolina in championing states' rights and nullification. The result, they believed, would be the secession of those states. See Miles; and Satz, 52–53.

[18]*Phoenix*, Aug. 11, 1832.

[19]In his veto of the bill to recharter the Second Bank of the United States, Jackson said: "The opinion of the judges has no more authority over Congress than the opinion of Congress has over the judges, and on that point the President is independent of both. The authority of the Supreme Court must not, therefore, be permitted to control the Congress or the Executive when

acting in their legislative capacities, but to have only such influence as the force of their reasoning may deserve." In other words, Jackson believed that the president was not obligated to enforce decisions of the Court.

[20]On Mar. 3, 1832, Chief Justice Marshall had delivered the Court's majority opinion which declared the Georgia laws unconstitutional and ordered the release of the missionaries. *Worcester* v. *Georgia*, 6 Peters 515. Lumpkin disregarded the decision, and Jackson made no move to enforce it. The president reportedly said, "John Marshall has made his decision, now let him enforce it." Marquis James, *The Life of Andrew Jackson* (New York, 1938), 603. Actually, legal technicalities prevented Jackson from acting even if he had wanted to do so. See Satz, 48–50. Finally, the missionaries followed the advice of the American Board and suspended legal action. In return, Gov. Lumpkin ordered their release in Jan. 1833. Worcester and Butler had served one year and four months in the Georgia penitentiary. By the time they were released, Elias Boudinot was advocating treaty negotiations with the federal government.

[21]See pp. 151n 80.

[22]Georgia passed discriminatory legislation which was enforced in that part of the Cherokee Nation within the state. No Indian could sue or testify in a case involving a white, nor could an Indian enter into a binding contract with a white. *Acts of Georgia* (1828): 88–89.

[23]Psalm 91:6.

[24]*Phoenix*, Sept. 29, 1832.

[25]Worcester, the American Board missionary who had defied Georgia and spent over a year in the penitentiary, wrote about Boudinot in 1836 from his new station in the west: "His extreme anxiety to save his people from the threatening union led him to unite with a small minority of the nation in forming a treaty with the United States: an act, in my view, entirely unjustifiable, yet, in his case, dictated by good motives." Quoted in Bass, 218.

[26]By "country," Boudinot meant the land itself and not the Nation.

[27]In 1832, Henry Clay, who was sympathetic to the Cherokees, was the National Republican candidate for president. William Wirt, the Cherokees' lawyer who successfully took *Worcester* v. *Georgia* to the Supreme Court, was the Anti-Masonic party's candidate. They were defeated by the incumbent, Andrew Jackson.

[28]Before adoption of the Twentieth Amendment to the U. S. Constitution in 1933, presidents were inaugurated on Mar. 4 instead of Jan. 20. In this case, the Cherokees were hoping that Clay or Wirt would be inaugurated on that day.

[29]Boudinot referred to the likelihood that the Cherokees would be allowed to remain, which he believed was remote. Although Boudinot's diatribe against Ross is replete with error and exaggeration, he was correct that Ross did not tell the Cherokees how seemingly hopeless their situation was. Ross's biographer concluded that "he occasionally left his people too uninformed of Washington proceedings to make intelligent decisions." Moulton, 70. Rather than intentionally dishonest, Ross probably was incredibly sanguine about the eventual outcome and reluctant to trouble his people unnecessarily.

[30]The Cherokees held their land in common, and an individual could use as much land as he wished if he did not infringe on someone else's right to land.

Under this system, the land could not be sold, and the Council could place restrictions on the sale of improvements. If the Cherokees came under state law, they would have to receive individual allotments, or reservations, which could be sold, mortgaged, and the like, according to state statutes.

[31]The Creeks, who received individual allotments and came under state law according to the terms of their 1832 removal treaty, lost most of their land through fraud. Although they were on the brink of starvation, the dispossessed refused to go west. Finally, civil war, provoked by whites and reminiscent of the Red Stick war, erupted and many Creeks were deported as a military measure. See Mary Elizabeth Young, *Redskins, Ruffleshirts, and Rednecks: Indian Allotments in Alabama and Mississippi, 1830–1860* (Norman, Okla., 1961).

[32]Ross had retained the Georgia firm of Underwood and Harris in an attempt to stay evictions in individual cases resulting from the Georgia land lottery. Although the fees were supposed to be paid from "public moneys," the Cherokee treasury was empty, and so Ross, Martin, and other wealthy men (who benefited from the suits) helped finance litigation. Woodward, 164–67.

[33]By suing in Georgia courts, the Cherokees tacitly admitted, Boudinot believed, that they were subject to the laws of Georgia.

[34]This resolution represents an attempt to reconcile the factions. The first five men were members of the Ross party; the second five were members of the Treaty Party.

[35]Ross objected to negotiating with the U.S. commissioner who had arrived in the Nation in the summer of 1835 because his credentials came from the secretary of war instead of the president. Ross preferred to negotiate in Washington with the secretary under the watchful eye of Congress.

[36]After Georgia prohibited meetings of the Council, the Cherokees assembled at Red Clay just across the state line in Tennessee.

[37]As Boudinot explained below, the brackets are his.

[38]"The majority of the persons by whom the negotiations were to be carried on" were members of the Ross party because that party commanded the loyalty of the majority of Cherokees. Even three of nineteen negotiators was a generous number, in proportion to the Treaty Party's support.

[39]Ross made the appointment after approval by the Council in order to satisfy some Cherokees who felt that they were not adequately represented. See Moulton, 69–70.

[40]Boudinot was reminding his readers that Ross spoke Cherokee so poorly that his remarks were delivered in English and translated into Cherokee. Ibid., 2.

[41]This resolution extracted Ross from a delicate and potentially embarrassing situation. In Feb. 1835, Ross had agreed to cede Cherokee lands for $20 million provided that the government allow the Indians five years to resettle and pay their losses and claims. When Secretary of War Lewis Cass refused to accept that amount, Ross agreed to abide by a decision of the U.S. Senate provided that he be furnished the minutes of the proceedings. Case reneged on his promise of the minutes, and, as a result, Ross refused to accept the Senate's offer of $5 million. In an address to the Cherokees assembled at Red Clay in May 1835, Ross did not really discuss his promise to cede Cherokee

lands and focused instead on the actions of the Treaty Party. The 1,000 present signed a protest against an earlier meeting with Commissioner Benjamin F. Curry at John Ridge's home which only Ridge partisans had attended. Ibid., 60–63.

[42]Ross had been exploring the possibility of Cherokee emigration to Mexico. By holding out for more money, he could purchase land instead of accepting the territory that the U.S. government offered in exchange and move his people beyond the reach of the federal or state governments.

[43]John F. Schermerhorn was one of two U.S. commissioners sent to negotiate a removal treaty with the Cherokees. Schermerhorn's colleague, Gov. William Carroll of Tennessee, was ill and unable to participate in most negotiations. Schermerhorn alone was present at the signing of the Treaty of New Echota. In accepting this treaty, he violated instructions from Secretary of War Lewis Cass, which forbade a treaty with only part of the Nation. See James William Van Hoeven, "Salvation and Indian Removal: The Career Biography of John Freeman Schermerhorn, Indian Commisisoner" (Ph.D. diss. Vanderbilt Univ., 1972).

[44]See pp. 229n 35.

[45]Although Jackson threatened not to receive the members of Ross's delegation, they did meet with Cass on Jan. 2 and with Jackson the following day. Jackson suggested that they draw up a proposal on which the government could act. Before the delegation could do so, however, word of the Treaty of New Echota reached Washington. Moulton, 73.

[46]Schermerhorn estimated that 500 Cherokees were present—hardly a "respectable portion" of a population of over 16,000. Even this figure may have been an exaggeration because when a vote was taken on the treaty, only 82 voted (and 7 of those voted against the treaty). Ibid., 74.

[47]George Lowrey.

[48]The assumption that Ross did not have the authority to cede land was based on a series of laws. The articles of government enacted in 1825, which Ross signed as president of the National Committee, prohibited the principal chief from making treaties "without the express authority of the legislative Council," and an 1829 law prescribed the death penalty for anyone who entered into a treaty "contrary to the will and consent" of the Council. The Constitution of 1827 gave "the sole power of deciding on the construction of all Treaty stipulations" to the Council. Furthermore, the first article of the Constitution established the boundaries of the Nation, and consequently, a land cession would have entailed a constitutional amendment enacted by a two-thirds vote of each legislative house. *Laws*, 45, 118–30, 136–37. Moulton suggests that Ross used his lack of authority to extract himself from his 1835 promise to accept the Senate's award for cession (61).

[49]U.S. House, "Memorial and Protest of the Cherokee Nation" (H. Doc. 286, 24th Cong. 1st sess.).

[50]*Letter from John Ross . . . in Answer to Inquiries from a Friend Regarding the Cherokee Affairs with the United States* (n.p., 1836), and *Letter from John Ross, Principal Chief of the Cherokee Nation, to a Gentleman of Philadelphia* (n.p., 1837).

[51]Under the provisions of the Cherokee Constitution of 1827, elections should have been held in Aug. 1832. Because Georgia law prohibited elec-

tions, the Council voted to continue in office those persons elected in 1828 until elections could be held.

[52]Payne assisted Ross in preparing the pamphlets. Moulton, 82.

[53]Boudinot probably had no political ambitions. His cousin, John Ridge, however, aspired to the position of principal chief. Perhaps it is only a coincidence, but Ridge's change of heart on the removal issue came shortly after the Council cancelled the 1832 election in which he hoped to defeat Ross. Eaton, 59–60.

[54]While Ross was evicted from his elegant home in Georgia and forced to live in a log cabin in Tennessee, those Cherokees disposed to negotiate continued to enjoy their improvements that temporarily were withdrawn from the lottery. Gov. Wilson Lumpkin of Georgia instructed the enrolling officer to "assure Boudinot, Ridge, and their friends of state protection under any circumstances." Georgia Governor's Letterbook, 1833, Georgia Department of Archives, Atlanta, Ga.

[55]The Treaty of New Echota provided for preemptions for those Cherokees who wanted to remain and were "qualified to take care of themselves and their property." Most of those who signed the treaty would have "qualified." The treaty also named a committee of 13, which included at least six treaty negotiators and John Ross, to decide who could remain. The Supplemental Articles signed on Mar. 1, 1836, declared preemption rights void. Kappler, 2:444–45, 448.

[56]Ross's property at Red Hill and Head of Coosa was appraised at $23,665.75. He was clearly among the wealthiest men in the Cherokee Nation. Moulton, 80.

[57]The document that Boudinot signed in Oct. 1835 gave a delegation of 20 the power to negotiate at Red Clay or in Washington and protested the amount of $5 million offered by the Senate for cession of Cherokee lands. Boudinot did not go to Washington with the delegation. Instead, he went to New Echota and signed a treaty accepting the $5-million offer. Wilkins, 270–71.

[58]John Ridge and Stand Watie, Boudinot's brother, were in Washington with Ross when the Treaty of New Echota was signed, and their names appear on a letter to Cass protesting the treaty. When the Treaty Party delegation arrived with the document, however, both signed it.

[59]Originally published in the *Knoxville Register*, Payne's account was reprinted in other newspapers and periodicals. See Clemens de Baillou, ed., *John Howard Payne to his Countrymen* (Athens, Ga., 1961).

[60]As can be seen below, Boudinot's version was not accurate.

[61]Payne's statement actually was as follows: "They [U.S. agents] forcibly fell upon our own newspaper press, and upon the types invented by one of our own people, in order to make those very types of ours tell lies of one Cherokee to another, in his language, and which we have no instrument for answering, excepting that which they have unwarrantably taken from us to turn against ourselves. By strategems of this nature, a few were led to misunderstand their brothers and fall off from them." De Baillou, 55.

[62]Ridge referred to the Cherokees' supposed promise to the United States that "provided you will let them live together, they will come under your laws" and the appeal that "if they do sell their native land for money, it must

be enough to secure them another in exchange, where they may be permanently free." Ibid., 59. In the spring of 1835, Ross actually met with a Mexican official to discuss the possibility of removal to Mexico. Moulton, 62.

[63]Payne wrote: "They [U.S. agents] say our chiefs do not belong to our nation, because a grant of the land upon which the ancestors of one of them had lived, was made to him as a free donation, under our treaty." De Baillou, 55.

[64]Under the terms of the treaty of 1819, John Ross and 30 others received reservations, that is, a fee simple title to a tract of land within ceded territory. The reservations were granted on the condition that the reservees notify the agent within six months "that it is their intention to continue to reside permanently on the land reserved." Kappler, 2:178, 180. Ross promptly informed the agent that he planned to "occupy and enjoy permanently" his 640-acre reservation in Tennessee. Actually, Ross never lived on the land. Moulton, 78.

[65]Reservations were supposed to be awarded to individuals who lived within the ceded territory, who preferred to remain in their homes and come under state jurisdiction rather than move within the shrinking boundaries of the Nation, and who were recognized as "persons of industry and capable of managing their property with discretion." Kappler, 2:178. All too frequently, however, the United States granted reservations as bribes to those who would negotiate land cessions, and it was this practice to which Boudinot objected. The most infamous Cherokee reservee was Doublehead, whom Major Ridge helped execute in 1807. Wilkins, 35–38.

[66]John Watts, who received the reservation jointly with Ross, had removed under the terms of the treaty of 1817, which required migrants to relinquish all land claims in the east. Kappler, 2:141. In 1817 the Council provided that "the authority and claim of our common property shall cease with the person or persons who shall think proper to remove themselves without the limits of the Cherokee Nation." *Laws*, 5. Consequently, Watts had no claim as a citizen of the Cherokee Nation to a reservation under the treaty of 1819.

[67]The government of the United States, of course, had been refusing to pay the Cherokees money owed under these past treaties.

[68]Money was loaned at 6 percent interest per annum for six months to individuals who could give bond and "two good and sufficient securities." The law provided that the property of those who defaulted be sold at auction. *Laws*, 50.

[69]Under the circumstances, little else could be done.

[70]The Census of 1835, or Henderson Role (Record Group 75, National Archives, Washington, D. C.), listed 16,542 Cherokees, 201 intermarried whites, and 1,592 black slaves. For a statistical analysis of this census, see McLoughlin and Conser.

[71]This treaty, negotiated between the United States and the western Cherokees at Fort Gibson on the Arkansas River, granted land to the Cherokees in what is today northeastern Oklahoma and provided them with a 7-million-acre "perpetual outlet west." Kappler, 2:385–88. Article three of the Treaty of New Echota joined the lands of two distinct Cherokee groups, each of which had its own chiefs and laws. The result was confusion and conflict when the eastern Cherokees arrived in the spring of 1839. The Treaty

Party aligned itself with the western, or Old Settler, Cherokees in an attempt to dilute Ross's constituency, and virtual civil war raged until 1846. See Gerard Reed, "Postremoval Factionalism in the Cherokee Nation" in *The Cherokee Indian Nation: A Troubled History*, ed. Duane H. King (Knoxville, Tenn., 1978), 148–63.

[72]The Indian Removal Act, *U.S. Stat.*, 4:411–12.

[73]In retrospect, Boudinot seems exceedingly naive when expressing such confidence in the land title guaranteed by the United States. Ross, on the other hand, appears prophetic. Following the Civil War, the United States forced the southern Indians, who had signed treaties with the Confederacy, to grant rights-of-way to railroads. The federal government pledged large land grants to railroads contingent upon the extinguishment of the Indian land titles. Whites streamed into the Indian nations as railroad workers, cowboys, tenants, or merely squatters and joined the railroads in agitating for Indian land. Finally, at the end of the 19th century, Congress voted to allot the Indians' land to individuals, dissolve the Indian governments, put the railroads in possession of their land grants, and open the remaining land to white settlement. In 1907 Oklahoma became a state in which Indians were a minority. See Angie Debo, *And Still the Waters Run: The Betrayal of the Five Civilized Tribes* (Princeton, N. J., 1940); H. Craig Miner, *The Corporation and the Indian: Tribal Sovereignty and Industrial Civilization, 1867–1907* (Columbia, Mo., 1976); and Theda Perdue, *Nations Remembered: An Oral History of the Five Civilized Tribes, 1865–1907* (Westport, Conn., 1980).

[74]Ross had requested the federal government to remove intruders and protect the Cherokees.

[75]Early in 1835 Ross indicated his willingness to cede a portion of the Cherokee lands in Georgia if the federal government promised to protect the Indians on the land they continued to hold and to extend the privileges of citizenship to the Cherokees when they had "progressed" sufficiently. Moulton, 60. Boudinot, who personally had experienced white racism (see pp. 9-10), believed that the Indians would never be accepted as equals and would remain an oppressed minority. Consequently, he opposed any proposal of ultimate assimilation.

[76]Ross's overseer permitted the property of the principal chief to be appraised, apparently contrary to his wishes. Moulton, 80.

[77]Ross had demanded $20 million for the Cherokee territory in 1835. In 1838, he presented the figure of $13 million to the War Department as the amount for which the Cherokees would remove. The Treaty of New Echota provided for only $5 million, but the federal government ultimately allowed $6,647,067 for removal. Moulton, 60–61, 94–95.

INDEX

CPSIA information can be obtained
at www.ICGtesting.com
Printed in the USA
LVHW040712130122
708384LV00002B/140